The Music Producer's Creative Guide to Ableton Live 11

Level up your music recording, arranging, editing, and mixing skills and workflow techniques

Anna Lakatos

BIRMINGHAM—MUMBAI

The Music Producer's Creative Guide to Ableton Live 11

Group Product Manager: Rohit Rajkumar

Publishing Product Manager: Vaideeshwari Muralikrishnan

Senior Content Development Editor: Rakhi Patel

Technical Editor: Simran Ali

Copy Editor: Safis Editing

Project Coordinator: Manthan Patel

Proofreader: Safis Editing

Indexer: Rekha Nair

Production Designer: Shankar Kalbhor

Marketing Coordinator: Nivedita Pandey

First published: March 2023

Production reference: 1090323

Published by Packt Publishing Ltd.
Livery Place
35 Livery Street
Birmingham
B3 2PB, UK.

ISBN 978-1-80181-763-9

www.packtpub.com

To the memory of my mother, Judit Bereczky, for her love and sacrifices and teaching me how to be persistent and true to myself. To my loved ones, who always support and inspire me, fueling my determination.

– Anna Lakatos

Foreword

With the advent of computer music software, music-making has become ever more accessible. No longer is an aspiring artist reliant on a record company to pay for studio time – hit records can be made in bedrooms and released online. Since Ableton produced their first version of Live back in 2001, Live has grown to be one of the most popular **Digital Audio Workstations (DAWs)** used by composers, producers, sound designers, performers, and artists all over the world. Ableton prides itself on maintaining the ethos of accessibility, useability, and transparency, helping you to realize your musical ideas as quickly as possible. The more you use Live, the more you will discover a huge community of like-minded producers, willing to help and support you through your musical journey.

In my role as Head of Education and Curriculum at Point Blank Music School in London, Anna Lakatos has been my friend and colleague for over five years and is also a fellow Ableton Certified Trainer. I have had the pleasure of observing Anna in the classroom on many occasions, meticulously planning her lessons to ensure students are learning effectively and solving problems for themselves. This book perfectly encapsulates her process, providing a structured approach to mastering Ableton Live, and allowing you to build on techniques, whilst giving you the confidence and motivation to progress. You will benefit from the experience and transferrable skills that Anna brings as an accomplished audio engineer, electronic musician, singer, and live performer.

In the first part of the book, Anna kicks off with the fundamentals, helping you navigate the main areas of Live, ensuring that you are familiar with the terminology and workflow. Essentially, DAWs recreate traditional hardware such as mixing desks and outboard equipment, so it's important to understand how these relate to the software. You'll then hit the ground running learning about audio recording, editing, and the concept of warping, which is one of the most useful and important features of Live. It means you can easily change the tempo (speed) of your tracks without losing audio quality. The topic of MIDI is covered next, which includes sequencing, editing, and MIDI effects. This is crucial when it comes to programming drums and instrumental parts.

In the second part you'll get to apply the functionality of Live in a creative way, learning techniques such as comping, audio effects, device racks, and slicing to MIDI. Don't worry if this terminology sounds unfamiliar at first, you'll soon get to know how it will benefit your productions. You will then build on this knowledge so you can start arranging your ideas into finished compositions and be able to start crafting fully-fledged mixes with automation and modulation techniques.

In the third and final part, you'll study how to personalize Live and take your music out of the studio and onto the live stage. You'll learn how to connect external hardware such as synths and controllers, and even how you can create your own plugins with Max for Live. Techniques such as file management and troubleshooting are also covered to ensure that you'll be an efficient and autonomous music maker.

I have no doubt that this book will break down any barriers to learning and get you up and running as an expert producer in no time, whatever your style or genre may be.

Ski Oakenfull

Musician and Producer.

Head of Education and Curriculum, Point Blank Music School.

Ableton Certified Trainer.

Contributors

About the author

Anna Lakatos, also known as **Anna Disclaim**, is a multi-talented electronic musician, singer, and audio engineer based in London. She has been active in the music industry since 2014, working as a recording engineer, mix engineer, and music producer, utilizing a range of digital audio workstations and analog outboard gear.

As an educator, Anna holds several positions, including as an Ableton Certified Trainer, university lecturer, module leader, and course developer on degree courses, such as BA (Hons) degrees in music production and sound engineering, music production and DJ practice, and music production and vocal performance. She also holds an Avid Pro Tools certification and is one of the UK's Native Instruments product specialists.

She studied audio engineering in London, where she specialized in object-based 3D sound for motion pictures as well as commercial music production, and is currently pursuing postgraduate studies at the University of London.

Her expertise has taken her to various festivals and events, including Dimensions and Outlook in Croatia, Sonar in Barcelona, Amsterdam Dance Event, and International Music Summit in Ibiza, to name a few, where she has facilitated masterclasses, and provided training and tech support to artists from top record labels and radio stations, including Universal Music, Ministry of Sound (Sony Music), Rinse FM, BBC Radio1, Ninja Tune, and more.

Anna has been recognized in industry publications such as *Future Music* and *MusicTech* magazines, and has contributed to content and masterclasses for leading companies, including Ableton, Native Instruments, ADAM Audio, Saffron Records, Music Hackspace, and Point Blank Music School.

For more information on her work, visit her website at https://www.annadisclaim.com/.

Writing a book is a journey, and it is only fitting to take a moment to acknowledge the people who have supported me along the way.

First and foremost, I would like to thank my loved ones for their unwavering support and encouragement. Their belief in me has been a constant source of inspiration and motivation.

I would also like to express my gratitude to my editor and publisher, who have helped shape this book into its final form. Their guidance, patience, and expertise have been invaluable.

I would also like to extend my thanks to the many people who have influenced my thinking and provided me with ideas and insights, including my colleagues, peers, and mentors.

Finally, I would like to thank my readers. It is your interest and support that makes this all worth it. Thank you for taking the time to read this book and for giving me the opportunity to share my ideas with you.

With heartfelt gratitude,

Anna Lakatos

About the reviewer

Charly Fariseo is a multi-instrumentalist, producer, composer, and live performer from San José, Costa Rica. He has been an Ableton Certified Trainer since 2017 and specializes in working on audio branding, sound design, and post-production for TV, radio, and web media. Charly teaches music production and performs as a solo artist and with different bands in various genres.

Charly is the founder and director of Rombos Sound Studio, a creative studio dedicated to innovating with sound. He has worked for Red Bull, Power Ade, ICT (Costa Rica Tourist Board), and many other brands. As an Ableton Certified Trainer, Charly has trained hundreds of students at all levels, from beginners to professional musicians and producers.

Table of Contents

Part 2: Creative Music Production Techniques with Ableton Live 11

6

Comping and Track Linking   151

7

Discovering Some of Live 11's Creative Audio Effects   163

11

Implementing Automation and Modulation   261

12

Getting Started with MPE in Ableton Live 11   285

Part 3: Deep Dive into Ableton Live

13

Exploring Tempo Follower, Follow Action, Max for Live, Working with Video, and Ableton Note   305

14

Exploring MIDI Mapping, External Instrument, and MIDI CCs   341

15

Playing Live   369

16

Interesting Mixing Techniques in Live 11   399

17

Troubleshooting and File Management · 417

Index · 427

Other Books You May Enjoy · 438

Preface

The Music Producer's Guide to Ableton Live will help you sharpen your production skills, and gain a deeper understanding of the Live workflow. If you are a music maker working with other **Digital Audio Workstations (DAWs)** or already working with Ableton Live, perhaps earlier versions, then you will be able to put your newfound knowledge to use right away with this book.

The book starts with some basic features and workflows that are more geared toward producers coming from another DAW who wish to use their transferable skills to learn to use Ableton Live 11.2. You will begin exploring the Live concept and learn to create expressive music using Groove and MIDI effects, as well as Live 11's new workflow improvements, such as note chance and velocity randomization. You will then discover some key features that can make composition and coming up with melodic elements easier, such as the Scale function and MIDI Transform tools. You will implement Live 11's new and updated effects into your current workflow as you learn advanced and creative music production techniques. Finally, you will gain knowledge of several production-related techniques with a focus on live performance capabilities.

By the end of this book, you will be able to implement advanced production and workflow techniques and take advantage of what the Live 11 workflow has to offer.

Who this book is for

If you are a music producer, enthusiast, or hobbyist with a basic understanding of using Ableton Live for simple projects and want to improve your skills to employ the best features and techniques to improve the quality of your projects, then this book is for you. This book is also for producers wishing to leverage their transferable skills to learn about Ableton Live who have prior expertise with another DAW.

What this book covers

Chapter 1, Taking a Quick Tour of Ableton Live 11

In this chapter, you'll receive a speedy overview of Live 11, designed to refresh or familiarize producers who have previously worked with other DAWs and are now transitioning to Live.

Chapter 2, Recording Audio in Ableton Live 11

This chapter will provide a comprehensive explanation of how to record audio in both the Session View and Arrangement View in Live. The chapter will cover the two recording buttons, routing setup, adjusting recording preferences, and an examination of the new Take Lanes feature in Live 11.

Chapter 3, Editing Audio and Warping

In this chapter, we will look at some editing techniques, and develop an understanding of how to work simultaneously in both the Session and Arrangement View. We will delve into the world of Warping and discover the power of Live's warp engine, which allows us to stretch audio to match the tempo of our song while preserving the original pitch.

Chapter 4, Exploring MIDI Sequencing Techniques

In this chapter, we will explore the different techniques we can use to sequence MIDI in Ableton Live. No matter what genre you make, how good your sense of rhythm is, or your music theory knowledge, you will find the techniques you feel the most comfortable with to develop the best workflow for you!

Chapter 5, MIDI Editing and MIDI Effects

In this chapter, we will take a look at MIDI editing functions, as well as MIDI effects, in order to correct timing errors, humanize patterns, and create more expressive musical parts.

Chapter 6, Comping and Track Linking

In this chapter, we will uncover some of the new editing functions in Live 11. We will explore how these features can be used both in a practical and creative manner, and learn how they can enhance and streamline our editing process. Take Lanes and Track Linking are powerful tools for establishing an efficient recording and editing workflow. However, Take Lanes are not limited to just practical use; they can also be utilized in innovative ways to generate new and unexpected outcomes quickly.

Chapter 7, Discovering Some of Live 11's Creative Audio Effects

In this chapter, we will jump into discovering some of the new and updated Audio Effects that Live 11 has to offer. These effects can be crucial parts of your sound design tools, as well as useful and creative tools for mixing. We will also take a look at some creative Sidechaining techniques that will give your musical parts a modern spin, and develop an understanding of insert and send effects for a more efficient workflow.

Chapter 8, Exploring Device Racks in Live 11

In this chapter, we will explore the power of the amazing Device Racks in Live 11, and all their new updated features too. Racks are important parts of the Live workflow and can open up a wide range of possibilities for production, sound design, and live performance!

Chapter 9, Audio to MIDI Conversion, Slicing to MIDI, and the Simpler Device

Have you ever struggled to identify the melody in an audio loop or played a bassline in your head that you couldn't recreate with MIDI?

Well then, this chapter is definitely going to be one to embrace! We will be looking at how to extract melodies and harmonies from audio and use them as MIDI and make edits, as well as manipulate the sounds. We will also look into extracting drum grooves and notes from audio loops, and replacing the sounds with our own!

Do you like chopped-up vocals and breaks? Then, let's discover some techniques to slice and dice audio with the Simpler device and even manipulate further the slices with Simpler's inherited subtractive synthesis features.

Chapter 10, Utilizing Arrangement and Organization Techniques in Our Ableton Live Project

In this chapter, we will take a look at some arrangement and project organization techniques to be able to lay down, organize, and progress your ideas in the most efficient way possible.

Chapter 11, Implementing Automation and Modulation

In this chapter, we will explore how you can add movement, variations, and interest to your transitions within your piece by using automation and modulation in Live. You will also learn how to manage and edit these parameter changes over time easily.

Chapter 12, Getting Started with MPE in Ableton Live 11

In this chapter, we will delve into **MIDI Polyphonic Expression** (**MPE**), the latest addition to Live 11, which allows for greater expression in your notes, the creation of evolving sounds, and a unique twist to your sound design toolkit. We will explore this exciting new feature in depth.

Chapter 13, Exploring Tempo Follower, Follow Action, Max for Live, Working with Video, and Ableton Note

This chapter will cover several topics, including the new Tempo Follow function and its integration with the improved Follow Action capabilities. We'll also explore some Max for Live devices that can help to enhance your music, as well as methods for integrating video into your Ableton Live projects. Additionally, we'll delve into the new music-making iOS app, Ableton Note, and learn how to synchronize projects between Note and Live via Ableton Cloud.

Chapter 14, Exploring MIDI Mapping, External instrument, and MIDI CCs

In this chapter, we will take a look at how we can control device parameters with an external MIDI controller for live performance or recording automation. We will go over setting up MIDI mapping and understanding MIDI CCs. Additionally, we will delve into incorporating external synthesizers into Live and how they can enhance your workflow.

Chapter 15, Playing Live

In this chapter, we will delve into the world of live performance in Ableton Live. We'll examine the various Clip Launch options and how to set up dummy clips to automate parameters on other tracks. We'll also explore Ableton Link, allowing us to jam with others while staying in sync. Additionally, we'll take a closer look at the Ableton Push 2 and discuss output routing and monitoring options in Live.

Chapter 16, Interesting Mixing Techniques in Live 11

In this chapter, we will dive into the world of mixing and discover techniques for enhancing the sound of our tracks in Ableton Live. We will also explore the basic steps involved in creating a balanced and polished mixdown and what it takes to prepare our mix for mastering. Whether you're just starting out or are a seasoned producer, this chapter will provide valuable insights into the art of mixing and mastering.

Chapter 17, Troubleshooting and File Management

In this chapter, we will delve into crucial techniques for managing files and resolving issues, as well as discovering how to handle third-party plugins within Live.

To get the most out of this book

You will need to install Ableton Live 11.2.7 Suite or later version.

Some features in earlier versions might not be available.

The book was written and illustrated with macOS screenshots. Some of the keyboard shortcuts are different on a Windows machine as included in the book.

However, you can access the extensive list of keyboard shortcuts for both macOS and Windows here: `https://www.ableton.com/en/manual/live-keyboard-shortcuts/`

Software/hardware covered in the book	Operating system requirements
Ableton Live 11.2.7 Suite	macOS or Windows

For additional built-in Live lessons, you can navigate to View | Help View inside Live. It is suggested to download a couple of additional Live Pack content (which are part of the Live 11 Suite license) besides the Core Library for a greater selection of sounds and devices.

Download the project files

You can download the project files for this book at `https://packt.link/lpTRI`

In certain chapters, there exist both **Incomplete** and **Completed** versions of the projects, enabling you to access the required resources to either undertake the instructions by yourself or follow along with the pre-made projects. This allows for flexibility in how you engage with the materials and provides opportunities for practice and reinforcement of the concepts.

Download the color images

We also provide a PDF file that has color images of the screenshots and diagrams used in this book. You can download it here: `https://packt.link/R9PWZ`

Conventions used

There are a number of text conventions used throughout this book.

Bold: Indicates a new term, an important word, or words that you see onscreen. For instance, words in menus or dialog boxes appear in **bold**. Here is an example: "Choose the **Edit Infor Text** option from the contextual menu."

> **Tips or important notes**
> Appear like this.

Get in touch

Feedback from our readers is always welcome.

General feedback: If you have questions about any aspect of this book, email us at `customercare@packtpub.com` and mention the book title in the subject of your message.

Errata: Although we have taken every care to ensure the accuracy of our content, mistakes do happen. If you have found a mistake in this book, we would be grateful if you would report this to us. Please visit `www.packtpub.com/support/errata` and fill in the form.

Piracy: If you come across any illegal copies of our works in any form on the internet, we would be grateful if you would provide us with the location address or website name. Please contact us at `copyright@packt.com` with a link to the material.

If you are interested in becoming an author: If there is a topic that you have expertise in and you are interested in either writing or contributing to a book, please visit `authors.packtpub.com`.

Share Your Thoughts

Once you've read *The Music Producer's Creative Guide to Ableton Live 11*, we'd love to hear your thoughts! Scan the QR code below to go straight to the Amazon review page for this book and share your feedback.

https://packt.link/r/1801817634

Your review is important to us and the tech community and will help us make sure we're delivering excellent quality content.

Download a free PDF copy of this book

Thanks for purchasing this book!

Do you like to read on the go but are unable to carry your print books everywhere? Is your eBook purchase not compatible with the device of your choice?

Don't worry, now with every Packt book you get a DRM-free PDF version of that book at no cost.

Read anywhere, any place, on any device. Search, copy, and paste code from your favorite technical books directly into your application.

The perks don't stop there, you can get exclusive access to discounts, newsletters, and great free content in your inbox daily

Follow these simple steps to get the benefits:

1. Scan the QR code or visit the link below

https://packt.link/free-ebook/978-1-80181-763-9

2. Submit your proof of purchase
3. That's it! We'll send your free PDF and other benefits to your email directly

Part 1:
The Live Concept
and Workflow

Upon completing Part 1 of this book, you will have a solid grasp of the fundamentals of Live, including the recording, editing, and warping of both audio and MIDI. Additionally, you will gain the skills to add more creativity to your music by utilizing Groove and MIDI effects, as well as some of Live 11's new workflow enhancements such Note Chance and Velocity Randomization. This part will also introduce you to several key features that simplify the process of composing music and help you generate melodic ideas, such as the Scale Mode and Scale settings, as well as MIDI transform tools.

This part comprises the following chapters:

- *Chapter 1, Taking a Quick Tour of Ableton Live 11*
- *Chapter 2, Recording Audio in Ableton Live 11*
- *Chapter 3, Editing Audio and Warping*
- *Chapter 4, Exploring MIDI Sequencing Techniques*
- *Chapter 5, MIDI Editing and MIDI Effects*

1
Taking a Quick Tour of Ableton Live 11

If you are reading this book, you've most probably already used Ableton Live and are here to brush up on the basics and sharpen your skills or even find the most suitable workflow for yourself. Or, you might have been using a different **Digital Audio Workstation (DAW)** and are looking to make the switch to the wonderful world of Ableton Live. Perhaps you are planning to dive into performing your music and you heard that Live is a popular choice among established live performers. Either way, you are in the right place!

The Live 11 update has definitely brought some amazing workflow improvements as well as some new devices to spike the community of users' creativity.

In this book, we will be using the Live 11 Suite version, although there are other, more limited, versions available (Lite, Intro, and Standard). I will guide you through some best practices, tips, and tricks to show you how you can get the most out of the software to create the music you always wanted.

In this chapter, we will take a quick tour of Live 11. This should provide a refresher or an introduction to the interface so you can have a more comfortable music-making journey.

By the end of this chapter, you will know how to set up Live, have developed an understanding of Live's linear and non-linear workflows, and understand how to save your projects, export your tracks, and work with Templates.

This will be important in order to find all the tools you need and develop a convenient and fast workflow that enables your creativity to flow.

We are going to cover the following topics in this chapter:

- Introduction to Live concepts
- The preferences
- A tour of the interface
- Session View versus Arrangement View
- Exporting audio, saving a project, and templates

Technical requirements

In order to follow along with this chapter, you will need the following:

- A computer with at least 8 GB of RAM and at least an Intel Core i5 processor
- A pair of headphones
- A copy of Live 11 Suite
- **Chapter 1** Ableton Live project

Don't own Live 11 Suite? You can download a fully functioning trial version from the Ableton website: `https://www.ableton.com/en/trial/`.

Introduction to Live concepts

Live originally started out as a *loop arranger (or loop sequencer)* before it became a fully realized DAW, and became popular upon its release in 2001.

Its unique approach to music-making can be a little intimidating to those coming from a traditional DAW background, especially when you first open the software. Sometimes, you might need to change your thinking and approach to producing music in this kind of environment; however, the workflow that you are about to embrace will definitely benefit your creativity in the long run.

Live is widely used among producers and performers due to its previously mentioned unique workflow. But what makes Live so unique? Well, I guess you already met Session View when you first opened up the program. This view will enable you to compose and perform your music in a non-linear environment (without a timeline) so you can just focus on your ideas and playing, in contrast to a grid-based timeline's linear approach.

The time will come when you will need to lay down your ideas in a traditional linear way to form your final arrangement, but that's why there is the other view – Arrangement View.

Furthermore, there is now **MIDI Polyphonic Expression** (**MPE**) support in Live 11, and we will also discover the amazing world of Racks (which will enable you to create complex and layered instruments, as well as providing you with track-based parallel effect processing, macro controls, and more), which can benefit both production and performance workflows.

Live also offers a bunch of tools to humanize your music (by adding further movement to sequences and fluctuation to values), generate ideas quicker, and even help you out with some areas that might not be your strongest suit, such as music theory.

You can carry out the entire production process in Live, from laying down your first initial ideas to forming your arrangement and doing your final mixdown.

Of course, you will not have to stop there. Once you are finished with your tracks, you can use Live to take them to the stage or design a set specifically for a live performance.

Let's have a look at how to set up Live's preferences in the best possible way to suit your workflow. To follow along in this chapter, you can use the **Chapter 1** Ableton Live project. You can also access the same project from within Ableton Live itself:

1. Navigate to **Help | Help View**
2. Click on **What's New in Live 11** on the right side of the screen in the Help View.
3. Click on **Live Set** within the first paragraph of text in the Help View.

Live will automatically open up the demo project.

Setting up the preferences

In the preferences, you can set up how Live operates on its own or with external devices that you connect to the computer.

The first thing that we will have to set up is the audio preferences:

1. Navigate to **Live | Preferences...** (**Options | Preferences...** on Windows) or use the key command, *Cmd + ,* (*Ctrl + ,* for Windows).
2. Click on the **Audio** tab.

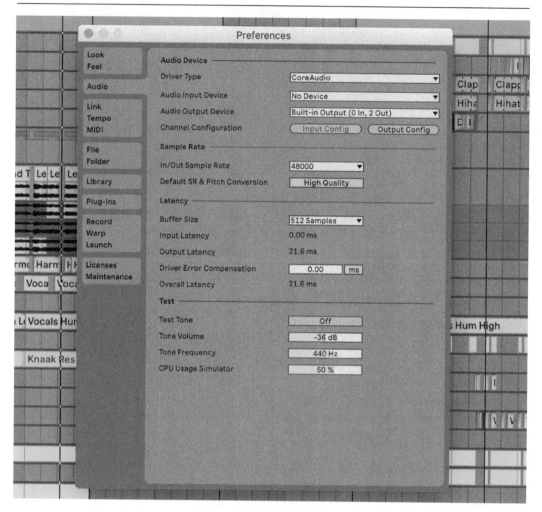

Figure 1.1 – Audio preferences

3. For **Audio Output Device,** you should choose the device that you want to use to play sound through. This could be external headphones, your audio interface, or your computer's built-in output.

4. You can define the **Sample Rate** that you'd like to use (generally, for music, 44.1 kHz is fine. If you are working on audio for a motion picture or other multimedia, then choose 48 kHz, but this would be in your project brief anyway). We will revisit the sample rate in *Chapter 2, Recording Audio in Ableton Live 11.*

5. **Buffer Size** is related to latency. The lower the buffer size, the more pressure you are putting on the CPU, so the sooner you will experience audio dropouts. However, the higher the buffer size, the more latency you are introducing. For now, we can set the buffer size to **256 Samples**. We will come back to this again in *Chapter 2, Recording Audio in Ableton Live 11.*

You should now be set to hear sounds in Live.

Let's just briefly look at what you can set in the other tabs within **Preferences**; however, don't worry too much about remembering what these do as we will keep on coming back to **Preferences** throughout this book:

- **Look Feel**: You can set up different and customize functions such as playback head behavior, display zoom, track and clip color assignments, and change the theme of the software interface.

- **Link Tempo MIDI**: You can set up Ableton Link and Tempo Follower here. You can also find the MIDI preferences here.

- **File Folder**: Here, you will find file management functions related to things such as analysis files, the temporary audio recordings folder, and cache.

- **Library**: You can set browser behavior and library content locations here, both for Packs and User Library.

> **What are Packs?**
>
> Packs are curated content libraries, which can be one-shot samples, device presets, or loops. You can find many of them to purchase on the Ableton website. Alternatively, the ones that are part of Live Suite will show up in your browser to be downloaded directly from there.

- **Plug-Ins**: This is the place where you can manage your third-party plugins' behavior and location.

  If your third-party plugins are not showing up, you should check whether their folder is set properly here and then rescan them.

- **Record Warp Launch**: Under this tab, you can set up functions such as the recorded file type, the bit depth, count-in, **Exclusive Arm and Solo** (this function will define whether you are able to arm or solo multiple tracks at the same time. If you set them to **Exclusive**, you can still solo and arm multiple tracks while holding down the *Cmd* (*Ctrl* for Windows) key), how session automation is being recorded, warping behavior, fades, launch modes, and global quantize.

- **Licenses Maintenance**: Here, you can authorize Live, set automatic software updates, and send usage data.

Now that the preferences have been covered, we can take a look at the different elements of the interface so you will be able to navigate Live quickly.

Tour of the interface

Let's begin to take a tour of Live!

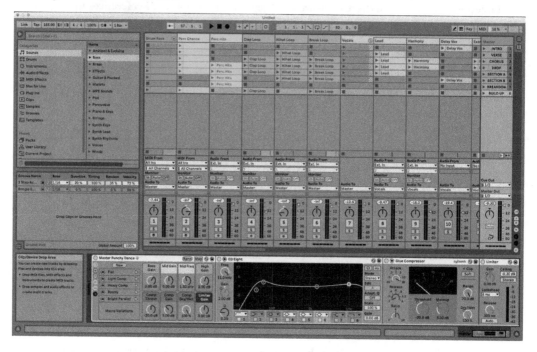

Figure 1.2 – Session View accessible by the Tab key

We are going to go through all the crucial parts of the interface, and in the next section, we will conclude with how Session View and Arrangement View operate in this **parallel workflow**.

But first, let's look at the parts of the interface that you can display regardless of whether you are working in Session View or Arrangement View.

The browser

In the browser, we can access all our samples, loops, synthesizers, samplers, audio and MIDI effects, as well as third-party plugins, grooves, Packs, templates, Max for Live devices, User Library content, project content, and custom collections of these.

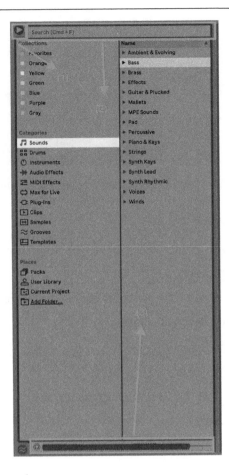

Figure 1.3 – The browser

This is where you are going to start your music-making. The unfold button (triangle) shown in *Figure 1.3(1)* shows and hides the browser.

Categories

There are two columns in the browser: the **browser sidebar** on the left and the **content panel**. When we click on something under **Categories**, it will expand the content of that category and show subfolders in the content panel.

For example, if you click on the **Instruments** category, Live will show you all the available instrument devices you can use. Furthermore, each of these devices will have a small triangle next to them, which will further expand the instrument types and presets (*Figure 1.4*).

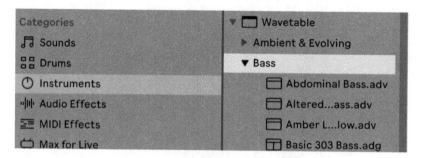

Figure 1.4 – Bass presets of the Wavetable instrument

Let's briefly cover the different categories:

- **Sounds**: Instrument presets, categorized by sound type rather than instrument type
- **Drums**: Drum presets/drum racks
- **Instruments**: Instrument devices and presets, categorized by instrument type
- **Audio Effects**: Audio effect devices and presets
- **MIDI Effects**: MIDI effect devices and presets
- **Max for Live**: Max for Live devices and presets
- **Plug-Ins**: Third-party AU/VST/VST3 instruments and effects
- **Clips**: Clips installed in Live
- **Samples**: Audio files
- **Grooves**: Live's grooves
- **Templates**: Different project templates

Places

Now that we've looked at the categories, let's go through what we can find under **Places**:

- **Packs**: Library content and installed content of Live which we looked at under *Preferences* already.
- **User Library**: Your own content. Your personal, saved presets of devices and effects, for example, will be found here.
- **Current Project**: You can access here all the files that are part of the currently active project that you are working on and open them.

- **Add Folder…:** Here, you can add custom folders to Live's browser. For example, if you have a personal samples folder on your computer, you can simply add it so that those external files will be part of your browser and you can take advantage of the **Preview** function (*Figure 1.3(3)*).

  Preview will enable you to hear the selected media in the browser before loading it into your session. You can activate it with the small headphone button on the left of the waveform display (*Figure 1.3(3)*). You can preview the media in real time or synced with the current tempo of the project. The preview can also be routed to a separate output, so if you are looking for a sample, loop, or instrument preset in the browser when playing live, it will not interrupt the music playing through your main output.

Collections

Collections allows us to organize any media within the browser into custom-made folders, so if you are working on a project that requires you to use the same device, preset, or sample over and over again, it's a good idea to tag those items into a collection folder.

You can simply navigate to the item, *Ctrl* + click (right-click for Windows), and choose the appropriate collection folder from the drop-down menu (*Figure 1.5*).

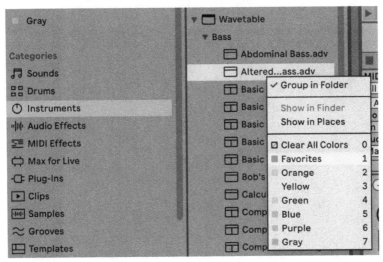

Figure 1.5 – Choosing a collection folder

You can also rename a collection folder by *Ctrl* + click (right-click for Windows) on it or selecting the folder and hitting *Cmd + R/Ctrl + R* (*Figure 1.6*):

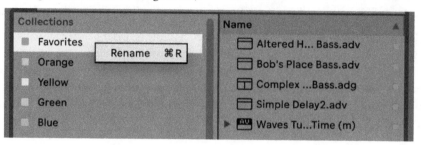

Figure 1.6 – Renaming a collection folder

In order to speed up the browsing process, we can also use the **Search** field in the browser (*Figure 1.3(2)*).

We can type in bass, for example, and it will show us everything in the browser with this keyword within the selected category.

If we would like to browse in all the categories at the same time, then we can select **All results**, or press *Cmd+F* (*Ctrl + F* for Windows) (*Figure 1.7*).

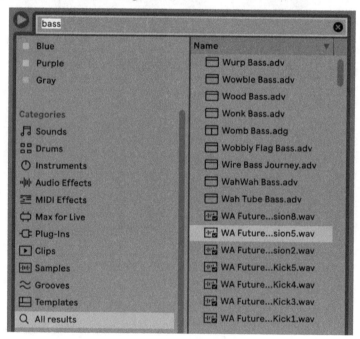

Figure 1.7 – Searching for bass in the browser

Now that we have gone through the browser, let's have a look at the other areas of the interface…

Figure 1.8 – The interface

Groove Pool

The Groove Pool (*Figure 1.8(1)*) allows you to add a more humanized feel (additional movement and fluctuation of values) to your clips by using grooves. Live comes with a rather large number of grooves, which you can either drop into the Groove Pool from the browser and then later add to your clips, or drop the Grooves straight onto a clip. They will appear in the Groove Pool, where you can adjust the parameters. More on this in *Chapter 5, MIDI Editing and MIDI Effects*.

Help View

Now, this is a quite crucial area if you are only beginning your journey in Live.

The Help View (*Figure 1.8(2)*) explains the functionality of each parameter in Live. You simply need to hover your mouse over the parameter and the Help View will display the appropriate information regarding the chosen parameter.

I strongly suggest displaying the Help View, as even for a seasoned Live user, it can be useful when the time comes to provide a little reminder of some functionalities.

You can hide and show the Help View by simply clicking on the small triangle button underneath the Help View box.

Clip View/Device View

This area (*Figure 1.8(3)*) will display either the device chain on the chosen track or the Clip View, which will be either the sample editor or the MIDI editor, depending on the chosen track's type.

You can simply double-click on the track head to display the Device View or double-click on the audio or MIDI clip to display the Clip View. Additionally, you could use the **Clip View selector** or **Device View selector**, as shown in *Figure 1.9*.

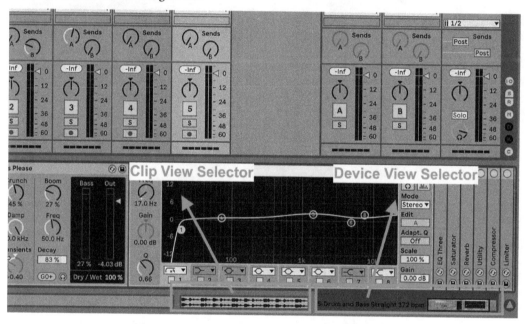

Figure 1.9 – Clip View Selector and Device View Selector

Control Bar

In the Control Bar, you can find the transport controls (*Figure 1.8(4)*). This area holds crucial functions, such as start playback, stop, and record, in both Session View and Arrangement View. Additionally, you can set the tempo here and switch on and off the metronome, among other functions.

Let's quickly have a look at these:

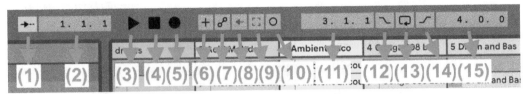

Figure 1.10 – Control Bar and transport controls

- The **Follow** button will make the screen scroll along with the position of the playback head to always display the current play position of the song (*Figure 1.10(1)*).

- **Arrangement Position** will display the current position of the playback head in the arrangement (*Figure 1.10(2)*).

- The **Play** button (*Figure 1.10(3)*).

- The **Stop** button (*Figure 1.10(4)*).

- The **Arrangement Record** button, when pressed, records clips in Arrangement View. There's more on this in *Chapter 2, Recording Audio in Ableton Live 11, Chapter 4, Exploring MIDI Sequencing Techniques,* and *Chapter 10, Utilizing Arrangement and Organization Techniques in our Ableton Live project (Figure 1.10(5))*.

- When the **MIDI Arrangement Overdub** button is enabled, recording MIDI over an already existing MIDI clip will add the new notes to the clip, not overwrite them. There's more on this in *Chapter 4, Exploring MIDI Sequencing Techniques (Figure 1.10(6))*.

- When the **Automation Arm** button is enabled, manual parameter changes will be recorded to the clips in Session View and Arrangement View. There's more on this in *Chapter 11, Implementing Automation and Modulation (Figure 1.10(7))*.

- The **Re-enable Automation** button will re-enable manually overridden inactive automation. There's more on this in *Chapter 11, Implementing Automation and Modulation (Figure 1.10(8))*.

- The **Capture** button pre-records MIDI and "captures" the notes you just played, even if you didn't hit the record button. There's more on this in *Chapter 4, Exploring MIDI Sequencing Techniques (Figure 1.10(9))*.

- The **Session Record** button enables you to record (and overdub MIDI) audio and MIDI clips in Session View (*Figure 1.10(10)*).

- **Loop Start/Punch in Point** in Arrangement View displays the start of the Arrangement loop or Punch recording. More on this in *Chapter 2, Recording Audio in Ableton Live 11 (Figure 1.10(11))*.

- **Punch-In Switch** in Arrangement View will prevent Live recording anything prior to the punch in point. There's more on this in *Chapter 2, Recording Audio in Ableton Live 11 (Figure 1.10(12))*.

- **Loop Switch** in Arrangement View activates the Arrangement loop. There's more on this in *Chapter 2, Recording Audio in Ableton Live 11 (Figure 1.10(13))*.

- **Punch-Out Switch** in Arrangement View will prevent Live recording anything after the punch out point. There's more on this in *Chapter 2, Recording Audio in Ableton Live 11 (Figure 1.10(14))*

- **Loop/Punch-In Region Length** in Arrangement View displays the length of the Arrangement loop or punch-region. More on this in *Chapter 2, Recording Audio in Ableton Live 11 (Figure 1.10(15))*.

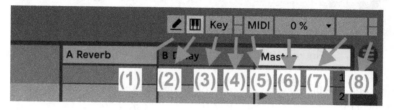

Figure 1.11 – Control Bar

- **Draw Mode Switch** is useful for drawing in MIDI notes as well as envelopes for automation and modulation. This can be also turned on and off by pressing the **B** button (*Figure 1.11(1)*).

- **Computer MIDI Keyboard** enables you to use your computer keys to input MIDI notes (*Figure 1.11(2)*).

- **Key Map Mode Switch** enables you to map Live's parameters to your computer keys (*Figure 1.11(3)*).

- **Key/MIDI In and Out Indicators** will flash when Live is sending or receiving MIDI messages belonging to remote control assignments made in Key and MIDI Map Modes. There's more on this in *Chapter 14, Exploring MIDI Mapping, External Instruments, and MIDI CCs (Figure 1.11(4))*.

- **MIDI Map Mode Switch**, when turned on, enables you to carry out MIDI mapping. There's more on this in *Chapter 14, Exploring MIDI Mapping, External Instruments, and MIDI CCs (Figure 1.11(5))*.

- **CPU Load Meter** can be seen in *Figure 1.11(6)*. Clicking on the small arrow will give you additional options, such as switching the CPU load meter between **Average** and **Current** and configuring your audio preferences (*Figure 1.12*).

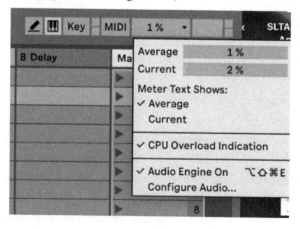

Figure 1.12 – CPU Load Meter

- **Overload Indicator**: This lights up when the CPU is overloaded because Live was not able to load audio fast enough. When this happens you will experience audio dropouts. It might be because your computer is not powerful enough to handle all the audio processing you are trying to do, or you need to increase your buffer size because it is currently set too low (*Figure 1.11(7)*).

- **MIDI Track In Indicator/MIDI Track Out Indicator**: These will flash when Live's tracks are receiving or sending out MIDI messages (*Figure 1.11(8)*).

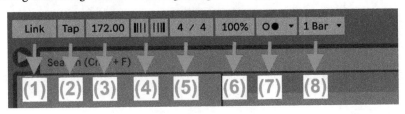

Figure 1.13 – Control Bar

- The **Link** On/Off switch triggers Ableton Link on and off. There's more on this in *Chapter 15, Playing Live (Figure 1.13(1))*.

- **Tap Tempo** is where you can set the tempo, by tapping this button. Live's playback will follow the tempo of your tapping (*Figure 1.13(2)*).

- **Tempo** is where you can manually type in the tempo for your project (*Figure 1.13(3)*).

- **Phase Nudge Down/Up** can be useful when you are trying to synchronize Live to a source that isn't locked to one tempo, to temporarily increase or decrease the tempo of Live (*Figure 1.13(4)*).

- **Time signature Numerators** will allow you to type in the time signature of your song (*Figure 1.13(5)*).

- **Global Groove Amount** defines the global intensity of all grooves in the Groove Pool (*Figure 1.13(6)*).

- *Figure 1.13(7)* shows **Metronome** and **Metronome Settings**. Here, you can enable and disable the metronome. By clicking on the small arrow, you can also enable **count-in** and apply further settings to the metronome, such as sound and rhythm.

- *Figure 1.13(8)* shows **Quantization Menu**. This is the magical function that keeps everything in time in your session. Global Quantize controls the global launching behavior of Live. We will be looking at this in more detail a bit later in this chapter.

So, now that we have had our first proper tour of Live, we can continue to have a look at Session View and Arrangement View. This is super important in order to take full advantage of the creative workflow that Live has to offer.

Session View versus Arrangement View

The time has come; we can begin to discover the magic of the non-linear Session View, the linear Arrangement View (*Figure 1.14*), and their relationship in Live.

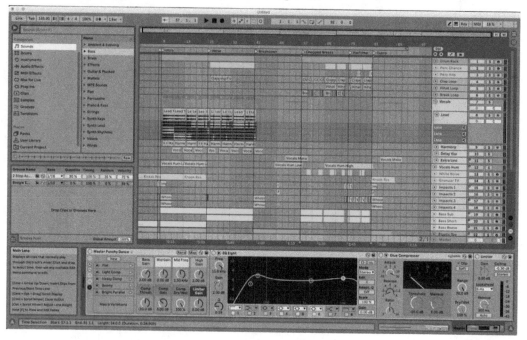

Figure 1.14 – Arrangement View

Session View

Let's quickly take a tour of **Session View**!

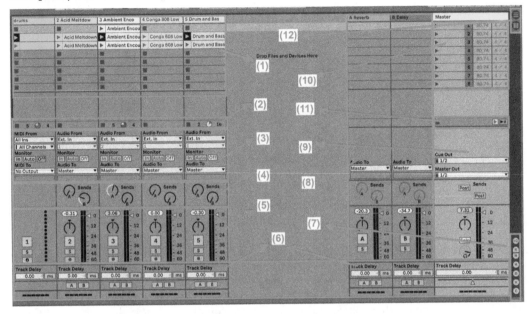

Figure 1.15 – Session View

Track Title Bar and clip slots

In *Figure 1.15*, for example, under the **Ambient Enco** track, there are three clips that belong to the track and will play back **Ambient Enco**. These clips can be triggered by the small launch button with the play symbol on it. Each track can have one clip triggered at a time. So, for instance, if you'd like the **Ambient Enco** track to play two different clips at the same time, you would have to duplicate the track so the two clips are placed on two different tracks. How the clips will be launched timing-wise will be defined by the **Global Quantize** settings. If **Global Quantize** is set to **1 Bar**, as in *Figure 1.16*, then Live will always wait for the next bar before it triggers the clip and plays it back.

This way, you can't fall out of time and clips will stay in sync within Session View.

Figure 1.16 – Global Quantize is set to 1 Bar

Each clip slot without a clip has a small square symbol instead of the launch (play) button. These squares are small "stop" buttons, so when you press on one of them, the clip that is currently playing on that track will stop. The timing of the clip-stopping during playback will also be defined by the global quantize settings, so even this will happen "on time."

Give this a try:

1. Go to the browser and navigate to **Samples**.
2. Type drum into the search bar and find a drum loop.
3. Preview a few loops until you find something decent.
4. Drag and drop a drum loop from the browser to an empty clip slot on an empty audio track.
5. Make sure the **Global Quantize** setting is set to **1 Bar**.
6. Now, launch the clip with the launch button on the clip slot.
7. Once you have heard it play through, at any time, press on the stop button underneath an empty clip slot.

You should hear that the loop playback stopping is synced to your tempo at the next bar.

Clip Stop button and Track Status Display

Here, you will also find another Clip Stop button, which if you press will stop the playback of the currently triggered clip of the track (*Figure 1.15(2)*). Now, if you're wondering why we need multiple stop buttons, well, just imagine a simple scenario. What if there are no more empty clip slots displayed in Session View? You might still need to stop the playback on that track. So, you can use this Clip Stop button, which is always displayed and available.

The Track Status Display will show you the status of your currently triggered clip.

This is super useful as you will be able to see when the clip that you triggered is about to end so you can trigger the next clip at the right time.

In and Out section

This is where you can route your inputs and outputs for both MIDI and audio on the tracks (*Figure 1.15(3)*). This is also where you can set up input monitoring. There's more on this in *Chapter 2, Recording Audio in Ableton Live 11*.

Sends section

You can use this section to send the signal to a return track for parallel processing. We will come back to this in later chapters of this book (*Figure 1.15(4)*).

Mixer section

Here, you will find the Track Volume Fader, the Meter, Track Pan, the Track Activator (which you might know as "mute"), the Solo button, and the Arm (record enable) button (*Figure 1.15(5)*).

Track Delay, Crossfade Assign, and CPU Load Meter

Track Delay (*Figure 1.15(6)*) allows you to pre-delay or delay the track output.

With Crossfade Assign, you You could actually set up Live for Djing, mimicking two decks. You could have one track that you assign as Deck A and another track that you assign as Deck B. The crossfade setting to transition between the two "decks" can be found in the same section but on the Master track. If the track isn't assigned to any "decks," the crossfade has no effect.

CPU Load Meter allows you to display how much CPU an individual track is consuming. This is super useful when you start experiencing audio dropouts due to CPU overload as you can easily find which track is contributing most to the dropouts and deal with it.

Hide Show section

You can customize what you are displaying by hiding some of the previously listed controls (*Figure 1.15. (7)*). You can hide and show the I/O, sends, returns, the mixer, Track Delay, crossfade, and track CPU metering.

Return Tracks

You can have up to 16 Return Tracks in Live Suite (*Figure 1.15(8)*). When you create a new Return Track, the corresponding Send will be created on the tracks. This is a concept that you might come across in other DAWs, Return Tracks popularly being called as AUXes and the Sends "Buses."

I/O on the Master track

Let's look at *Figure 1.15(9)*. I wanted to talk about this separately so we can discuss the Cue. Again, this is something that can be extremely useful for performing. We will come back to this when we look at live performances later in this book, but since you use the Cue to control the output of the browser's **Preview** function, it is important to know about it. You can route out the Master to, for example, your speakers, which are your main outputs, but you can also route out the Cue to a separate pair of outputs. Besides the **Preview** of the browser, you can decide whether you want to hear other tracks in the Cue too. Once you have sorted the routing, then you can click on the Cue button. This will turn the Solo buttons on the tracks into little headphone buttons, which will send the tracks into the Cue when you select them. You can then switch it back to Solo when you want to. See *Figure 1.17*. We will come back to Cue again in *Chapter 15, Playing Live*.

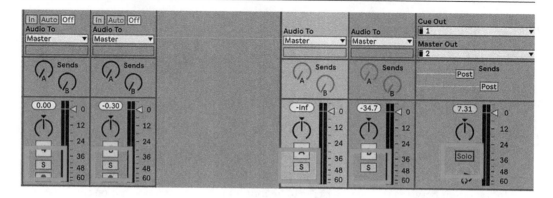

Figure 1.17 – Cue and Solo buttons

Scenes, Scene Tempo, and Scene Time Signature

Let's look at *Figure 1.15(10)*. Scenes represent a selection of clips across all the tracks. Take a look at *Figure 1.18*.

Figure 1.18 – Scene

You will see that we have three different scenes. The first one was renamed **Intro** (you can right-click (*Ctrl* + click for Windows) on a Scene and choose the **Rename** option, or select the Scene and press (*Cmd* + *R* (*Ctrl* + *R* for Windows) and type in the name) and it only has one clip to play back on the **Ambient Enco** track. The next Scene, named **Intro pt2**, has three different clips across three different tracks to be played back, and the **Verse** Scene has even more. When you press the **Launch** button on the Scene, it will launch all the clips that are part of that Scene. This is how you will be able to progress your ideas into some sort of structure before moving to Arrangement View. Or you can structure a live performance where you will be launching clips, scenes to have a little jam session.

But how do we create these Scenes?

Well, you can use a simple copy-paste technique to insert the clips into the clip slots to form scenes, or you can do the following. If you have clips in Session View that you you have launched and you would like to form a Scene out of these triggered clips you can simply Ctrl + click (right-click for Windows) on the last engaged Scene and chose **Capture and Insert Scene** from the contextual menu (Figure 1.19):

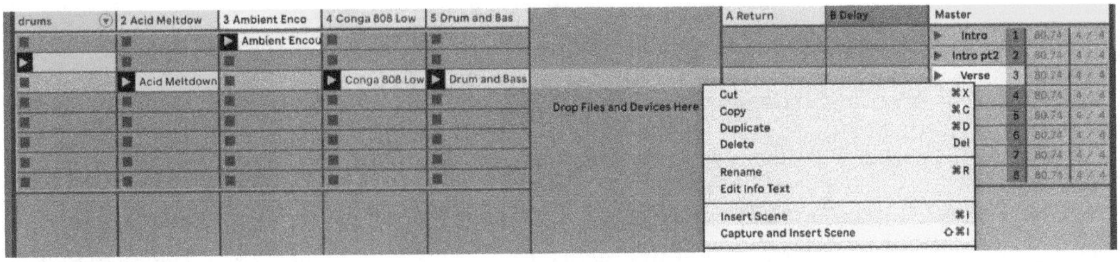

Figure 1.19 – Capture and Insert Scene

This will form a brand-new Scene, including all the clips that were launched across multiple Scenes (*Figure 1.20*).

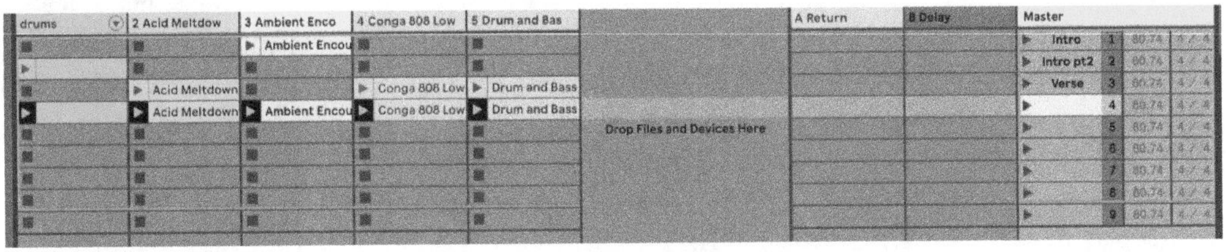

Figure 1.20 – Brand-new Scene formed after selecting the Capture and Insert Scene option

You can always copy and paste or duplicate previous Scenes (see from the contextual menu in *Figure 1.19*) in order to add a new clip from an additional track to the copied or duplicated Scene to progress your ideas/track.

We will be working in Session View quite a bit throughout this book, so you will get to understand the full potential of this workflow!

Scenes can represent a part of your track, but when you are preparing a Set for a live performance, sometimes a Scene will represent full tracks. For example, *Scene 1* will hold all the elements of *Track 1*, and *Scene 2* will hold all the elements of *Track 2*. The two tracks you are performing might have totally different tempos. Obviously, you wouldn't want to spend time on stage typing in the tempo of the next Scene/track. You would essentially want the Scene to switch to the appropriate tempo for the track when you trigger it. This is exactly why there is the option to enter the tempo separately for each Scene. This works the same for time signature changes too; each Scene can have its own Scene Time Signature.

Even in production, sometimes you might want to switch things up with a cheeky tempo change, such as dropping to half-time after the breakdown and then going back to the original tempo in the next section, or having a lovely middle-8 with a time signature change. Being able to change the tempo for each Scene will enable you to do these kinds of things.

Stop All Clips, Enable Follow Actions Globally, and Back to Arrangement

Let's have a look at what functions we can access on *Figure 1.15(11)*.

The **Stop All Clips** button will globally stop playing back all clips in Session View.

The **Enable Follow Action Globally** button allows you to enable Follow Action. Follow Action is a rather large topic. We will be looking at it in *Chapter 13, Exploring Tempo Follower, Follow Action, Max for Live, Working with Video, and Ableton Note*.

We then have the **Back to Arrangement** button. This is the right time to start talking about Arrangement View. A pretty standard workflow can be that you start laying down your ideas in Session View's non-linear loop-based environment, where you can focus on playing live and quickly capturing your idea without worrying abot the timeline.. But eventually, you will want to move into Arrangement View to form a full arrangement in a linear environment where you can just press play at the beginning of the track and it will play through from left to right. The Arrangement View is also where you would do your micro-edits and add additional ear candy. Once you've done that, move your clips to Arrangement View; the original clips you started out with will still remain in Session View too. When any clips in Session View are triggered, the Back to Arrangement button will light up to indicate that you aren't playing back your arrangement in Arrangement View (*Figure 1.21*). If you press this orange button, Live will only play back whatever is supposed to be playing in Arrangement View. So, you can only play back a given track in either Arrangement View or Session View; otherwise, you would have some serious chaos.

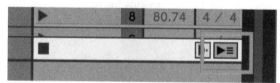

Figure 1.21 – Back to Arrangement button

If you don't know already, I am sure you are dying to know how to get the clips and Scenes from Session View into Arrangement View. Hold your horses; we will get to that a little later!

Arrangement View and Session View selectors

Let's have a look at the preceding functions shown in *Figure 1.15(12)*.

So, you have probably figured out by now that the Ableton logo is actually made out of the symbols of Session View and Arrangement View. Pretty amazing, eh?

If you press one of these buttons (in the top-right corner of the screen below the CPU Load Meter), it will switch between the two views. There is another, perhaps more convenient, way to toggle between the views, by simply pressing the *Tab* key on your computer keyboard.

So, let's click the Arrangement View selector and take a look at **Arrangement View** (*Figure 1.22*)!

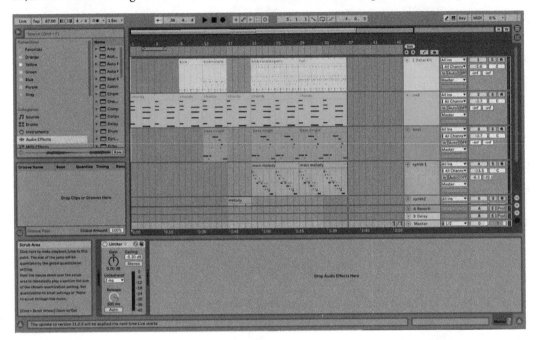

Figure 1.22 – Arrangement View

Now, I want you to look at *Figure 1.22* and *Figure 1.23*. Hopefully, you have clocked that the tracks are the same in both views, just in a non-linear manner and a linear manner. The elements of this track were composed in Session View and then the Scenes were transferred into Arrangement View, where the idea can be further developed.

Figure 1.23 – Session View

You can get your clips and Scenes into Arrangement View from Session View by either simply copy-pasting them or actually recording them in real time into Arrangement View by pressing the **Arrangement Record** button in the Control Bar and launching the Scenes or clips. You are basically jamming out your arrangement and capturing it in real time (*Figure 1.24*)!

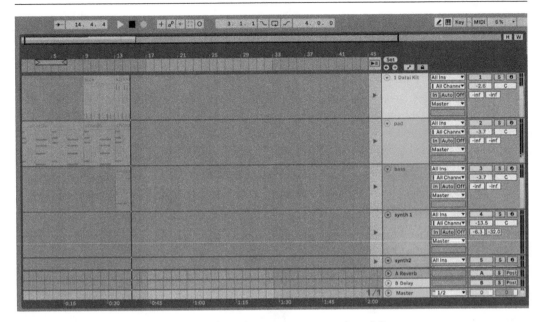

Figure 1.24 – Capturing an arrangement in real time

This is something that we are going to cover in depth in *Chapter 10, Utilizing Arrangement and Organization Techniques in Our Ableton Live Project.*

Arrangement View

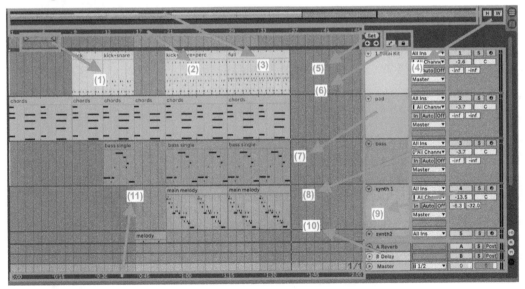

Figure 1.25 – Arrangement View

For now, we are going to quickly explore the controls in Arrangement View.

- *Figure 1.25(1)* shows **Loop/Punch-Recording Region**. You can drag left and right to extend this selection.

- *Figure 1.25(2)* shows **Beat-Time Ruler**. If you hover your mouse over this area and start dragging up and down, it will allow you to zoom in and out. Alternatively, if you click into the clip area, you can use the - and + symbols to zoom in and out. You can also move your mouse left and right over this area in order to scroll over the timeline.

- *Figure 1.25(3)* shows **Clip Overview/Zooming Hot-Spot**. You can resize this view by dragging the view's edge up and down, just like the majority of the areas in Live. This view will give you an overview of the clips in your timeline.

- *Figure 1.25(4)* shows **Optimize Arrangement Height** and **Width**. If you click on these, the tracks' height and width will be optimized so they can fit into Arrangement View.

- *Figure 1.25(5)* shows **Set/Delete Locator**, **Previous**, and **Next Locator**. These buttons will allow you to create and delete locators to organize your arrangement's structure, and also navigate between them.

- *Figure 1.25(6)* shows **Automation Mode** and **Lock Envelopes**. These switches will enable you to display the automation lanes for all tracks or the track content, as well as be able to copy clips without or with their automation.

- *Figure 1.25(7)* shows **Track Name**.

- *Figure 1.25(8)* shows **In/Out Section**. This is the same as in Session View; here is where you can perform signal routing and choose monitoring options.

- *Figure 1.25(9)* shows **Mixer Section**. Again, the same as in Session View, the only difference being the design of the parameter controls. Instead of a pan pot, fader, and send pots, you can see sliders here, but they control the same parameters.

- *Figure 1.25(10)* shows **Return Tracks** and **Master**. Once again, they are the same tracks that you see in Session View, but they will always be placed at the bottom of the screen permanently.

- *Figure 1.25(11)* shows **Time Ruler**.

Of course, there will be times when you go straight to Arrangement View to start a project and do not use Session View. In this case, just like in Session View, you can drag and drop media from the browser to the appropriate track, but this time not to a clip slot but into the timeline.

Now, you should feel more comfortable with Live 11's interface. In the next section, we are going to look at how we can export audio out of Live, save our work, and use templates before we can dive in and start making music.

Getting your work out

This section is super important in order to speed up your workflow with templates, to save your project properly so you never lose any files, and, of course, to export your track so it can see the light of day.

Exporting audio

In order to export your audio from Live's Arrangement View, take the following steps:

1. Select the desired portion of audio (perhaps the whole track). Make sure if it is the whole track that you leave some extra space at the end for any time-based effect tail (such as reverb and delay).

2. Then, you can either go to **File | Export Audio/Video...** or use the *Cmd + Shift + R* (*Ctrl + Shift + R* for Windows) key command to bring up the **Export Audio/Video** window (*Figure 1.26*).

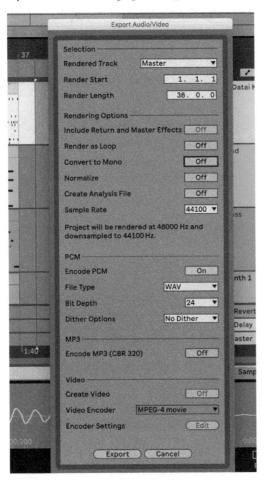

Figure 1.26 – Export Audio/Video window

3. Under the **Selection** section, the first option you can set is **Rendered Track**. Here, if you'd like to render your whole track, then you'd select **Master**.

4. Make sure that **Render Start** and **Render Length** match your desired selection, and that you don't have any clips selected in **Track Display**. You can also choose to render any of your Return Tracks, a single track of your project, only selected tracks, or all individual tracks, which allows you to export stems.

5. You will also find additional rendering options, such as **Include Return and Master Effects**, which you can select when you are rendering single, selected, or all individual tracks. You can also enable **Convert to Mono**. If you are looking to export something as a mono signal, you have control over creating an analysis file with the export, changing the sample rate, rendering as a loop, and normalizing.

6. In this window, you can also choose your desired file type, change the bit depth, and set **Dither Options** if you need to. You can also export an additional MP3 file at the same time.

    Live can be used to edit audio for videos, and can actually host video in the timeline. Therefore, you have options for exporting your video work from here too.

7. Once you are happy with your settings, just hit the **Export** button and sit back while the magic happens.

It's always a good practice to check your exported audio by playing it back, to make sure everything is included that you want to export, because an accidental timeline selection or a muted or soloed track can mess up your exporting.

Saving your work

When you start working in Live, you create a Set, which is an `.als` file. This file can be found inside the **Project** folder (*Figure 1.27*).

Figure 1.27 – Project folder

This will include other crucial media related to your Set (*Figure 1.28*) or multiple Sets in the Project folder.

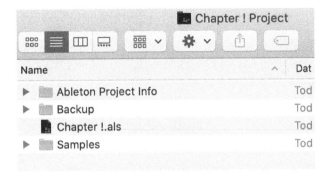

Figure 1.28 – Crucial files in the Project folder

It is extremely important that when you are transferring your work to a USB stick, an external hard drive, or another computer, you move the Project folder, not the Set .als file. If you move the Set, you will end up with loads of offline/missing files. If that happens though, don't worry; we will cover what to do in *Chapter 17, Troubleshooting and File Management*. Your project folder will include, of course, the Set(s), the **Samples** folder (including imported, recorded, and processed files), the **Backup** folder, and the **Ableton Project Info** folder.

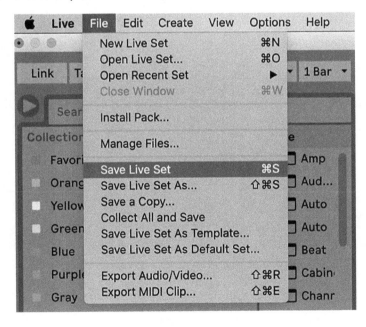

Figure 1.29 – Saving a Live Set

Let's investigate the saving options (*Figure 1.29*):

- **Save Live Set** allows you to save the Set to a location on your computer or portable drive. You can set the location, and a Project folder will be created. However, the samples you are using in your project will not be saved in the Project folder. So, if you move the project, or the folder that holds the samples that you are using in your Set, to a different computer, those files will be missing and will need to be relocated.

  Additionally, you can use this option to save minor changes you last made to your already existing project as long as that change didn't include bringing in any new media into the Set.

- **Save Live Set As...** allows you to save the current version of your Set to a new location or save it into the same **Project** folder under a different name, even if you are working on an already existing project. In doing so, you would have two different Sets within the same Project folder.

- **Save a Copy...** allows you to save a copy of your current Set.

- **Collect All and Save** is probably the most important saving option. This is the function that will allow you to save your Set and collect all the corresponding media with the Set into its Project folder. In order to avoid missing files, it is recommended to always use **Collect All and Save** when you finish your work for the day. It is especially important to do this before you try to move your work to portable data storage or send it to someone.

Upon clicking **Collect All and Save**, the following dialog box will appear (*Figure 1.30*):

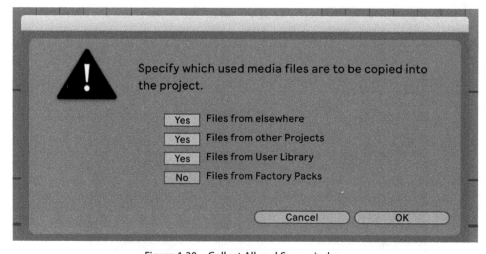

Figure 1.30 – Collect All and Save window

Here, you can select where exactly you'd like to collect the files from.

Saving your work might seem a very easy task but it is definitely something you should do properly to avoid lost work and disappointment. File management is a crucial part of any media work, regardless of whether you are a hobbyist or a professional.

Saving templates

Templates can really speed your workflow up for specific types of work!

If you are, for example, editing loads of voice-overs for videos or recording loads of vocals and you find yourself having to set up the same chain of devices on tracks for your session, that's when it's probably a good idea to save a template. You could have one for all your voice-over work and all your vocal recording work. When you open these templates, the saved data will automatically be loaded up, so you don't have to set up the same track count and devices over and over again.

If you look at *Figure 1.29*, you can see that you also have options to save templates.

Save Live Set As Template… will save your set into your User Library (*Figure 1.31*).

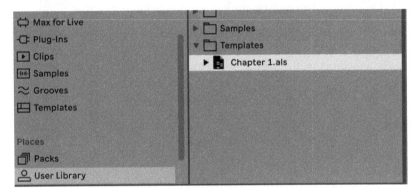

Figure 1.31 – Saved template in User Library

Ableton also provides some of its own templates that are already made for you, which you can find in your browser, under the **Templates** tab (*Figure 1.32*).

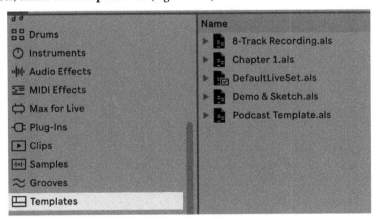

Figure 1.32 – Premade templates in the browser

Lastly, you can also select **Save Live Set As Default Set…**, which means every time you open Live, this Set will load up by default.

This is something that should you also consider doing if you find yourself always using the same devices on your Master track (of course, with different settings) or if you have a specific reverb device preference for your Return Track, so each time you sit down to produce, all of these settings will be automatically loaded for you.

Summary

This brings us to the end of *Chapter 1*. By now, you should be comfortable with finding your way around the Live interface, have a solid idea of the Live workflow, know how Session View and Arrangement View work, and know how to finish up your work by exporting and saving it.

In the next chapter, we are going to take a look at how we can record audio in both Session View and Arrangement View.

2

Recording Audio in Ableton Live 11

Recording audio is a crucial part of music production. We all know the importance of capturing the magic of musical performances, which could be vocals or any instruments being played by a human that will translate a lot of emotions and energy and add a lot to your track. However, there is more to it than just that.

We can also approach this with a more creative mindset and think about sampling old records, recording Foley sounds and working these into our music, or recording analog synthesizers.

It is crucial that the recorded material is captured appropriately and of great quality. Therefore, this chapter will be important for gaining an understanding of the technical aspects of recording in Live, as well as developing a seamless workflow.

By the end of this chapter, you will be able to set up Live to record audio. You will also develop an understanding of how to record in both **Session View** and **Arrangement View**.

Furthermore, the Live 11 update brought in the long-awaited function of Take Lanes in order to be able to create the perfect comp from the takes to provide a more fluid recording and editing workflow.

We are going to cover the following topics:

- Setting up for recording
- Routing and monitoring
- Recording audio in **Session View**
- Recording audio in **Arrangement View**
- Using Take Lanes

Technical requirements

In order to follow along with this chapter, you will need the following:

- A computer with at least 8 GB of RAM and an Intel Core i5 processor
- A pair of headphones
- A copy of Live 11 Suite
- An audio interface
- A microphone
- An instrument or your voice
- **Chapter 2** Ableton Live project

Setting up Live for recording

Let's head to where we need to start:

1. After opening Live, navigate to **Live | Preferences (Options | Preferences** on Windows)or use the *Cmd +* , (*Ctrl +* , for Windows) shortcut.

2. Choose the **Audio** tab:

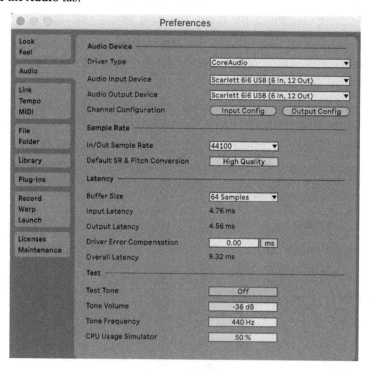

Figure 2.1 – The Audio tab in Preferences

Now, you should see the audio preferences (see *Figure 2.1*):

- For **Audio Input Device**, you should choose where your microphone is connected to.

  This could be your audio interface where you plugged your microphone in with an XLR cable, or if you are recording an instrument, then your quarter-inch jack cable.

  If you are using a USB microphone, that will also show up here. Alternatively, if you don't have a microphone, you can use your computer's built-in microphone.

- For **Output Device**, you should choose where your headphones are connected to – again, this could be your audio interface or your computer's built-in output.

- **Input Config** and **Output Config** enable you to set up your **Channel Configurations**. Only the selected channels will be available in Live later to route through them. You should always disable the channels that you won't use to ease your CPU's workload.

- **Sample Rate** will define the range of frequencies captured in digital audio, meaning the number of samples captured in one second by your converter.

  Think of it this way: when you are, for example, singing, you are creating vibrations that you are trying to capture with your microphone and your audio interface (or converter). Your voice is an analog signal that you need to convert into digital in order to see the waveform of it in your **Digital Audio Workstation (DAW)**.

  However, the higher the sample rate and the more "snapshots" you are taking, the more space will be used on your computer. The current standard sample rate for music is 44.1 kHz, and audio for videos is 48 kHz. So, let's set it to 44.1 kHz.

- Now, we are going to move on and set the **Buffer Size** setting! This is extremely important to avoid latency, which can quickly turn our recording experience into a nightmare.

  The smaller the buffer size, the higher the CPU load, but also, the lower the input latency.

- The input latency will define the time between you saying a word into your microphone (or hitting a key or pad on your MIDI controller) and this incoming signal hitting your computer and you hearing it through your headphones while you are waiting for it.

  Without going into too much detail, just remember that when you are recording, you should have a low buffer size to decrease input latency, and when you are producing (using loads of software instruments, effects, or devices that need loads of processing power), you need to increase the **Buffer Size** setting in order to avoid audio dropouts, but this will increase input latency.

> **Note**
>
> Now, you might ask how you are supposed to record, for example, vocals after you finished producing the full backing track where you already need a high buffer size to be able to play it back without glitches.
>
> In this case, it is a common practice to export the backing tracks out as a stereo bounce and load it into a new empty session, and record on top of that. Once you are done, you can move the recorded audio into the full production session.

Let's set the buffer size to **64 Samples** for now while we are recording, and we will increase it later as we progress the track.

With that said, we can leave the audio preferences now, and start looking at the track I/O section.

Routing and monitoring

Let's head to the **Audio From** tab in **Session View** (see *Figure 2.2*):

Figure 2.2 – The Audio From section

Here, we can select where we would like to get the incoming signal from in order to record it. You can see the same in **Arrangement View** too (see *Figure 2.3*):

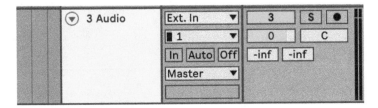

Figure 2.3 – The Audio From section in Arrangement View

To capture the signal of the device you have connected to your interface, we will select **Ext. In** (external in). Underneath, you will be able to select the channel into which you plugged your microphone or instrument, enabled in the preferences. So, if you are connecting to input channel 1 on your interface, then choose that in this tab.

For the **Audio To** section, we are going to leave it set to **Master** – however, this is the area where you can route the audio to a different track or to a different output of your audio interface if you need to.

Now, we are going to **arm** the track by clicking on the track record button (see *Figure 2.4*), which will enable the track record:

Figure 2.4 – Arming the track with the track record button

Make sure you add enough gain on your audio interface so that you will start seeing the incoming signal appearing on the meter in gray (see *Figure 2.4*). This means the signal is coming in, but we cannot hear it yet.

For that, we will set up our **Monitor** section, as it is currently set to **Off**.

Set **Monitor** to **Auto**, which will monitor the signal when the track is armed and stop monitoring when we play it back. If you set it to **In**, monitoring will be on during recording and playback as well.

Now, we can see the signal coming through the meter in green and we can also hear this incoming signal (see *Figure 2.5*):

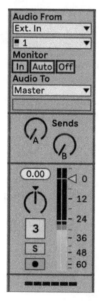

Figure 2.5 – Signal shown through the meter

> **Tip**
>
> Here is a tip for you for setting up the appropriate level of gain for the incoming signal on your interface. It is a well-known fact that you should avoid clipping at all costs – therefore, the meter should never turn red, indicating clipping and experiencing distortion.
>
> However, sometimes, you set up the gain while you are saying "check one two" into the microphone and set a nice, healthy level. Then, when you start recording, you still experience clipping.
>
> A good technique for setting the right level is to always play the loudest part of your song with your instrument or the loudest you will need to sing and set a healthy level for that part, so when you start quieter, for example, at the verse and then you get louder for your chorus, you have left enough headroom to play or sing comfortably without clipping.
>
> Setting your levels too low is also not a good idea, as that means you will have to increase the gain of the clip later and you will have loads of noise that you are bringing up with the additional volume boost.

Now that we have set this up, we are ready to begin recording!

Importing and recording audio in Session View

We have learned in the previous chapter about the non-linear workflow of **Session View**. First, we will have a look at how we can record audio in this environment to be able to focus more on playing and capturing ideas without worrying about any linear timelines.

Let's begin:

1. First, we are going to drop a drum loop into an empty Clip Slot on the first audio track so that we have some rhythm to record to (see *Figure 2.6*).

> **Importing audio into Live**
>
> You can drag and drop a loop into an empty Clip Slot from the **Samples** tab under **Categories** within the browser, where you can find all the samples from the Ableton Live Packs.
>
> Alternatively, if you have added a folder with your own sample collection (see *Chapter 1*) under **Places** within the browser, then you can browse within your own samples.
>
> Furthermore, if you type drums into the search bar and then hit *Cmd+F* (*Ctrl + F* for Windows), this will show you **All results** from across the whole browser.

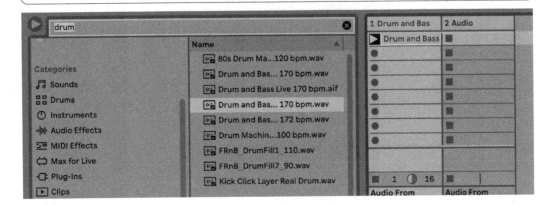

Figure 2.6 – Drum loop dropped into an empty clip slot

2.   After you have connected your microphone or instrument, choose the appropriate input, select **Auto** for the monitoring option, and arm the track (*see Figure 2.7*):

Figure 2.7 – The track is armed and an incoming signal is shown through the meter

3.   We can set up the metronome and count-in to support our recording workflow.

4. So, let's enable the metronome and select a **1 Bar** count-in (*see Figure 2.8*):

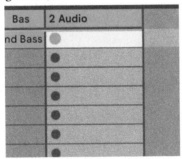

Figure 2.8 – Setting up a one-bar count-in

Now, we have two options for recording audio onto a clip slot.

1. We simply press the record button on the clip slot, which will trigger the count-in, and then the recording starts (see *Figure 2.9*):

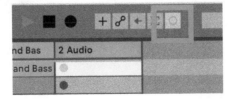

Figure 2.9 – The record button on the clip slot

We can stop the recording by pressing on the same record button on the clip slot, stop the playback using the stop button, or use the *spacebar* on your keyboard.

2. We can select the empty clip slot in which we would like to record and then press the **Session Record** button (see *Figure 2.10*):

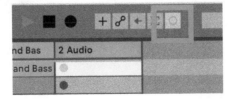

Figure 2.10 – The Session Record button

Again, we can stop the recording by pressing on the same **Session Record** button or stopping the playback.

> **Note**
>
> You will notice that the recording will start and stop in sync with your session tempo – this is due to the **Global Quantize** setting, which is set to **1 Bar** by default.
>
> As we discussed in the previous chapter, this will allow you to launch clips on time, as Live will always wait for the next bar to start playback if it is set to **1 Bar**. As you can see, this applies to recording as well (see *Figure 2.11*):

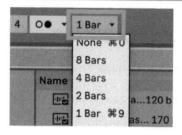

Figure 2.11 – Global Quantize settings

Now that we have looked at recording in **Session View**, let's have a look at how it is done in **Arrangement View**!

Importing and recording audio in Arrangement View

Let's open a new Live set by navigating to **File | New Live Set**.

A window will pop up asking you whether you'd like to keep temporary recording files (see *Figure 2.12*) – you should select **Delete**:

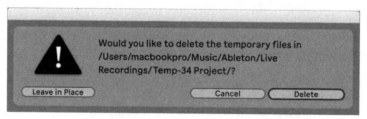

Figure 2.12 – Pop-up window

Once that is done, follow these steps:

1.   Now that we have an empty project open, let's hit the *Tab* key on the computer keyboard to switch to **Arrangement View**.

2.   Drag and drop a drum loop from the browser again to the first empty audio track.

3. Enable the metronome and one-bar count-in again.

4. Navigate to another empty audio track, set the appropriate input at the I/O section and the monitoring to **Auto**, and arm the track (see *Figure 2.13*):

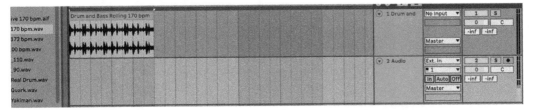

Figure 2.13 – I/O, monitoring, and track arming set up

5. Now, we are going to press the **Arrangement Record** button, and you will hear the count-in before the recording begins (see *Figure 2.14*):

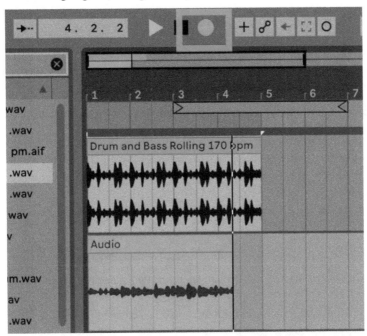

Figure 2.14 – The Arrangement Record button

Again, to stop the recording, you can either press the **Arrangement Record** button again and the playback will continue but the recording will stop, or you can stop the playback, which will also stop the recording.

You can change the behavior of the **Arrangement Record** button so that when you press it, the playback will not start automatically – you will manually have to press play.

To do this, just use the *Ctrl + click* (*right-click* for Windows) shortcut on the **Arrangement Record** button (see *Figure 2.15*):

Figure 2.15 – Changing the behavior of the Arrangement Record button

Recording with punch-in or punch-out

Punch recording can be useful to re-record parts of already recorded material without having to press the record button exactly where you want to start and stop recording, ensuring that you capture the beginning and the end of the section properly.

It is a fairly old recording technique, originating from the times when the recording was happening on a tape:

1. Punch-in and punch-out points can be used by either setting the loop brace or entering the values into the **Loop Star**, **Punch-in Point-Loop**, and **Punch-Region Length** settings on the control bar (see *Figure 2.16*):

Figure 2.16 – Loop Start, Punch-in Point-Loop, and Punch-Region Length settings

2. Next, the Punch-in and Punch-out buttons should be activated (see *Figure 2.17*):

Figure 2.17 – Punch-in and Punch-out buttons

The Punch-in and Punch-out buttons will prevent recording prior and after the punch-in and out points.

> **Important**
>
> The loop switch needs to be deactivated!
>
> Place your cursor and the playback head before the punch-in point for as long as you would like a "count-in" and begin recording.
>
> You can also punch yourself in and out manually if you wouldn't like to use the previously mentioned settings by beginning playback and manually switching the **Arrangement** button on and off. For this, it is practical to map the record button, for example, to a button or pad on your MIDI controller, so that you do not need to reach for your mouse and click (we will cover MIDI mapping in *Chapter 14, Exploring MIDI Mapping, External Instrument, and MIDI CCs*).

We have now covered the simple workflow of recording audio in Live's **Session View** and **Arrangement View**.

> **Tip**
>
> To avoid having loads of clips called **Audio 1, Audio 2**, and so on across multiple tracks, it is a good idea to rename the track first before starting to record, as the clip name will inherit the track's name.
>
> To rename a track, simply press *Ctrl + click* or *right-click* on the Track Title Bar and choose the **Rename** option, or hit *Cmd + R (Ctrl + R on Windows)* shortcut after clicking on the Track Title Bar.

Next, let's have a look at something useful that we can do in **Arrangement View** to get that perfect take of our recordings!

Using Take Lanes in Live 11

Something exciting came along with the Live 11 update – a long-awaited function to be able to perform comping.

Comping will enable us to record multiple takes of audio within the same track and then pick the best parts of each take to create the perfect comp!

If you never carried out comping before, just think about it this way: you loop the section of the song where the singer is supposed to be singing the verse. You can let the singer sing that verse a couple of times on a loop record without any interruption and capture every single take they have performed in multiple Take Lanes.

Then, you can go into the Take Lanes and pick the best part of each. For example, maybe the beginning of the first take was pitchy, the second part was great, and, in the second take, the first part was great, but in the second part, the singer missed the last word.

Now, you are able to combine the great parts of both takes in a super fast, seamless way.

This feature is only available in **Arrangement View**. For this, we will need to use Take Lanes, so let's have a look at how this works:

1. Open a new Live Set.

2. Pick an audio track, connect a microphone and set the appropriate input in the I/O section, arm the track, and set the monitoring to **Auto**.

3. Use *Ctrl + click* (*right-click* on Windows) on the track name and select **Show Take Lanes** (see *Figure 2.18*).

4. You can also use the *Option + Cmd + U* (*Ctrl + Alt + U* for Windows) key command:

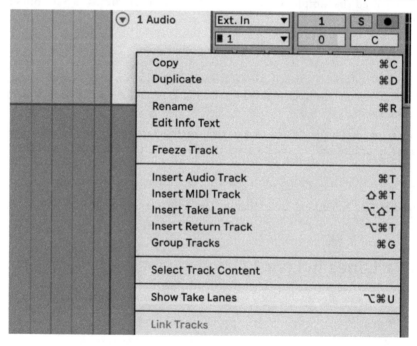

Figure 2.18 – Show Take Lanes

5. Set a two-bar-long loop on the timeline (see *Figure 2.19*):

Figure 2.19 – Two-bar loop set on the timeline

6. You will record three different takes. For the first one, I'd like you to say "I hate spinach." For the second one, say "You love music," and for the third take, "We use Ableton Live.".

7. Now, begin to record. We don't need to stop recording between takes. When the playback head gets to the end of the looped area, the loop will simply begin again, and so will the recording. Live will move each take onto a new Take Lane.

8. You can set up the metronome so that you can say the sentences with the same tempo and rhythm.

    After you have done this, you should have the takes on different Take Lanes (see *Figure 2.20*):

Figure 2.20 – Multiple takes on Take Lanes

9.   After you have done this, you can save this project. We will come back to this in the next chapter when we will look at how to comp!

With this, we have arrived at the end of this chapter. By now, you should be able to comfortably record audio in both **Session View** and **Arrangement View**, as well as use Take Lanes.

Summary

Recording audio is a crucial part of music production to capture performances and any unique audio to use creatively in your production.

Recording in **Session View** will allow you to just jam and capture your performance quickly in a loop-based environment. This is also going to be useful if you are planning to record audio as part of a live performance on stage.

Recording in **Arrangement View** will allow you to purposefully record audio material in a more arrangement-focused way and take advantage of Take Lanes and comping.

In the next chapter, we will be focusing on how you can edit your recorded material in both **Session View** and **Arrangement View**.

3

Editing Audio and Warping

Working with audio can bring a lot of joy to music production. It can involve your own recorded material, pre-made loops, and re-sampled material; it doesn't really matter. Live can provide you with many tools to make the most of your experience of audio editing in a corrective and creative way.

Getting audio into Live is one thing, but knowing how to fit the audio into the track, re-work pre-made loops by slicing and dicing, making sure that unwanted noise and breaths are properly edited out of vocals, and fading out a guitar chord, for example, is another.

These are all crucial skills that a music producer needs to have to be able to create efficiently.

In this chapter we are going to cover the following key topics:

- Exploring the Clip View, Sample Box, and the loop
- Audio editing functions
- Understanding warping in Live

Technical requirements

In order to follow along with this chapter, you will need the following:

- A computer with at least 8 GB of RAM and an Intel Core i5 processor
- A pair of headphones
- A copy of Live 11 Suite
- **Chapter 3** Ableton Live Project

Exploring the Clip View

This is the place where we can adjust clip properties. We can display this by double-clicking on a clip in the Session or Arrangement View, or alternatively, we can click on the Clip Overview (Figure 3.1).

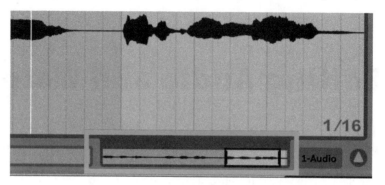

Figure 3.1 – Clip Overview

By doing this, we will also display the Sample Editor in the case of an audio clip (Figure 3.2).

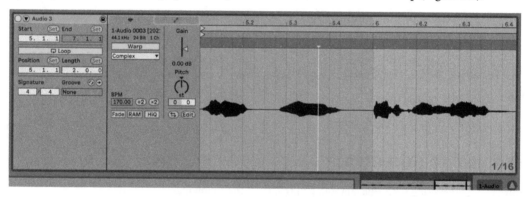

Figure 3.2 – Clip View and Sample Editor

If we are working in the Session View, we can further display **Follow Action** (which we will cover in *Chapter 13, Exploring Tempo Follower, Follow Action, Max for Live, Working with Video, and Ableton Note*), **Launch Modes**, and **Clip Quantization** (which will be covered in *Chapter 15, Playing Live*) by clicking on the triangular toggle button (*Figure 3.3*).

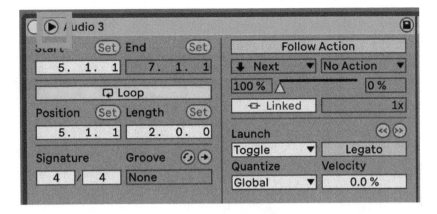

Figure 3.3 – Displaying Follow Action, the Launch modes, and clip Quantize options

Let's see what we can set up in the Clip View and how to use the Clip properties:

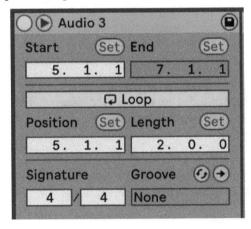

Figure 3.4 – The Clip View

- Here, in Figure 3.4, we can set up the **Start** and **End** positions of the clip, which means that a portion of the clip will be played back when we launch the clip. We can type a number into these boxes or drag the numbers up and down.

- The **Loop** button enables us to loop the set portion of the clip.

- **Position** and **Length** affect the looped section.

  Let's say we have the clip right now playing back from bar 6, but we only want to loop the section from bar 5. In this case, we will enter this under **Position**.

You will notice that the playback will start from bar 6; however, the clip will then be looped from bar 5 (*Figure 3.5*).

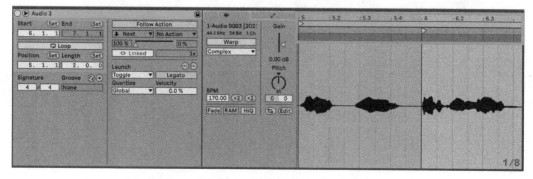

Figure 3.5 – The playback Start and Loop Position

You can also see that these settings are represented at the clip display where you can clearly see the loop brace and the start of the playback in the scrub area (the top right of *Figure 3.5*). You can also adjust these values by moving the start and end points in the scrub area and the loop brace.

> **Note**
>
> This is super useful if you have recorded, for example, the same pattern of shakers for four bars and you feel like the first or the second two bars of the recording are better. You can just play back/loop the preferred two bars.

- We can also enter the clip's time **Signature**; however, this will be there just for reference and will not affect the playback of the clip.

- **Groove** enables us to add some movement to our clips via the Groove Pool, which we will cover shortly in this book.

The Clip View tabs

We can choose from two different tabs to display at the same time here, which will display different properties.

The **Sample** tab displays options to change the gain and pitch of the selected audio clip or reverse it.

Also, here you will find **Warp** functions, which we will be looking at later in this chapter (*Figure 3.6*).

Figure 3.6 – The Sample tab

The **Envelopes** tab displays the envelope-related properties of the selected clip. You can apply modulation and automation in the clip's envelope. We will look at these in *Chapter 11, Implementing Automation and Modulation* (*Figure 3.7*).

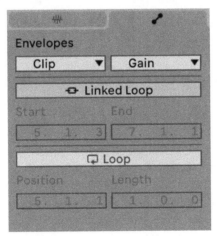

Figure 3.7 – The Envelopes tab

The Clip View is an excellent place to make independent adjustments to audio material on a clip-by-clip basis.

Let's say you would only like to adjust the volume of one vocal phrase, not the whole vocal take; then, as long as this phrase is split into an individual clip in the Arrangement View, we can control everything we looked at previously for that one vocal phrase/clip without affecting the rest of the vocals (*Figure 3.8*).

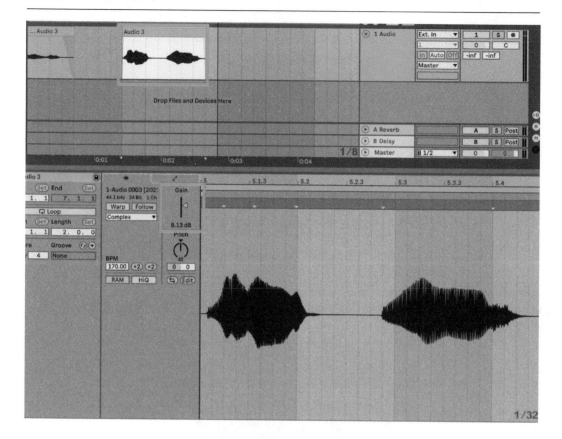

Figure 3.8 – Adjusted clip Gain in the Arrangement View

In the Session View, you might have different vocal parts on the same track in different clip slots. For example, one scene will trigger the verse vocal clip, and the next scene will trigger the chorus vocal clip. The chorus vocal clip might be too loud compared to the verse vocal clip. If we drop the volume via the fader of the track, we are dropping the volume of the verse vocals as well. So, in this case, it's a good idea to just select the chorus vocal clip and adjust **Gain** in the Clip View (*Figure 3.9*).

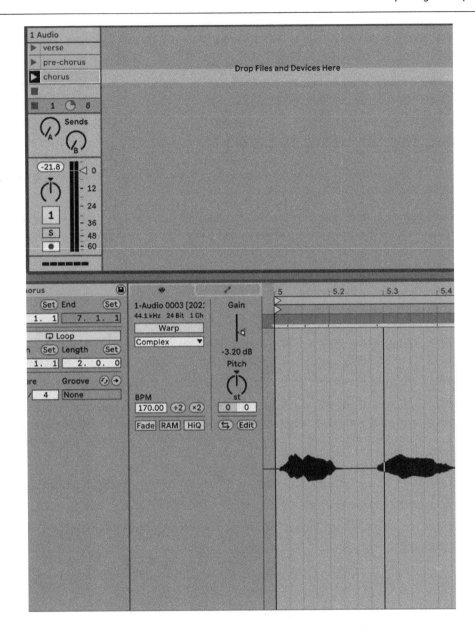

Figure 3.9 – Adjusted clip Gain in the Session View

We can also manipulate **Pitch** here, **detune** or **reverse** the sample, and **Edit** it with a third-party audio editor. Furthermore, we can apply **Fade** in the Session clips to avoid clicks and pops on the clip edges.

There are also options for **high-quality mode (HiQ)**, which will affect the sonic quality of audio when the clip is transposed.

The clip **RAM** mode provides the option to load the audio file into RAM, not reading it directly from the hard drive.

Now we have had a look at what we can display for clips in the Clip View, we will check out how we can apply further physical edits to audio material in Live 11.

Audio editing functions in Live 11

There are different ways to how you should approach editing in the Session and Arrangement Views. It is important to understand what the two views are focusing on.

As we previously discussed, the Session View is good for laying down ideas in a non-linear fashion, which can speed up your workflow tremendously; however, eventually, you will move into the Arrangement View to define your arrangement and, therefore, the majority of your editing work as well.

This is reflected in the editing capabilities of the two views.

Editing audio in the Session View

It is a fact that the editing possibilities are rather limited in the Session View. But if we really reflect on what the Session View is used for and its music-making nature, it is quite understandable. This is not where you will be carrying out all your micro edits and getting really bogged down on refining these.

In fact, the only slicing and dicing you can do here is crop a sample. Let's say you have recorded four bars of audio, but you only wanted to keep two bars of it. You already learned how you can adjust the loop and start points of a clip; however, you might eventually want to commit to this selection to ease your CPU usage as well.

In this case, you *Ctrl + click* (*right-click* for Windows) on the audio clip with its loop brace and the **Start** and **End** times set in the Sample Editor and choose **Crop Sample** (*Figure 3.10*).

From this point, the Sample Editor will only display the selected audio and crop everything outside of this area.

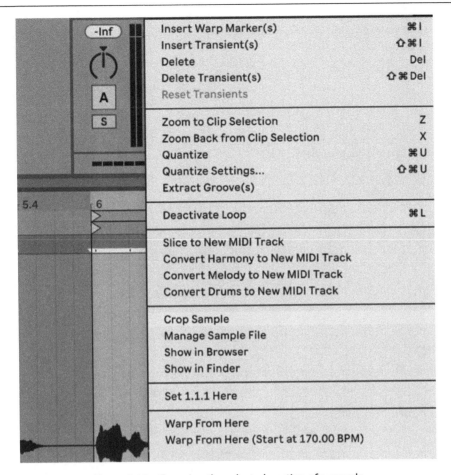

Figure 3.10 – Cropping the selected portion of a sample

Now let's look at what we can do in the Arrangement View and then later move between the two views should we need to carry out more complex editing of audio material that we would rather use in the Session View.

Editing audio in the Arrangement View

The Arrangement View certainly provides you with all the tools to carry out all the heavy-duty editing of your work.

For this example, I would copy the vocals from the Session View that I recorded there, drop them in the Arrangement View, edit them, and then move them back into the Session View as I would like to carry on working there. However, in this case, I don't want to wait until I have laid down the majority of the elements of my track before I get to edit these vocals because these edits are important to continue the composition.

Let's look at some more editing options, for example, how to use fades in order to avoid clicks and pops at the clip edges.

Fades

Follow these steps to adjust the fade at the clip edges:

1. Let's copy the vocal clip from the Session View, then navigate to the Arrangement View, and paste the clip to the appropriate track.

2. Press the **Back to Arrangement** button (*Figure 3.11*), and let's begin.

Figure 3.11 – The Back to Arrangement button

3. To trim off the silence from the end of the clip, if we hover our cursor over the clip edge, we will see it turn into this trim symbol. Now, we can start dragging the clip back until we have removed the silence (*Figure 3.12*).

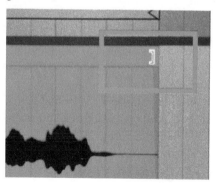

Figure 3.12 – Trimming back a clip

4. After this, go ahead and adjust the fade at the end of the clip to smooth out the ending of the audio. We can also adjust the shape of the fade by moving the three little dots of the fade (*Figure 3.13*).

Figure 3.13 – The fade and its adjustable curve/shape

Remember, we briefly touched on fades when we looked at **Preferences** in the **Record**, **Warp**, **Launch** section in *Chapter 1, Taking a Quick Tour of Ableton Live 11*. There, we can set up the option that Live will create fades on the clip edges (*Figure 3.14*).

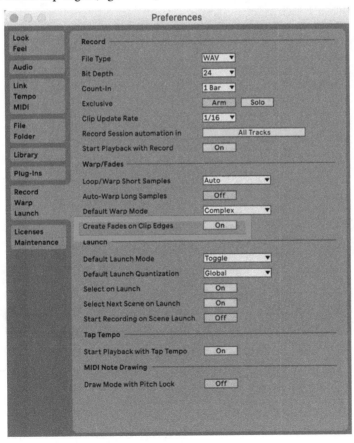

Figure 3.14 – Preferences

This is a fantastic option to enable. For example, each time we split a clip, there are always going to be fades created at the edges, which we can further shape and increase the size of if we need to.

Split

We can also go ahead and remove some silence in between the words. For that, use **Split** to split the clip at multiple places (*Figure 3.15*), trim off the silence, and adjust the fade at the clip edges.

To split a clip, just put your cursor where you'd like to apply the cut, *Ctrl + click* (*right-click* for Windows), or hit the key command *Cmd + E* (*Ctrl + E* for Windows):

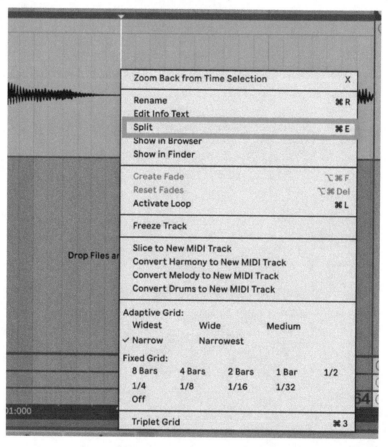

Figure 3.15 – Splitting a clip

Once this is complete, you should end up with something similar to *Figure 3.16*.

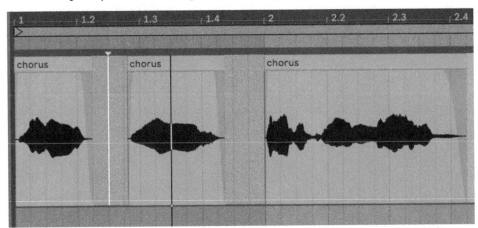

Figure 3.16 – Audio edits that have had split, trim, and fade applied

At this point, we cannot transfer back the edited audio into the Session View since we now have multiple clips on our timeline, and one clip slot can only hold one clip at a time in the Session View.

So, somehow, we need to create a consistent clip out of these edited clips.

Consolidating

We can make a selection on the timeline in the Arrangement view (this can contain silence as well) and turn this selection into one continuous clip by consolidating it:

1. First, make the selection (*Figure 3.17*).

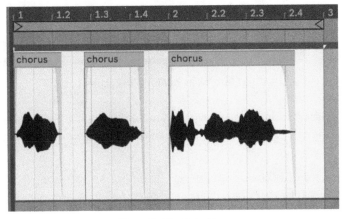

Figure 3.17 – Selection

2. Then *Ctrl + click* (*right-click* for Windows) and select the **Consolidate** option from the context menu or use the key command *Cmd + J* (*Ctrl + J* for Windows) (*Figure 3.18*).

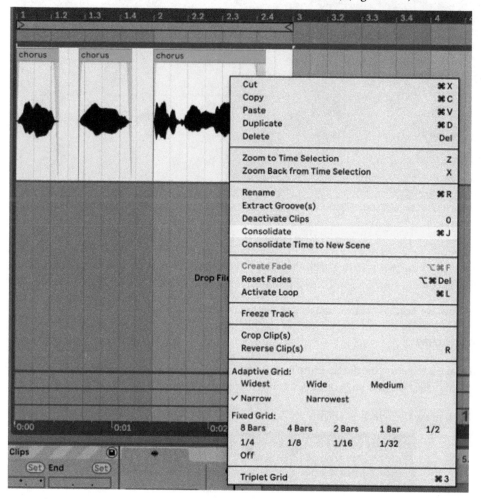

Figure 3.18 – The Consolidate option in the context menu

Once the process is finished, you will end up with a continuous clip that you can transfer back into the Session View. All the edits, silences, fades, trims, and everything we did up till now are part of this continuous clip.

Notice that I have selected extra silence after the clip that I previously trimmed off; this is simply because the original clip was two bars long, but the end contained noise, so I replaced it with silence, so it can perfectly loop in the Session View (*Figure 3.19*).

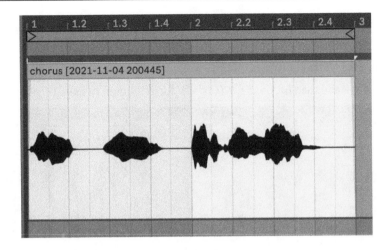

Figure 3.19 – Consolidated clip

Duplicate, Copy, Paste

These simple editing functions work much like in any other **digital audio workstation** (**DAW**) and can be activated by general key commands.

In the next example, I have brought in a drum loop. I'd like to take the last hits from the loop and repeat it for a bar after the initial loop. Follow these steps for how to do this:

1. Selected the portion of audio we'd like to repeat.

2. Then hit *Cmd + D* (*Ctrl + D* for Windows) as many times as needed to fill out the next bar with the duplicated audio (*Figure 3.20*).

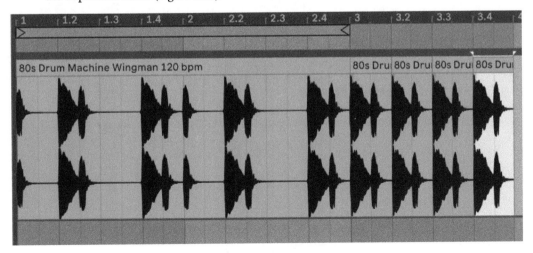

Figure 3.20 – The loop and duplicated audio

Now there are four bars of audio, and we want these four bars of content to repeat again from bar **8**.

3.   Select all four bars, then hit *Cmd + C* (*Ctrl + C* for Windows) to copy.

4.   Navigate to bar **8** and then hit *Cmd + V* (*Ctrl + V* for Windows) to paste (*Figure 3.21*).

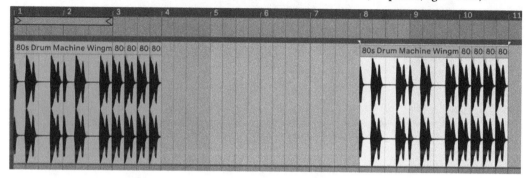

Figure 3.21 – Copy and pasted selection on the timeline

We can also copy and paste, or in other words, move a duplicate of a clip to somewhere else by selecting the clip, and while we are dragging it to the new location, we hold down the *Option key* (the *Alt* key for Windows).

All these functions can be accessed by *Ctrl + click* (*right-click* for Windows) and choosing from the context menu in case you cannot remember the shortcuts.

You have probably noticed while you were trimming clips or dragging and dropping selections or clips on the timeline that, for example, when you move a clip, it snaps to the grid. Sometimes, especially with edited vocal clips, you might want to land a clip between the grids.

We can temporarily suspend the grid while moving a clip by holding down the *Cmd* key (the *Alt* key for Windows).

Let's have a look at what else we can change regarding the grid!

The grid in the Arrangement View

If you *right-click* within the timeline, you will see some options for our grid settings (*Figure 3.22*):

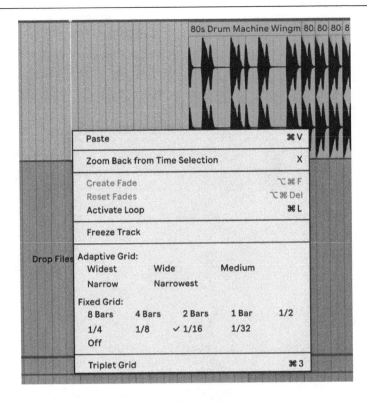

Figure 3.22 – The grid settings

- You can set up **Adaptive Grid**, meaning the grid resolution will change depending on how much you zoom in and out of the timeline

- Or you can select **Fixed Grid**, which means it doesn't matter how much you zoom in; your grid resolution will be fixed to the value that you chose

- Or, of course, you can select **Off** for your grid

This is super important to know if you'd like to maximize your speed while you are working!

By now, you should feel comfortable carrying out editing tasks in both the Session and Arrangement View, so we will dive into the world of audio warping in the next section of this chapter!

The world of audio warping in Live

Live has a real strength when it comes to working with audio. Warping allows you to stretch the audio to your song's tempo while maintaining high audio quality.

At the sample box, you can set **Warp** to on and off on a per-clip basis (*Figure 3.23*).

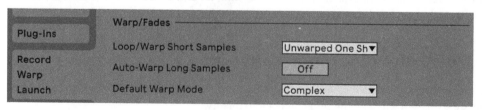

Figure 3.23 – Sample Box with warping enabled

Warp switched on enables you to loop your audio clip in the Session View; otherwise, once the clip is launched, it will play through once, but then it will stop until you launch it again.

It is important that you tell Live how to deal with audio in terms of warping when you import some into your Set.

These settings can be found in **Live | Preferences | Record Warp Launch (Options | Preferences |Record Warp Launch** on Windows) (*Figure 3.24*).

Figure 3.24 – Warp settings in Preferences

There are some considerations to note about these settings. For example, perhaps you don't like to warp one-shot samples due to their nature; long samples could be anything from a full track (if you are DJing with Live, for example, then you'd like this setting to be on) an ambient loop, in which case you'd probably want to turn it off. Even if you have any of these settings off, you can still warp the imported audio in its Sample Box.

In this window, you can also choose the default **Warp** mode.

Even if you set the default **Warp** mode in **Preferences**, again, this is something that can be changed for each clip independently in its Sample Box.

Let's take a closer look at the differences between these **Warp** modes!

The different Warp modes in Live

You will need to judge which **Warp** mode suits the audio best based on the sound characteristics of the material (*Figure 3.25*).

Figure 3.25 – The different Warp modes in the Sample Box

If you look at a drum loop and a loop of a pad sound, you will see significant differences in their waveform (*Figure 3.26*). You will see there are way more transients in the drum loop than in the pad loop. This will be super important for Live when preserving the audio for warping.

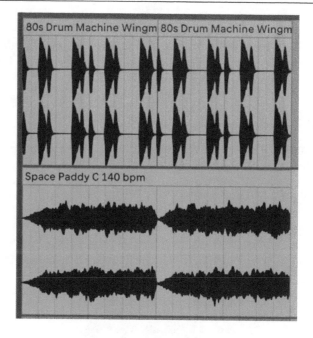

Figure 3.26 – The waveform of a drum loop and a pad loop

Because of their different sound characteristics, you will need to choose different Warp modes for the two clips to maintain the sound quality.

The Beats mode

The **Beats** mode was designed for more rhythmical and percussive audio material. There are further settings you can set for this **Warp** mode (*Figure 3.27*):

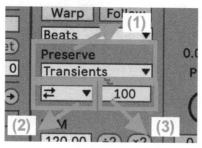

Figure 3.27 – Preserve, Transients Loop Mode, and Transient Envelope

- **Preserve:** Granulation Resolution: This allows you to choose how the audio material will be divided into chunks (segments) that will be aligned to the tempo (*Figure 3.27 (1)*).

  This algorithm will divide the audio up by transients or beat divisions.

- **Transients Loop mode**: This defines what happens to the audio in terms of looping once each segment is played to its end.

  If it's set to the first option (**off**), the segment will play to its end and then stop. If it's set to one of the other two options (**Loop Forward**, **Loop Back-and-Forth**), the audio will play to its end and then loop either forward or back and forth, depending on the setting (*Figure 3.27 (2)*).

- **Transient Envelope**: This setting controls the amount of fades at the end of the divided segments to avoid pops and clicks (*Figure 3.27 (3)*).

Experimenting with these settings can result in some surprising, interesting, and sometimes stuttered/choppy outcomes.

The Tones mode

The Tones mode is best suited for melodic monophonic sounds where you can easily identify the pitch for the notes, such as bass, vocals, and instruments playing a single-note melody.

You can adjust **Grain Size** (*Figure 3.28*) to determine the size of grains used for time stretching the audio.

Again, this is something worth experimenting with for some happy accidents.

Figure 3.28 – Grain Size

The Texture Mode

This mode is suitable for audio that does not have a clear single pitch that can be identified but rather is used for polyphonic material. This can be instruments playing chords or more ambient synth sounds.

This mode has some great parameters to adjust, not just to maintain clarity but also for sound design purposes.

Again, **Grain Size** determines the size of grains used for stretching the audio, and **Flux** introduces randomness in the grain selection process (*Figure 3.29*).

This is something highly recommended for experimenting with for sound design purposes.

Figure 3.29 – The Grain Size and Flux settings

The Re-Pitch mode

This mode alters the pitch of the audio while syncing to the session tempo. The slower the tempo is, the lower the pitch will get, and the higher the tempo, the higher the pitch will be.

The Complex mode

If we look back through the previous **Warp** modes, besides **Re-Pitch**, all the other modes could cover an entire song's worth of elements, drums, bass, synths/pads, pianos, vocals, and more. But what about entire songs? As mentioned before, Live is a great tool to DJ with, where you can play entire songs that have all the previously mentioned elements in them. If that's the case, the Complex mode is the mode to use.

This mode can handle complex audio material with multiple elements and pitch information.

It is important to note that it is one of the most CPU-heavy **Warp** modes!

The Complex Pro mode

Complex Pro is an even more CPU-heavy **Warp** mode, fairly similar to the Complex mode. However, it works with a more defined result and also provides some extra parameters to adjust.

This is a great mode if you don't just want to time stretch the audio but also want to transpose it. Let's take some vocals as an example.

You want to create some harmonies, so you copy the lead vocals to a new track and then adjust the copied audio, let's say, by 5 semitones. You will hear quite an unnatural artifact with the transposition; however, with the Complex **Pro** mode, you can adjust the **Formants** and **Envelope** settings (*Figure 3.30*).

When you start adjusting the **Formants** settings, you will hear that Live starts to maintain the pitch and provide a more realistic **throat sound** to the transposed audio.

The **Envelope** settings will help maintain the spectral characteristics of the sound.

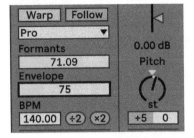

Figure 3.30 – The Formants and Envelope settings while transposing audio

Let's also have a look at some additional settings we can adjust in the Sample Box related to warping.

Tempo leader and Follower

You might have noticed that this button only becomes available in the Arrangement View (*Figure 3.31*).

Figure 3.31 – Tempo leader and Follower switch in the Sample Box

By default, it will be set to **Follow**, which means the audio clip follows the Set's tempo and is stretched/warped to it.

If you press this button you can set it to **Lead**, which enables the audio to play in this natural, original tempo like it isn't warped. Additionally, the Set's tempo will sync with this clip's tempo. If you have more than one **Leader** set up in the session, the one that's at the bottom of the Arrangement View at the time will get priority.

The Seg. BPM

The **BPM** box contains some important information that will affect the warping process (*Figure 3.32*).

When you import audio into Live, Live guesses the **original tempo** of the audio material. It is correct most of the time; however, sometimes it doesn't get it right.

Figure 3.32 – The Segment BPM box

If you know the tempo of the audio material and you can see that Live is clearly not displaying the right tempo, you can type the correct number in the box.

Most of the time, when Live makes a mistake, it either doubles or halves the number.

This mistake can make Live **over-warp** your audio, so if that's the case you can just press the **Halve** or **Double Original Tempo** buttons (*Figure 3.33*).

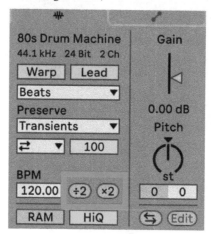

Figure 3.33 – The Halve or Double Original Tempo buttons

> **Remix tip**
>
> You might actually want to halve or double the tempo on purpose. Let's say you are working on a remix, and you are trying to go from 170 BPM (the original tempo of the vocals) to 80 BPM because that's your preferred tempo for your Set. If you let Live stretch the vocals for you from 170 to 80 BPM, you will end up with extremely slow vocals. Instead, you can halve the Seg. BPM to 85 BPM, so Live would only need to work with that remaining 5 BPM difference so that you will end up with much more natural sounding and useable vocals.

You can also change the Seg. BPM and stretch audio in the Arrangement View by holding down the *Shift* key while dragging out the audio clip (*Figure 3.34*).

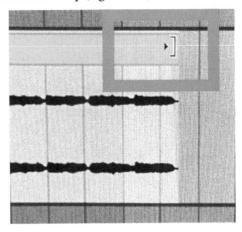

Figure 3.34 – Shift and drag the clip edge to time stretch a clip

In the following example, I stretched a one-bar-long sweep audio sample to be two bars long (half time). You can see the original one-bar-long sample on the left and the stretched version on the right (*Figure 3.35*).

Figure 3.35 – A stretched audio sample in the Arrangement View

We have now covered many settings that we can adjust, mainly in the Sample Box and **Preferences**, to ensure we take full advantage of warping's potential.

It is time to go ahead and look at what we can do in the Sample Editor while we are working with transients and look at further warping possibilities.

Working with transients

When we import audio into Live we will see its waveform either in the Arrangement View or in the Clip View. The waveform of audio has a bunch of transients, the peaks (the loudest parts) of the waveform.

Live's warping is based on working with the transients of any audio material.

These transients are marked with **Transient Marks** (*Figure 3.36*).

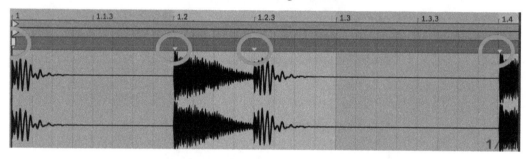

Figure 3.36 – Transient Marks in the Sample Editor Clip View

These markers can be moved by holding down the *Shift* key and dragging the Transient Marks to the new location. While you hover your mouse over the Transient Mark, you will notice that it turns into a gray handle called the **Pseudo Warp Marker** (*Figure 3.37*).

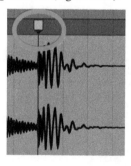

Figure 3.37 – The Pseudo Warp Marker

Warp Markers

If you don't hold down the *Shift* key to move the Transient Markers, and just move or double-click on the pseudo Warp Marker, Live will transform it into a yellow Warp Marker (*Figure 3.38*).

To delete a Warp Marker, just double-click on it again, or right-click and choose **Delete** from the context menu, or after selecting it just hit *Backspace* or *Delete* on your computer keyboard.

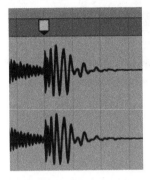

Figure 3.38 – Warp Marker

Let's say we would like to move one drum hit to a different location in the following drum loop (*Figure 3.39(1)*). We create the Warp Marker on the transient of the hit and move it to the right.

You will notice that everything on the right will shrink while everything on the left side of the Warp Marker will be stretched out. Now we are totally out of tempo (*Figure 3.39(2)*).

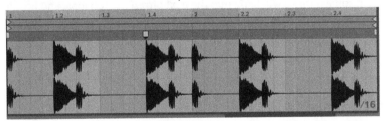

Figure 3.39 (1) – The original drum loop with the Warp Marker to be moved

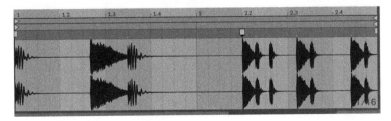

Figure 3.39 (2) – The edited loop with the Warp Marker moved

To resolve this, after performing an *undo* command (*Cmd + Z* (*Ctrl + Z* for Windows)), we will create two further Warp Markers around the initial Warp Marker that we would like to move. This will allow us to move that hit without affecting the other hits' locations around it. Now we can move the hit forward so it will play earlier in the sequence than it did before (*Figure 3.40*).

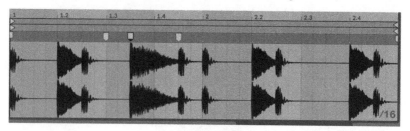

Figure 3.40 – Transient Marker moved to a new location without affecting the other hits

---

Remix tip

You should never be afraid of creating and moving Warp Markers. This allows you to modify drum loops and change their groove and it is also super useful when working on a remix. Let's say you are using an acappella from an R'n'B song, and you are planning to use it to create a house track.

Since the singer sang over the beats of the R'n'B song, which has a very different rhythm and groove to house beats (not to mention the other instruments the R'n'B song had to guide the singer), the length of the phrases of the acapella might not fit the four-on-the-floor straight-up beats. As a result, some phrases will hang into the next phrase, be too long, and just fall out of sync with the house beats, even though it is stretched to your new tempo properly.

This is when creating and moving Warp Markers comes to the rescue, as you can manipulate and modify some of the phrases to better fit your genre.

Other Warp commands in Live

There are other commands that can further help us with warping. We are going to take a look at these here.

Quantize

Quantize is something that you will definitely have encountered while working with MIDI if you are a seasoned producer. This command allows us to fix timing issues by snapping the notes to the grid. We can also set up which grid by defining the grid value.

In modern music production, we can do this to audio as well with the help of Warp Markers.

In the following screenshot (*Figure 3.41*), we can see that the drum hits have some swing, and the transients aren't aligning with the grid properly. It can be fine depending on what genre of music we produce and how much timing fluctuation there is, but for this example, we are looking for beats to be aligned to the grid, which is currently not happening.

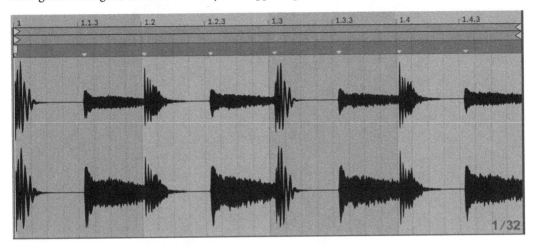

Figure 3.41 – Transients aren't aligned with the grid

We can obviously fix this by moving all the transients one by one, by creating Warp Markers and dragging them to the grid, but we can also enable Live to do it for us. Let's see how in the following steps:

1. By *Ctrl + click* (*right-click* on Windows), we can bring up the context menu, and see the **Quantize** and **Quantize Settings** options (*Figure 3.42*).

    Since we don't know what settings are currently set for quantization, we will head to **Quantize Settings** or use the key commands: *Cmd + Sfift + U* (*Ctrl + Shift + U* for Windows) for **Quantize Settings** and *Cmd + U* (*Ctrl + U* for Windows) for **Quantize**.

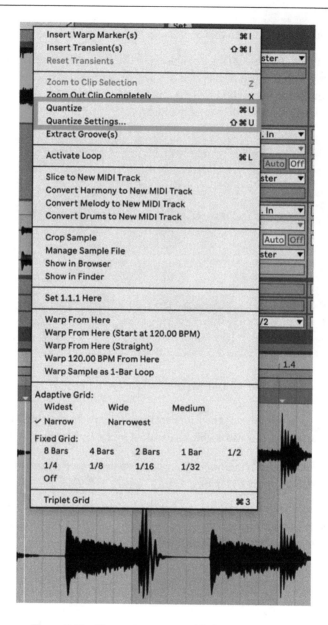

Figure 3.42 – The context menu with Quantize options

2. Once we are in the **Quantize Settings** tab, we can set up **Quantize To**, which defines the grid value that we intend to quantize to, and **Amount**, which defines how much quantization we will apply (*Figure 3.43*).

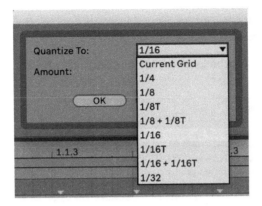

Figure 3.43 – Quantize settings window

> **Tip**
>
> Unless your genre desires very straight-up beats with no swing whatsoever, it's a good idea to try to quantize first with a smaller value than 100% (for example, 80%). This will move the notes 80% closer to the grid but keep some of the time shifts, which can give a bit more of a human feeling to your beats.

3. For this example, go ahead with quantizing to **1/16** and with 100% amount. The result is shown here (*Figure 3.44*).

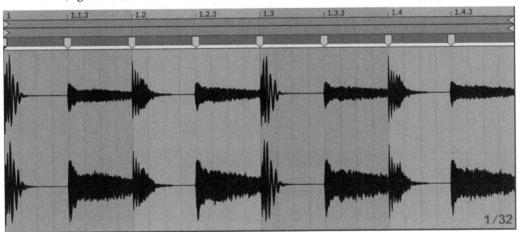

Figure 3.44 – Quantized audio

Notice that Live created a Warp Marker for every single transient, and they were moved to the grid so that they are totally **on time** and aligned with the grid.

You have probably noticed in the context menu that there are other **Warp**-related commands as well (*Figure 3.45*).

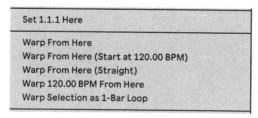

Figure 3.45 – The context menu with other Warp commands

Let's have a look at them!

Warp From Here

Let's say you are again working on a remix using an acappella.

When you first drag the acappella into Live, it will most probably be silence at the beginning of the file, where the other instruments played in the original track within the intro (*Figure 3.46*).

That is normal. However, Live now takes that silence into consideration as it starts warping from the very beginning of the file. So even though the acappella is already warped to your Set's tempo, it is still out of sync.

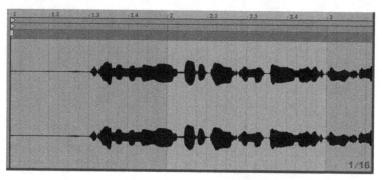

Figure 3.46 – Silence at the beginning of the acappella that is affecting the warping

To resolve this, we will go and find the beginning of the acappella, which we would like to place on the downbeat on the *1*.

We will zoom in and find where the acappella starts, and then once we have that, we will go ahead, *Ctrl+ click* (*right-click* for Windows), and choose **Warp From Here** from the context menu, and then we adjust the loop start from that point (*Figure 3.47*). Now start playback, and either put some drums underneath the acappella or just simply switch the metronome on.

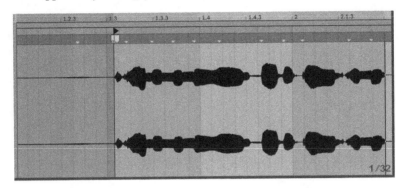

Figure 3.47 – Acappella alignment after Warp from Here

If it's still not perfectly in sync, don't be afraid to add further Warp Markers and adjust their location.

However, if you look at *Figure 3.47* again, you will see that where we started to warp from, and where the loop starts from, is not **1.1.1**. To resolve that too, we will *Ctrl + click* (*right-click* on Windows) again and choose **Set 1.1.1. Here**, and we will see now our warp point and playback point are at **1.1.1** (*Figure 3.48*).

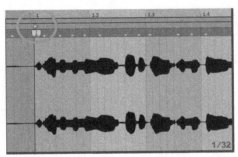

Figure 3.48 – The Set 1.1.1. Here command's result

This is something that you will need to practice quite a lot of the time when you are working with audio that isn't cut as a perfect loop.

Warp From Here (Start at … BPM)

This will ask Live to start the Auto-Warp process using the tempo of your Set.

Warp From Here (Straight)

This command is pretty similar to the previous one; however, it also tells Live that the song has a straight, consistent tempo.

Warp ... BPM from Here

If you know the tempo of the audio in question, then you can use this command, so Live will interpret the material as it matches the Set's tempo.

Just make sure you type the tempo into the **Tempo Controller** box in the Control Bar.

Warp Selection as 1 bar Loop

Live will suggest a certain loop length to create a perfectly looping clip in this length.

At this point, you might have put quite a bit of time into warping certain audio so it is perfectly how you want it. So, what are the final steps?

Saving your warped audio for future use

You might even want to use this audio file again in a different Set, but you don't want to spend all that time again doing all this warping. In this case, you can save the file with all its Warp Markers and settings to be used again.

Just hit **Save Default Clip** in the Clip View (*Figure 3.49*).

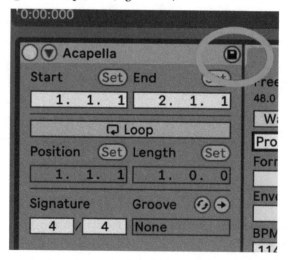

Figure 3.49 – The Save Default Clip button

And with this, we have arrived at the end of warping, which should now give you a great selection of tools to work with audio in Live.

However, it doesn't end here; there are two new functions that arrived with the Live 11 update, Track Linking and Take Lanes-comping, which we started to take a look at in the last chapter and we will pick up again in *Chapter 6, Comping and Track Linking*.

Summary

As you can see, there are many ways we can work with audio in Live, and even more now since the Live 11 update. Editing operations are important from a creative but also a corrective point of view to be able to work efficiently and create professional-sounding pieces.

In the next chapter, we are going to jump into the world of MIDI and look at how we can program and record MIDI information with Live.

4

Exploring MIDI Sequencing Techniques

We have already had a more in-depth look at how we can work with audio in Live 11 and now it is time to start exploring how we can utilize **Musical Instrument Digital Interface (MIDI)** for our production.

Working with MIDI can provide us with a lot of creative freedom and flexibility. When we are recording audio, if we would like to record, for example, a guitar solo, there needs to be someone who can play the guitar so we can record it. With MIDI, we can play any instrument ourselves, even just by using our computer mouse.

Also, what happens if we change our minds and we would like the same melody to be played by another instrument? It isn't so easy to make it happen with audio – however, with MIDI, we can change the instrument that is being played with the click of a button.

There are very few limitations that we will experience when working with MIDI and even a lack of music theory knowledge isn't one that we have to worry about. The modern technology of digital music-making offers us a great range of tools that can help us out even if we don't have a great deal of music theory knowledge.

MIDI technology is an absolutely crucial tool in the modern electronic musician's range of creative weapons for a quick, free, and efficient workflow.

We are going to cover the following topics:

- Importing and exporting MIDI into Live
- Programming MIDI – drawing notes and step input
- The grid settings in the MIDI editor
- Drawing MIDI notes in Arrangement View
- Real-time recording

- How to use Overdub and take lanes in Arrangement View
- Exploring Capture MIDI
- Discovering Scale Mode and Scale Settings in Ableton Live 11

Technical requirements

In order to follow along with this chapter, you will need the following:

- A computer with at least 8 GB of RAM and at least an Intel Core i5 processor
- A pair of headphones
- A copy of Live 11 Suite
- A MIDI controller
- **Chapter 4** Ableton Live project

MIDI notes don't actually carry any sounds – it is just protocol or data that is telling the instrument that you have inserted onto the MIDI track how to play them.

MIDI works the same way in Live as it does in other **Digital Audio Workstations (DAWs)**. However, there are quite specific tools that can help with your MIDI inputting and editing in Live 11, which we will be investigating closely within this book.

Now, let's get started and create something!

Importing and exporting MIDI Into Live

As a seasoned producer, you probably have some MIDI files handy as well, either because you downloaded them, you worked with someone who sent you MIDI information, or you sent some.

Either way, as long as the MIDI files are in the browser under **Places**, you can even pre-view MIDI clips in the browser. As with anything from the browser that you would like to add, just simply drag and drop it into an empty clip slot, or into the timeline in **Arrangement View**:

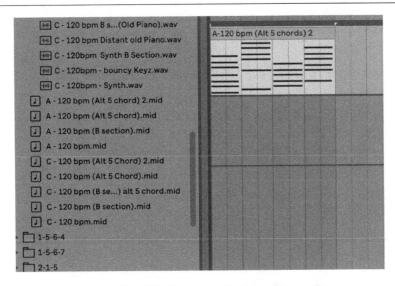

Figure 4.1 – The MIDI clip dragged into Arrangement View

Alternatively, you can drag and drop MIDI files from any folder of your computer if you don't feel the need to preview them in the browser first:

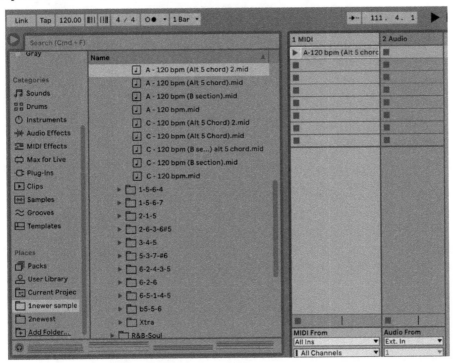

Figure. 4.2 – The MIDI clip dragged into Session View

In **Arrangement View**, you may be asked whether you want to import the tempo and time signature of the MIDI data.

If we try to import multiple MIDI clips into Live, Live will create a separate track for each MIDI clip to be accommodated.

Once you have the MIDI clip in Live, now it's time to *choose the instrument* that you would like the MIDI track to trigger and *insert it onto the track* by either double-clicking on the preset you like in the browser (which will insert the instrument onto the currently selected MIDI track) or dragging and dropping the instrument onto the track.

To export a MIDI clip, we can simply *Ctrl + click* (*right-click* on Windows) on the clip, and choose **Export MIDI Clip....**

Since we just learned how to work with pre-made MIDI clips, it's time to look at how to create our own MIDI sequences.

Programming MIDI – drawing notes and step input

The first technique we are going to explore is drawing notes and inputting steps. Let's start with some drums!

Create a new empty MIDI track, or use one of the already available ones in Live, and follow these steps:

1. Head to the browser, choose **Drums**, and find a preset that you really like (you will learn how to build your own Drum Racks in *Chapter 8, Exploring Device Racks in Live 11!*).

2. Insert it onto the MIDI track.

You will notice that you can see the Drum Rack in the **Device** area (see *Figure 4.3* and *Figure 4.4*):

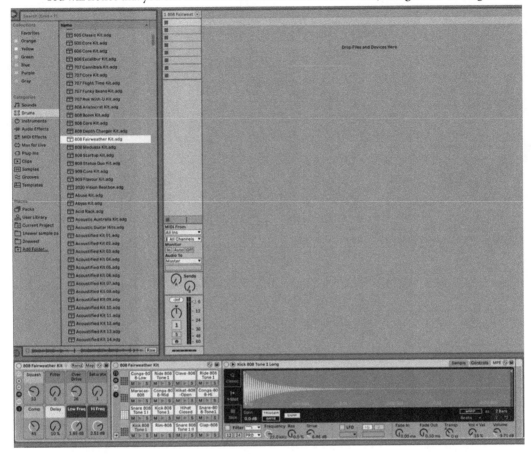

Figure 4.3 – The Drum Rack loaded in Session View

The Drum Rack is loaded in **Arrangement View** too:

Figure 4.4 – The Drum Rack loaded in Arrangement View

Now that we have a drum kit to work with, we can move on to how to add the MIDI notes to trigger the sounds.

First, we are going to have a look at how it is done in **Session View**!

1. Double-click on an empty clip slot – this will create a default 1-bar-long MIDI clip.

2. You will see the MIDI editor popping up at the bottom for the created MIDI clip straight away (see *Figure 4.5*).

3. You will also see each sound in the Drum Rack that you can trigger on the **Piano Roll**:

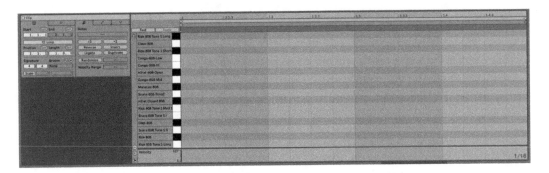

Figure 4.5 – The MIDI editor and the Piano Roll

4.   Click on the notes to hear the sounds that belong to that particular note.

5.   Remember, if you cannot hear the sounds, click on the **MIDI Editor Preview** button (see *Figure 4.6*):

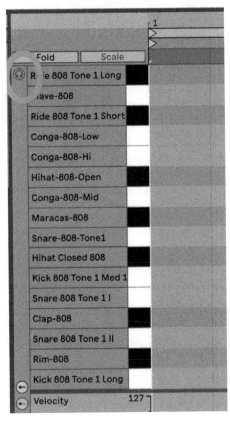

Figure 4.6 – The MIDI Editor Preview button

6. Now, we can look at the **Clip View** to customize our loop – we looked at this already in detail in *Chapter 3, Editing Audio and Warping*.

7. Let's change the loop **Length** value to **2** bars by entering 2.0.0. – this has now given us an extra bar to fill with our sequence.

8. Double-click on the grid where you would like to add the note and you will see that the note will appear (the length of the note will depend on the grid settings, which we will get to in a moment!).

9. Program a basic drum pattern that contains perhaps two different drum elements. In my example, I programmed a basic pattern with **Kick** and **Clap** elements (see *Figure 4.7*):

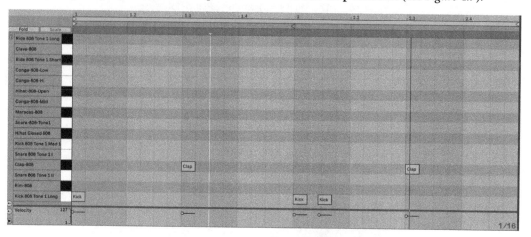

Figure 4.7 – A basic programmed drum pattern

I know it is very tempting to keep adding more notes until we get a nice groove, but before you do that, let me show you a different approach!

10. So, before we carry on, we will look at **Session View**. Navigate to the MIDI clip that we have been working on.

11. *Ctrl + click* (*right-click* for Windows) and choose **Duplicate**. Alternatively, after selecting the clip, you can use the *Cmd + D* (*Ctrl + D* for Windows) key command.

12. Now, you will see the same MIDI clip in **Session View** twice! This is great because if we carry on adding more notes into the second newly created clip, then, in the end, we will have both the first pattern and the second one with extra notes in it and we will be able to switch between them (see *Figure 4.8*).

This is a great technique to create variation, which is super important if you are jamming live or actually composing with a final arrangement in mind.

Variation is key in music production in order to keep your tune interesting and be able to create an arrangement easier.

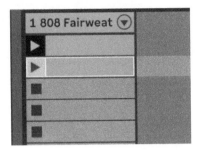

Figure 4.8 – The original and the duplicated clip in Session View

13. After you have launched the duplicated clip, you can head back into the MIDI editor to carry on sequencing the drums.

    The next step will be to program some repeated closed hi-hat sequences. Sure, we can click on the grid as many times as we need to add the notes, but there is a faster way to get this done – by using the **Pencil Tool**.

14. To enable the **Pencil Tool**, head to the top right-hand side of the screen (see *Figure 4.9*) or simply press *B* on your computer keyboard:

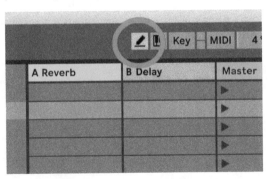

Figure 4.9 – The Pencil Tool enabled

You will notice that in the MIDI editor, your cursor will have turned into a little pencil icon.

15. Now, you can click on the downbeat of the sequence where the row is for the closed hi-hats and start dragging the mouse left to right across your screen. You will notice that you are creating repeated notes (see *Figure 4.10*). The length of the notes will be determined by your **Grid Value**:

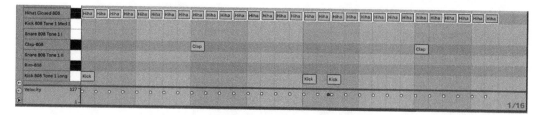

Figure 4.10 – Repeated hi-hat notes made with the Pencil Tool

Since I have now mentioned the importance of **Grid Value** and the grid settings twice, we are going to have a look at how you can change the grid settings for your clips.

The grid settings in the MIDI editor

In order to change the grid resolution in the MIDI editor, we simply *Ctrl + click* (*right-click* on Windows) and we will have a few options in the context menu:

- **Adaptive Grid**: This function means that when you are zooming in and out in the sample editor, the grid will adapt to its values. For example, using the **Narrow** option might make your grid **1/32** when you are fully zoomed out. As you start zooming in, you will start seeing smaller increments, such as 1/64 and so on (see *Figure 4.11*).

- **Fixed Grid**: This option will fix your grid value to a specific chosen value. For example, if you set it to **1/16**, it will always show you 1/16, no matter how zoomed in you are (see *Figure 4.11*).

- **Triplet Grid**: This will change your grid to be able to sequence triplets (see *Figure 4.11*).

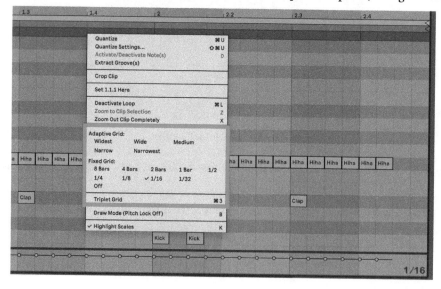

Figure 4.11 – Grid Settings in the Context Menu

> **Tip**
>
> You can toggle between the grid resolutions by using the shortcuts *Cmd + 1, 2, 3, and 4* (*Ctrl + 1, 2, 3, and 4* for Windows) respectively:

You can continue to create more clips of drum patterns with different variations.

The more clips you have, the more options you will have when it comes to the arrangement or jamming out to the content of your **Session View**.

> **Tip**
>
> For easier navigation, you can rename and re-color your different clips (see *Figure 4.12*):

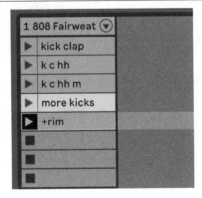

Figure 4.12 – Renamed and re-colored clips

To continue, we are now going to discover how to get started with this in **Arrangement View**.

Drawing MIDI notes in Arrangement View

Everything is going to be pretty similar to what we covered in the previous section, besides the environment where we are going to do it, and how to get started with it. So, follow along:

1. Navigate to **Arrangement View**.

> **Important note**
>
> Because in this practical example, we already have content and launched clip(s) in **Session View**, we are going to hit the **Back to Arrangement** button (see *Figure 4.13*):

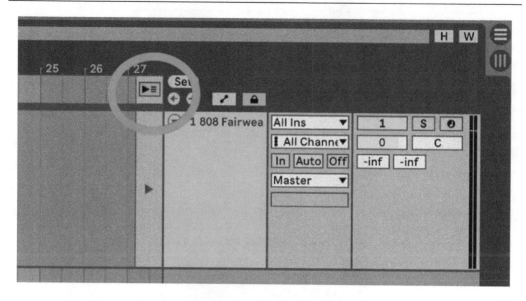

Figure 4.13 – The Back to Arrangement button

2. Double-click on where in the timeline you would like to insert the empty MIDI clip – that's where we are going to input our MIDI notes (for example, the first bar).

    Now, we see an empty MIDI clip created. In order to make our MIDI clip longer, we will do the same as we did in **Session View**.

3. Head to the **Clip View** and change the loop **Length** value, but you will also need to drag out the clip edge on the timeline after you amended the **Length** value.

    If you try to adjust the clip length in **Arrangement View** by dragging it out without first adjusting the **Length** value, you will just loop the same length of the clip. Alternatively, you can also create a new empty MIDI clip in the **Arrangement View**, by making a selection on the timeline (the selection should be as long as you would like the new empty MIDI clip to be) for the desired track, *right-clicking* (*Ctrl + clicking* on Windows) on the timeline selection you made and choosing **Insert Empty MIDI Clip(s)**, or using the shortcut: Shift + Cmd + M (*Shift + Ctrl + M* on Windows).

    From hereon, you will be working in the MIDI editor, so everything you learned previously in this chapter should be applied.

With this, for now, we are finished with using our mouse to insert MIDI notes. Next, we are going to focus on recording notes in real time, actually *playing* notes, which can provide a more organic and *human* feel to sequencing, but, of course, it will always depend on personal workflow preferences!

Real-time recording

In this section, we will explore how to record MIDI notes in real time in **Session View** and **Arrangement View**.

Recording MIDI notes in real time in Session View

In this practical example, we are going to play a bass line.

First, we are going to use our *computer keyboard* to record notes, as everyone at all times has access to that. Then, we are going to move on to see how we can work with a **MIDI controller**. So, let's get started:

1. Choose a bass preset from the browser.

2. Insert it into a new empty MIDI clip.

3. Enable the computer keyboard to act as a MIDI keyboard (see *Figure 4.14*) or use the *M* key command to enable and disable it.

> **Attention**
>
> As long as your keyboard is acting as a MIDI keyboard, some shortcuts will not work – for example, *A* to toggle **Automation** on and off – as at this point, Live is expecting to receive MIDI notes from your computer keyboard.

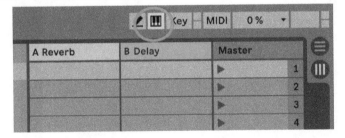

Figure 4.14 – The MIDI computer keyboard enabled

4. Now, arm the track in order to tell Live which track should be receiving the MIDI notes and start triggering notes on your computer keyboard.

    You can go up and down an octave by pressing *Z* to go down and *X* to go up.

Once you like what you hear and you know what melody you would like to play in, you can put on the metronome if needed; make sure you have count-in set up, and start recording by doing the following:

1. Hitting the **Session Record** button, which will start recording onto the selected clip slot or hit the record button on the clip slot in which you intend to record (see *Figure 4.15*).

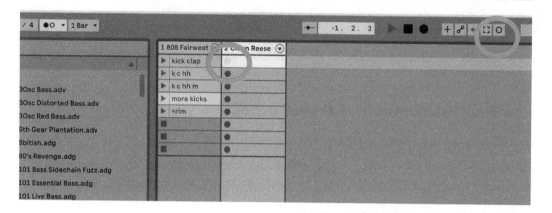

Figure 4.15 – The Session Record button and the record button for the clip

2. Live will keep on recording until you press on one of the record buttons again or stop playback altogether.

3. Again, to create variations, you can repeat the same task on an empty clip slot to record in another bass line that is triggering the same sound.

    In my example, I recorded nearly the same notes, but while I recorded the first pattern with long **legato** notes, in the second version, I did it in a more **staccato** style (see *Figure 4.16*):

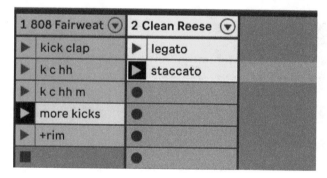

Figure 4.16 – A variation of clips

Moving on, let's repeat this task but now in **Arrangement View**.

Recording in real time in Arrangement View

In order to repeat the task here, follow the following steps:

1. Head to **Arrangement View**.

    Again, since in this practical example we already used for **Session View**, we are going to start by hitting the **Back to Arrangement** button.

2. Make sure the track is armed.

3. Click on the part of the timeline from which you'd like to record – for example, the ninth bar (however, if you would like to record from the beginning of the timeline at the first bar, then you can always move your cursor back to it by double-clicking the **Stop** button).

4. Make sure you have the **Metronome** function and the **Count-in** function on if needed.

5. Now, hit the **Arrangement Record** button (see *Figure 4.17*) and start playing.

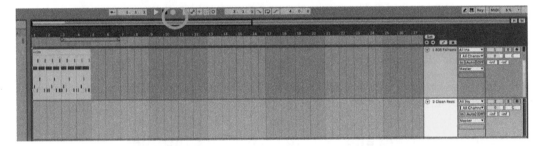

Figure 4.17 – Recording MIDI in Arrangement View

6. Again, to stop recording, you can hit the **Arrangement Record** button, or stop playback.

Now that we have recorded a melody into both views, let's talk a little bit about the relationship between the computer keyboard used to input MIDI and **velocity**.

You probably know that velocity defines the force that the note was played with. The harder you hit the note on the MIDI controller, as in, the more force/pressure you are applying, the higher the velocity will be – therefore, the note will be louder than if you barely touched the key, which will result in low velocity and a quieter note.

Velocity will play a big role in humanizing sequences (which we will talk about in greater detail within *Chapter 5, MIDI Editing and MIDI Effects*) – therefore, it is important to note that even though with the computer keyboard, you are able to achieve more human patterns, as you can capture your timing as you play, you are unable to capture velocity.

If we have a look at the bass line I played with the computer keyboard (see *Figure 4.18*), you will see that the velocity is flat (you will also see on the same picture – circled in red – which button you can toggle on and off to show or hide the velocity):

We can change the default velocity value with which the notes are being inputted by having the computer keyboard enabled as a MIDI keyboard and hitting the *C* key to decrease the default velocity and *V* to increase it:

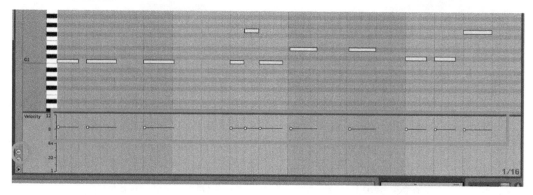

Figure 4.18 – Flat velocity and the show/hide velocity button

Your computer's keyboard is simply not capable of receiving and translating velocity information – it only takes *On* and *Off* messages.

For this reason, we are going to have a look at how you can hook up a MIDI controller that has velocity-sensitive pads or keys.

The benefits of using and setting up a MIDI controller

Using a physical MIDI controller will allow you to play more expressive and humanized sequences, while also providing you with a more tactile experience. Let's have a look at how we can set up a MIDI controller by following these steps:

1. Make sure the track is armed.

2. Connect your MIDI controller.

3. Head to **Preferences** (*Cmd + ,* or *Ctrl + ,* for Windows).

4. Navigate to the **Link | Tempo | MIDI** tab.

5. Make sure that if your MIDI controller needs any drivers, they are downloaded and installed. Otherwise, check this tab (**Link | Tempo | MIDI**) and make sure that the controller shows up under **MIDI Ports** and that the inputs are set up as shown in *Figure 4.19*:

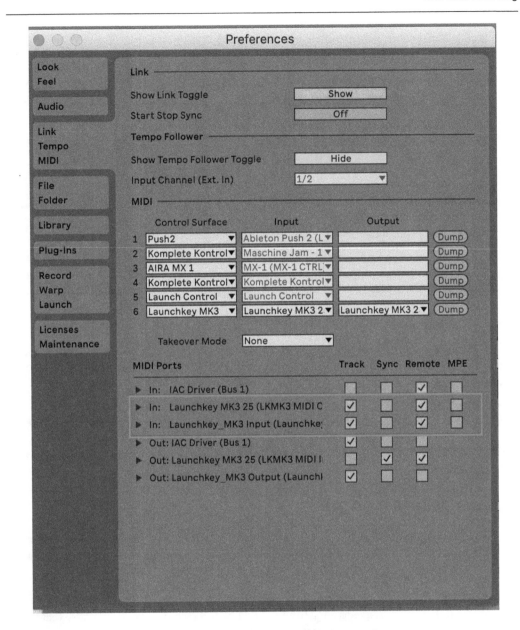

Figure 4.19 – Input settings for the MIDI controller

6. Now, start hitting the keys or the pads of your controller to hear the sound of the track that you are triggering.

We will look at MIDI controllers and their settings in more depth in *Chapter 14, Exploring MIDI Mapping, External Instrument, and MIDI CCs!*

Now, we can re-record the same bassline sequence, or record some drums using the MIDI controller, and we will see and hear that we are now able to control and capture the velocity of the played notes (see *Figure 4.20*):

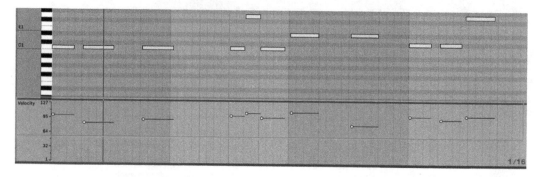

Figure 4.20 – Velocity of the notes recorded with a MIDI keyboard

Now that we have touched upon velocity briefly, and the simple pleasure of actually playing notes and capturing all the characteristics of human playing, we can move on to have a look at further MIDI recording techniques.

How to use Overdub and Take Lanes in Arrangement View

Both the Overdub and Take Lanes functions are crucial and super useful for your recording workflow in **Arrangement View**.

MIDI Arrangement Overdub

This function will enable you to add notes to an existing MIDI clip without writing over the content of it. This is something that happens automatically in **Session View**. However, in **Arrangement View**, it needs to be enabled.

Let's say you have some drums already programmed into a clip. Then, you realize that you'd like to add some extra hi-hats to the sequence. You head to the clip, start recording, and you notice that the already programmed notes are being replaced by the new hi-hats (see *Figure 4.21*):

Figure 4.21 – Recording without Arrangement MIDI Overdub enabled

This is happening if the overdub isn't enabled. So, let's hit the **Overdub** button to turn it on (see *Figure 4.22*).

Now, if you start recording again, you will notice that the new notes you are playing are being added to the already existing content (see *Figure 4.22*):

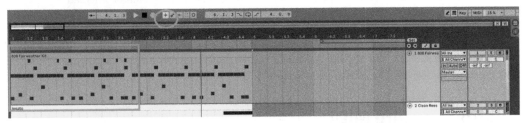

Figure 4.22 – Recording with Arrangement MIDI Overdub enabled (the MIDI Overdub button)

Now that we have learned how we can add new MIDI notes to existing content within MIDI clips, let's have a look at how we can loop records and use Take Lanes!

Loop recording and Take Lanes

This is something that you actually know how to do already since we looked at this feature in *Chapter 2, Recording Audio in Ableton Live 11*, in the *Using Take Lanes in Live 11* section with audio. In fact, it works exactly the same way:

1. Set **Loop Recording Region** in **Arrangement View**'s timeline.

2. Make sure the **Loop Switch** option is on.

3. Make sure that **Arrangement MIDI Overdub** is off (otherwise, instead of capturing multiple takes, you will keep adding new notes to the same MIDI clip).

4. Record a few times over the same loop.

5. Now you can go ahead and *Ctrl + click* (*right-click* on Windows) on the Track Title Bar (or use *Cmd + Option + U* (*Ctrl + Alt + U* for Windows)) to display the recorded takes (see *Figure 4.23*):

Figure 4.23 – Take Lanes displayed after loop recording without MIDI Overdub enabled

And with this, we have arrived at the end of the crucial MIDI recording features of Live.

However, there are still two fun and helpful features that can help us with MIDI inputting in Live! One of these is Capture and the other one is Scale Mode.

Exploring Capture MIDI

Have you ever spent some time jamming some melodies over some drums, or vice versa, and you came up with something really cool along the way, but you didn't press the record button?

Well, the good news is, even though you didn't press the record button, Live "captured" your MIDI notes along the way, as it is always "listening" to the armed MIDI tracks.

Let's try it!

In this example, I am going to come up with a different drum sequence to the existing bass line in **Arrangement View** – however, this feature works the same way in **Session View**:

1. First, mute the already programmed drums.
2. Then, bring in a different Drum Rack preset from the browser onto a new MIDI track.
3. Put the **Metronome** on and set the loop to embrace the clip of the bass line.
4. Next, start jamming some drums over the bass melody.

5. Then, stop playback and hit the **Capture MIDI** button (see *Figure 4.24*):

Figure 4.24 – The Capture MIDI button

Now, you can see the MIDI notes captured from my little jam, even though I never hit the record button (see *Figure 4.25*):

Figure 4.25 – Recalled captured MIDI data by the Capture MIDI function

This feature was revolutionary when it was first introduced in Ableton Live version 10! It can take off the pressure of having to "perform" well while the record button is on, and also ensure that if you just made a mistake by forgetting to press record, you haven't lost your idea!

Next up, we are going to take a look at something that can also help us, but more with the music theory side of things.

Discovering Scale Mode and Scale Settings in Ableton Live 11

This is a new feature in Ableton Live 11 that enables you when it is set up to easily write melodies within the chosen scale.

This feature can be enabled in the **Clip View** (see *Figure 4.26*):

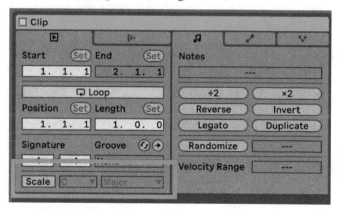

Figure 4.26 – Access to Scale Mode in the Clip View

Let's try it out:

1. Let's head to **Session View** for this task (although it works the same way in both **Session View** and **Arrangement View** since it's a feature that is applied to a MIDI clip).

2. Create a new MIDI track with an instrument playing a piano sound.

3. Now, create an empty MIDI clip.

4. Let's extend the clip to at least **2** bars.

5. Enable the **Scale** button (see *Figure 4.27*) in the **Clip View**.

6. Chose the preferred root note and scale types by using the drop-down menus next to the **Scale** button.

7. Now, you should see some changes both on the Piano Roll and the MIDI editor.

8. All the colored notes are the ones that are part of the chosen scales, so Live is indicating that you should use those (see *Figure 4.27*):

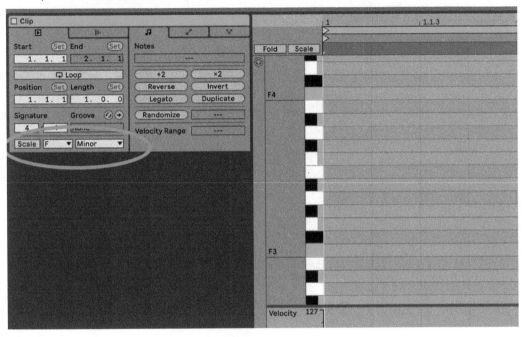

Figure 4.27 – Scale Mode enabled and the Piano Roll and MIDI editor displaying the appropriate notes

9. You also have the option not to display notes at all outside of your chosen scale by hitting the **Scale** button above the Piano Roll (*Figure 4.28*).

Now, you should only see the notes that are part of the chosen scale:

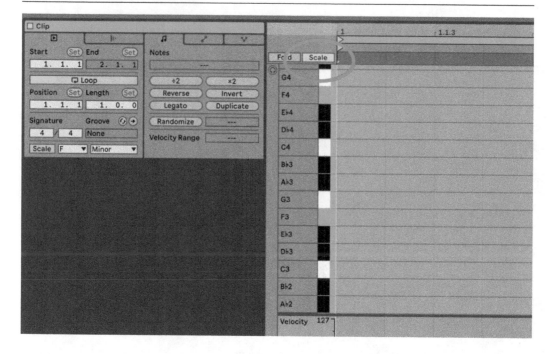

Figure 4.28 – With the Scale (Fold to Scale) button enabled, no notes outside of the scale are displayed

10. You can go ahead and add in some notes by drawing them in with your mouse, and the result will definitely sound pleasant since you cannot hit a wrong note that would result in being out of tune:

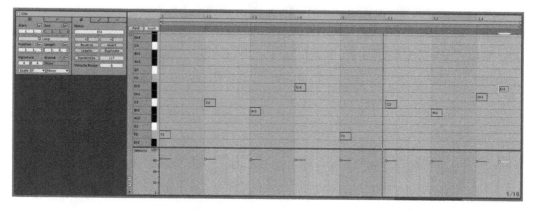

Figure 4.29 – Notes sequenced by staying entirely within the chosen scale

11. We can also choose how we would like to display **flats and sharps** on the Piano Roll, by *Ctrl + click* (*right-click* on Windows) on the Piano Roll to access the context menu:

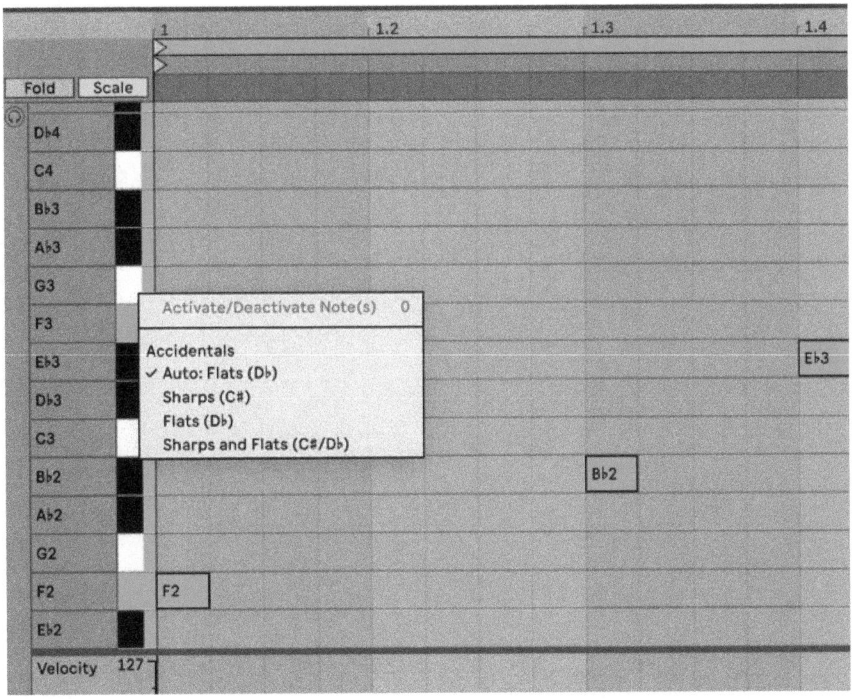

Figure 4.30 – The context menu to display options for flats and sharps on the Piano Roll

12. Now, save the project you have worked with in this chapter, as we will continue to learn how to edit the parts you have created in the next chapter!

The **Scale Mode** is a super useful feature that can provide you with a quick and safe workflow to come up with comprehensive melodies with the comfort of knowing that you will not hit the wrong note.

Summary

We have approached the end of this chapter.

Here, we have learned crucial MIDI sequencing techniques in both **Session View** and **Arrangement View** while we also discovered some helpful creative tools such as Scale and Capture.

We also discovered how to input MIDI notes with our mouse and the Pencil Tool, how to change the grid resolution while inputting notes, and how to record in real time while playing notes with our computer keyboard, as well as a MIDI controller.

We established the importance of the use of Overdub in **Arrangement View** as well as how to use Take Lanes with MIDI tracks as well.

Working with MIDI opens up a super fun world of possibilities and space for our creativity to bloom. It also allows us to work super fast and efficiently to come up with new musical elements for our composition.

In the next chapter, we are going to take a look at how we can edit MIDI information in a corrective and creative way and use some of Live 11's MIDI effects to achieve expressive musical elements.

5
MIDI Editing and MIDI Effects

In the previous chapter, we learned about various MIDI inputting techniques. We looked at using our mouse to input MIDI notes as well as how to play notes in real time.

Both techniques come with pros and cons, and there is no right way of sequencing MIDI; the right way is always going to be the one that we feel the most comfortable with.

This preference might be influenced by our key strengths as musicians and, perhaps, what genre we are producing.

In this chapter, we will explore these pros and cons further and learn how to correct errors with editing, and also have a look at how we can apply edits in a more creative way to improve our MIDI parts.

Furthermore, we will also be looking at some of Live's MIDI effects to further enhance our MIDI sequencing experience and, with that, the potential results.

In this chapter, we are going to cover the following topics:

- Basic MIDI editing functions
- Exploring Quantize, velocity, and Note Chance in Live 11
- The Groove Pool
- Utilizing the MIDI transform tools
- An introduction to multi-clip editing
- Exploring Live's MIDI effects

Technical requirements

In order to follow along with this chapter, you will need the following:

- A computer with at least 8 GB of RAM and an Intel Core i5 processor
- A pair of headphones
- A copy of Live 11 Suite
- The **Chapter 5** Ableton Live project

First, we are going to take a look at some basic MIDI editing techniques carried out in the MIDI Editor.

Understanding the basic MIDI editing functions

Here are some basic functions of MIDI editing that can be carried out in the MIDI Editor:

- **To move a note:** Just grab the note with your cursor and move it to the desired place within the MIDI Editor.
- **To move a note up or down a semitone:** Select the note(s) and hit the *up* and *down arrow* keys.
- **To move notes up and down a whole octave:** Select the note(s) and hit *Shift* + the *up* and *down arrow* keys.
- **To make a selection of all notes placed on the same semitone:** Select a semitone on the piano roll (*Figure 5.1*).

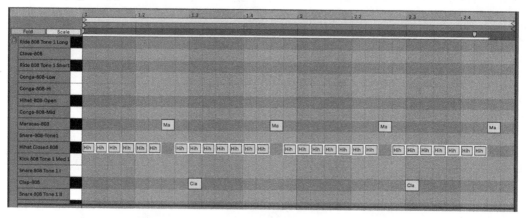

Figure 5.1 – All notes triggered by the same semitone are selected
after clicking on a semitone within the piano roll

- **To change the length of a note:** Simply drag the note out or in.

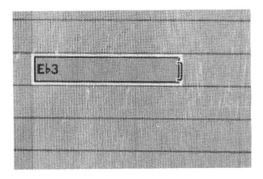

Figure 5.2 – Changing the note length

- **To deactivate notes**: Select the note(s), then *Ctrl + click* (*right-click* on Windows) on them, and chose **Deactivate** from the context menu. Alternatively, after you have made your selection, you can hit *0* to deactivate the note(s).

  Deactivating notes can be a better idea than deleting notes if you are unsure about how your composition will go, since you can always reactivate notes if you have changed your mind about them with a hit of a button.

Now that we covered simple editing techniques, in the next section, we are going to take a look at how we can correct timing errors and humanize patterns.

Exploring Quantize, velocity, and note chance in Live 11

First, we are going to correct the timing issues of some of the instruments in our project.

Quantize

If you decide to utilize real-time recording more in your production, you have probably already realized that it comes with certain pros and cons.

One of the pros is that you are able to capture the *human feel* of playing in terms of timing and velocity, being able to implement natural groove. However, this can be a drawback as well if the timing of your playing is not the greatest, as you could be way too late or early playing the notes, which results in greater timing errors.

These timing errors can be easily fixed by using the **Quantize settings**.

Quantize allows us to correct timing issues by *snapping* notes to the grid that are too late or too early (off the grid). This occurs according to our Quantize settings. These settings allow us to fine-tune the amount of quantization that we are looking to apply, as we might not always want to have "perfect" timing in all our sequences, losing all the natural groove we achieved with our human playing.

Now, let's have a look at how the **Quantize** function works on the legato and staccato patterns, which we sequenced in the previous chapter.

Using Quantize with the legato pattern

Let's have a look at it by following these steps:

1. In the **Chapter 5** project, navigate to the bass track (**Clean Reese**) in the Session View.

2. Select the clip called **legato** and double-click on it so that you can view the notes of the clip in the MIDI Editor.

3. Now, you can *Ctrl + click* (*right-click* on Windows) on the grid and choose **Quantize** from the context menu. Alternatively, you can use the *Cmd + U* (*Ctrl + U* for Windows) key command.

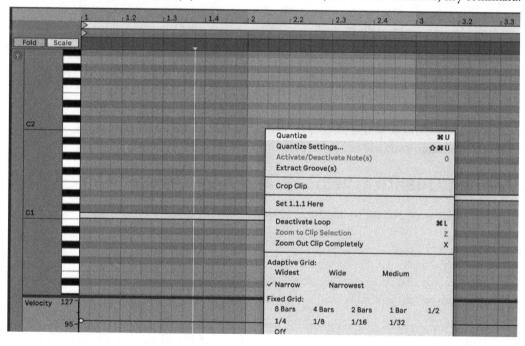

Figure 5.3 – The Quantize option in the context menu

Note that when you applied this command, the notes went from being off the grid (*Figure 5.4*) to snapping fully to the grid (*Figure 5.5*).

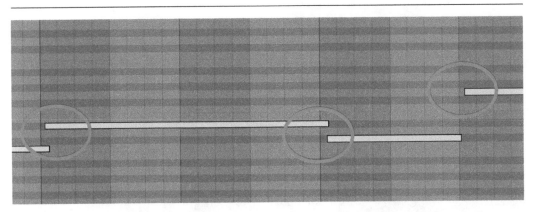

Figure 5.4 – Notes before applying quantization

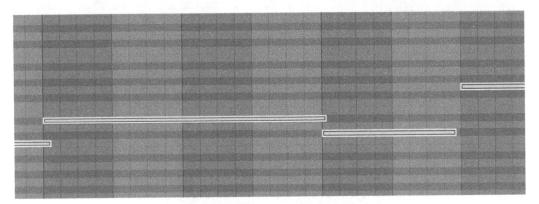

Figure 5.5 – Notes after applying quantization

Using Quantize with the staccato pattern

Now that we have fully corrected the timing errors on the legato pattern, we are going to move on to look at the staccato pattern:

1. On the same track, select the clip called **staccato**.

2. Now, before we Quantize again, we will bring up the **Quantize Settings….** You can *Ctrl + click* (*right-click* on Windows) again in the MIDI Editor, and this time choose, **Quantize Settings….** Alternatively, use the *Shift + Cmd + U* (*Shift + Ctrl + U* for Windows) key command.

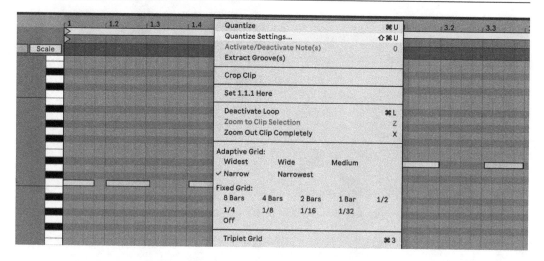

Figure 5.6 – Quantize settings in the context menu

3.   Now, you will see a pop-up window, where you can amend what grid value you would like
     to quantize to, how much quantization you would like to apply, and whether this should be
     applied to the note start or the note end, or both.

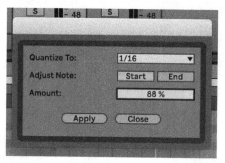

Figure 5.7 – The Quantize settings values

I chose **88%** for the amount, and **1/16** notes to adjust the note start; this way, I will keep some
of the natural swings that the pattern had, but the notes will move 88% closer to the grid value.

4.   Then, we can simply hit **Apply**!

Now that we have looked at how to Quantize, let's talk some more about velocity!

Velocity

We discussed in the previous chapter what velocity is – the force that MIDI notes are played with.
For example, if you hit a key harder (with more force) on your MIDI keyboard, it will result in higher
velocity and a louder note.

We also discussed that when we are using our mouse to input MIDI notes, even though we are sequencing with no timing errors (which is great!), we are adding each note at the same velocity, which results in a fairly flat sequence with absolutely no groove.

Let's take, as an example, a real-life drummer, playing repeated hi-hat notes in a 1/16 pattern. There is no way each note will have the same volume, as the drummer is a human being, incapable of hitting the hi-hat repeatedly with the exact same force. This is something that we are trying to mimic while making music on a computer, so we can emulate the human feel of playing. To do that, we are going to explore how we can manipulate the velocity of our MIDI notes.

Follow these steps:

1. In the Session View, navigate to the **808 Fairweather** track and double-click on the clip called **more kicks** to bring up its notes in the MIDI Editor.

2. Make sure you display the velocity at the bottom, as we learned to do in the previous chapter, by clicking on the **Show/Hide Velocity Editor** button.

    You will see the flat velocity for every single note in the sequence. We are going to work on the velocity of the hi-hats.

3. Click on the note that holds the closed hi-hats on the piano roll to select all the hi-hat notes at once. You will see that all the hi-hat notes became highlighted, as well as the related velocity markers of the notes (*Figure 5.8*).

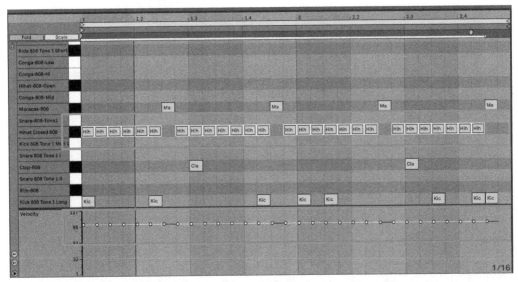

Figure 5.8 – All hi-hats and their velocity markers are selected

4. Now, you can grab one of the markers (make sure you only click on it once; otherwise, you will lose the selection) and move them up and down.

5. Note that all the selected note's velocity markers move together.

6. This is great, and it also shows how it would work with a single note selected to enable you to set different velocities to individual notes.

    Note also that as you decrease the velocity and the notes get quieter, the color of the notes also fade, and vice versa as you increase the velocity.

We have just learned how we can change the velocity of selected notes simultaneously or individually by moving the velocity markers.

Our original plan was to change the velocity of the hi-hat notes so that every single one of them isn't flat and identical.

You have probably already figured that you can just go and adjust the velocity marker of every single one of them, which is correct.

However, a new feature was introduced in Live 11 that enables you to randomize and further edit the velocity of notes with a more time-efficient technique.

Velocity randomization in Live 11

Let's discover how to use this new feature:

1. Make sure you still have all the hi-hat notes selected within the clip called **more kicks**.

2. Now, we are going to navigate to the Clip View and have a look at the **Tool** tab.

    Here, we are particularly interested in the **Randomize** button, the **Randomize** range, and **Velocity Range**.

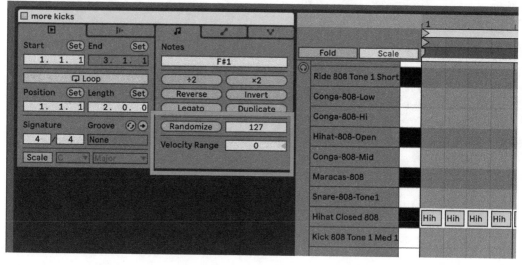

Figure 5.9 – The velocity settings in the Tool tab

3.   We will go ahead and randomize the velocity of the hi-hat notes. First, I will adjust the amount of randomization to be applied by the **Randomize** range slider, which currently shows **127** (*Figure 5.9*). I will set this to 37.

4.   Now, hit the **Randomize** button.

5.   If you check the velocity of the hi-hat notes we selected, you will see that the velocity has been successfully randomized. And if you then listen, you should hear a more "human," realistic hi-hat pattern playing.

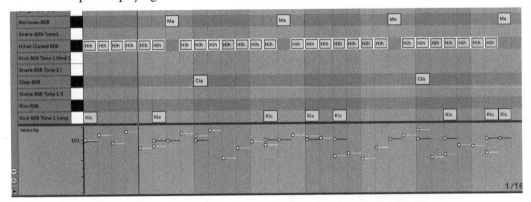

Figure 5.10 – The randomized velocity of the hi-hat notes

6.   To manipulate the velocity range for the selected notes, you can use the **Velocity Range** slider. I will set it to -22 to better fit my taste.

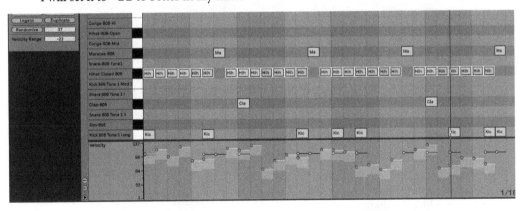

Figure 5.11 – The velocity range of the hi-hats adjusted

With this new feature in Live 11, we can save a great amount of time while we are adjusting note velocity, and randomization is always an exciting topic in music-making, in my opinion. Please note that these changes were only applied to the clip called **more kicks** as these settings are stored and can be applied differently to individual clips.

When Live 11 was released, there was another feature introduced that can inject some extra fun into our MIDI sequencing adventures – **note chance**.

In the next section of this chapter, we will be taking a close look at it!

Note chance

This new feature allows us to change the probability of selected notes that play back each time a clip repeats itself.

To display the **Chance** lane in the MIDI Editor, we will hit the **Show/Hide Probability Editor** button.

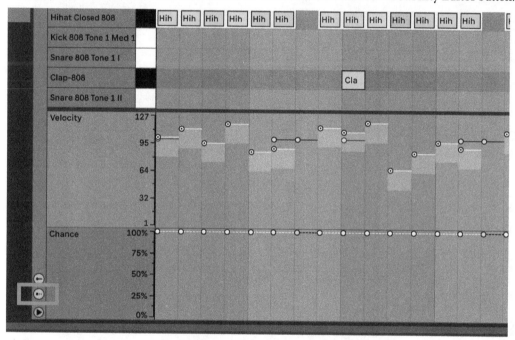

Figure 5.12 – Displaying note chance

Note

In *Figure 5.12*, we are displaying the note chance of our hi-hat notes, as they are still selected, to continue working on them.

A chance marker of a note set to 0% will result in the note never playing back, while one set to **100%** will always play back. This % range is the range for the probability of the note playing back when the clip repeats – the higher the number, the more likely the note will play back when the clip repeats itself.

Just like with velocity, we can also randomize the probability of the notes.

Follow these steps:

1. Make sure the hi-hat notes are still selected within the clip called **more kicks**.

2. Make sure you have selected the **Chance** expression editor lane (*Figure 5.13*).

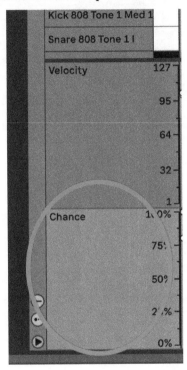

Figure 5.13 – The Chance expression editor lane selected

3. Navigate to the Clip View and the **Tool** tab again.

4. Set the **Randomize** range to your taste (I will set mine to 50%).

5. Hit the **Randomize** button.

6. Now, you should see the probability markers randomized, similar to how the velocity markers were randomized previously (*Figure 5.14*).

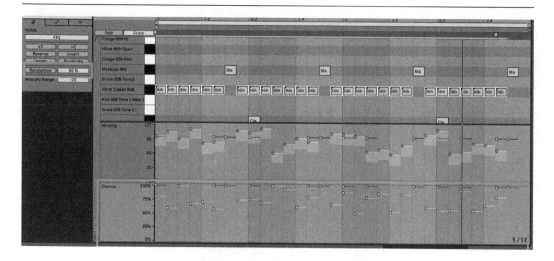

Figure 5.14 – The randomized note probability of hi-hats

If you play back the sequence, you will realize that each time the clip repeats, you hear a slightly different hi-hat pattern playing back.

You can add more randomization if you want, by adjusting further the **Randomization** amount slide and applying it as many times as you like. Please note that these settings were also applied only to the clip called **more kicks** as these settings are stored and can be applied to individual clips.

This feature can add great unpredictability and surprise to your music. It can also help you to come up with new sequences by capturing the changes introduced by the note probability randomization.

To do that, you can just simply record the output of this MIDI track to a new MIDI track.

Here are the steps:

1. Create a new empty MIDI track.

2. On the new MIDI track's **MIDI From** section, choose the **808 Fairweather** track (*Figure 5.15*).

3. Arm this new MIDI track.

4. Hit the **Clip Record** button to begin the recording (*Figure 5.15*).

Figure 5.15 – The note probability result of the more kicks clip of the
808 Fairweather track is recorded onto a new MIDI track

5. Let the clip that you are recording repeat itself a few times in order to capture the different variations of the hi-hat pattern as a result of its probability settings.

6. Now, you can check what you have recorded, and you will see that the MIDI notes of the hi-hats are never really the same!

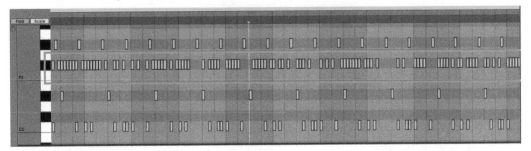

Figure 5.16 – The recorded result of the notes with note probability set

Now, we can see physical proof of note probability on the hi-hats working, not just hear it. We can now delete the track we just created with the recorded clip, or we can move this clip from this empty MIDI track back onto the **808 Fairweather** track as a new variation of our drum patterns.

Now that we have looked at some great tools to humanize and add some unpredictability to our MIDI sequences by learning about velocity and note probability randomization, we will further investigate how we can humanize and add more movement to our MIDI parts by discovering the Groove Pool in the next section.

Diving into the Groove Pool

Step-inputted or fully quantized sequences can lack the feel of real performance because they are "too perfect," "too on time," or just sound unnatural and quite robotic. The same can be said about certain audio loops as well. Applying **groove** will slightly change the timing and "feel" of a sequence.

To make things even more interesting, we can also extract a groove from real-life recorded material and apply it to our MIDI.

Let's have a look at how to do it:

1. Navigate to the clip on the **808 Fairweather** kit called **k c hh m**.

Figure 5.17 – The k c hh m clip selected

Note that this clip has a flat equal velocity on all the notes, which are all strictly arranged on the grid. If we play this back, it sounds super unnatural, flat, and just doesn't have any life. Let's breathe some in it!

2. To find the grooves, navigate to the browser and choose **Grooves** under **Categories** (*Figure 5.18*).

3. Choose the **2 Step Shuffled 16ths.arg** groove and drag and drop it onto the **k c hh m** clip.

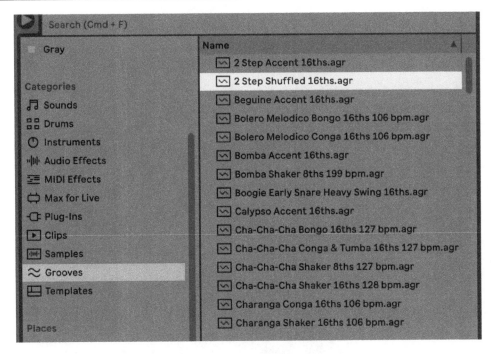

Figure 5.18 – Grooves in the browser

This is one of the quickest ways to audition and load grooves onto clips.

Now, you will notice that the Groove Pool opened up in Live. You can hide and show the Groove Pool with the button encircled in *Figure 5.19*.

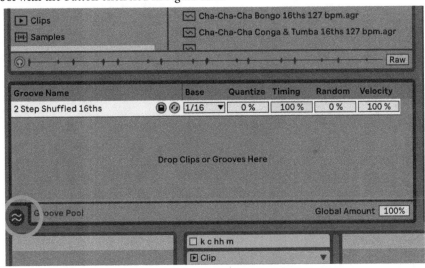

Figure 5.19 – The Groove Pool with the loaded groove and the Hide/Show button

You can also drag grooves directly into the Groove Pool from the browser.

4.   Now, navigate down to the Clip View, and you will see that the groove has been loaded onto the MIDI clip.

If we click on the chooser, we can see the list of grooves we have in the Groove Pool and choose from them. Since we only selected one, we only see that one in the dropdown.

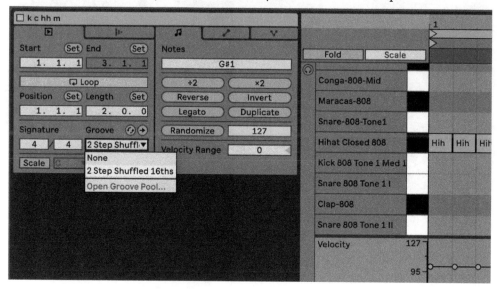

Figure 5.20 – The groove in the Clip View

5.   Now that we have the groove in the Groove Pool and on the clip, we can head to the Groove Pool to make adjustments (see *Figure 5.21*):

   • **Base:** The subdivision that the groove and the clip are set to.

   • **Quantize:** Pre-quantization is applied to the clip before the re-quantization of the groove. This happens with the value stated by the base.

   • **Timing:** How strongly the groove will be applied to all clips where it is assigned (*Figure 5.21*).

   • **Random:** The amount of fluctuation of timing that will be applied.

   • **Velocity:** The amount of groove accent that will be applied to the clip's velocities.

   • **Global Amount:** This controls the overall amount of all the preceding settings, applied to all grooves in the Groove Pool (*Figure 5.21*).

Once you have amended these settings to your taste and you reckon you will recall your amended groove in the future, you can save the settings in your **User Library** by hitting the little floppy disk button (*Figure 5.21*).

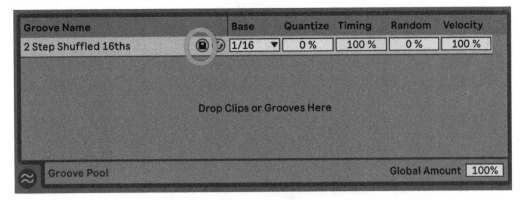

Figure 5.21 – The Groove Pool's settings

Next to the floppy disk button that saves the settings to the User Library, you will find the **Hot-Swap** button, which allows you to change presets quickly.

6. As you are adjusting the settings in the Groove Pool and playing back the clip, you can hear the effect of the groove on the clip in real time. However, you will see no change in the timing of the notes or the velocity in the MIDI Editor. In order to see these changes, you need to **commit** the groove to the clip.

7. Head to the Clip View and hit the **Commit** button:

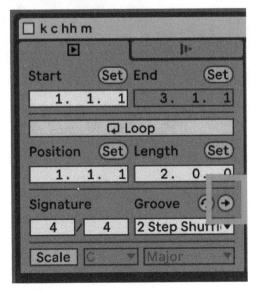

Figure 5.22 – The groove Commit button

8. Now, you will see the applied groove represented in the MIDI Editor, as the note timing has slightly changed, as well as the velocity of the notes (*Figure 5.23* and *Figure 5.24*).

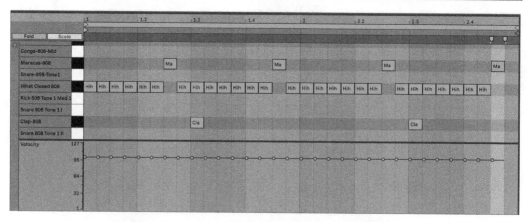

Figure 5.23 – The groove is not committed to the MIDI clip

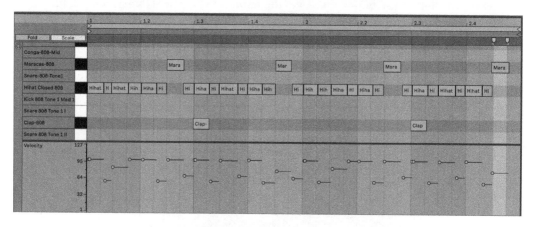

Figure 5.24 – The groove is committed to the MIDI clip

On the left side, next to the **Commit** button, we have another **Hot-Swap** button, which will again allow us to swap the grooves from the library fast.

> **Note**
> Grooves work exactly the same way with **audio clips** as they do with MIDI clips.

Applying different grooves to individual drum sounds

In the previous section, we worked with a MIDI clip that triggers a drum rack. You have probably realized that grooves were applied to the whole clip and every single note in it. Now, what would happen if you wanted to apply a different groove just to your hi-hat notes, for example, but these notes are in the same clip as the other notes? Well, all we need to do is extract the hi-hats from the drum rack so that they end up on their own track and, therefore, in their own clip!

We will be looking at **drum racks** in more detail in *Chapter 8, Exploring Device Racks in Live 11*, but for now, just follow these simple steps:

1. Head to the **808 Fairweather** track, and in the mixer, toggle the **Chain-Mixer Fold** buttons (*Figure 5.25*).

2. Once you have found the hi-hats chain, *Ctrl + click* (*right-click* for Windows) on the chain name and choose **Extract Chains**. Since we have only selected one chain, Live will only extract the selected chain, which is the hi-hats chain.

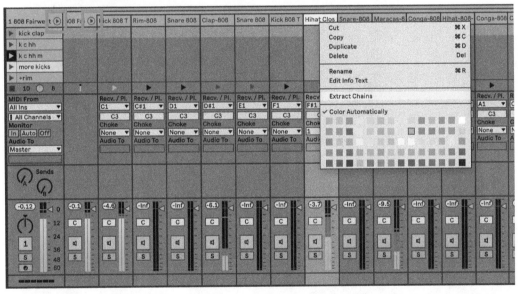

Figure 5.25 – The Chain-Mixer Fold buttons and the Extract Chains command in the context menu

Note that you now have a new **808 Fairweather** track with a drum rack on it. This drum rack only contains the extracted hi-hat sound, and the clips on this new track only contains the hi-hat notes extracted out from the original **808 Fairweather** track's clips.

Figure 5.26 – The new 808 Fairweather track only contains the extracted hi-hats

3. If you go back to the original **808 Fairweather** track and display the drum rack, you will see that the hi-hat sound has now disappeared from this rack (*Figure 5.27*).

Figure 5.27 – The original 808 Fairweather track, now without the hi-hat after extraction

4. Since the hi-hats are now living in their own dedicated track and in their own dedicated clips, you can apply a different groove to them.

In this section, we had a look at how we can work with grooves that come with the Ableton Live Library. In the next section, we will explore how we can extract grooves from existing audio loops and apply them to our MIDI clips.

Extracting grooves

In order to see how extracting grooves works in Live, we will use the track called **DRUM LOOP** and the audio clip inserted on this track:

1. *Ctrl + click* (*right-click* for Windows) on the **DRUM LOOP** clip and choose **Extract Groove(s)** from the context menu.

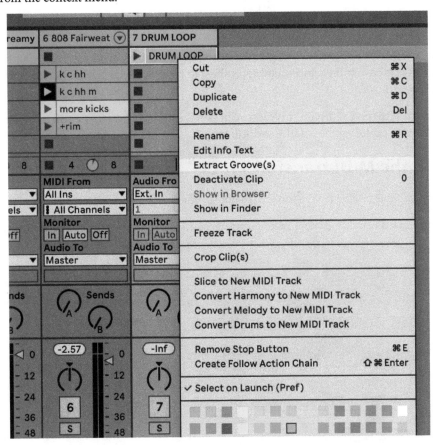

Figure 5.28 – The Extract Groove(s) command in the context menu

Now, you will find the extracted groove in the Groove Pool.

2.   You can apply it to any clips in Live now; you can also save it to your User Library, as we learned in the previous section.

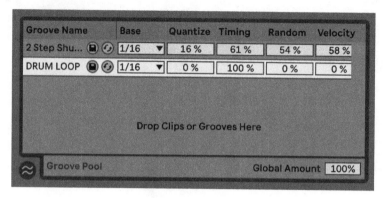

Figure 5.29 – The extracted groove in the Groove Pool

This is a super useful feature; you can just get your hands on audio and MIDI loops from your favorite artists, extract the groove of these loops, and apply them to your own sequences to breathe some new life into your own music.

We have arrived at the end of discovering Groove in Live. In the next section, we will revisit the Clip View and dive into exploring the MIDI transform tools.

Utilizing the MIDI transform tools

MIDI transform tools (*Figure 5.30*) allow you to quickly manipulate your MIDI sequences.

These can be applied to selected notes within a sequence and also allow us to adjust the time range.

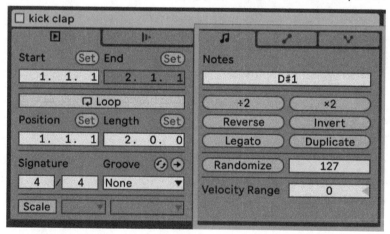

Figure 5.30 – The MIDI transform tools in the Notes tab

We already looked at what **Randomize** and **Velocity Range** do earlier in this chapter, so let's quickly have a look at the remaining tools:

- **The transpose slider**: This will transpose the selected notes.

- **The ÷2 and x2 buttons**: These will double or halve the playback speed. This is a super useful tool if you want to, for example, quickly test how your beats would sound in half-time, which can be a great technique to apply within your arrangement, even if the beats only drop by half just for a section of a song.

- **Reverse**: This command will reverse the selected notes, meaning that the last note will become the first one and the first note will become the last one.

- **Invert**: This command will also flip the selected notes so that the highest note will become the lowest note, and vice versa.

> **Note**
>
> When you invert the notes, some notes might end up outside of the scale you are working in. To get around this, you can use the Scale MIDI effect device (which we will cover later in this chapter) or edit the notes using the **Scale** function in the MIDI editor that we explored in *Chapter 4, Exploring MIDI Sequencing Techniques*!

On the Clean Reese track, I duplicated the staccato clip (*Figure 5.31*).

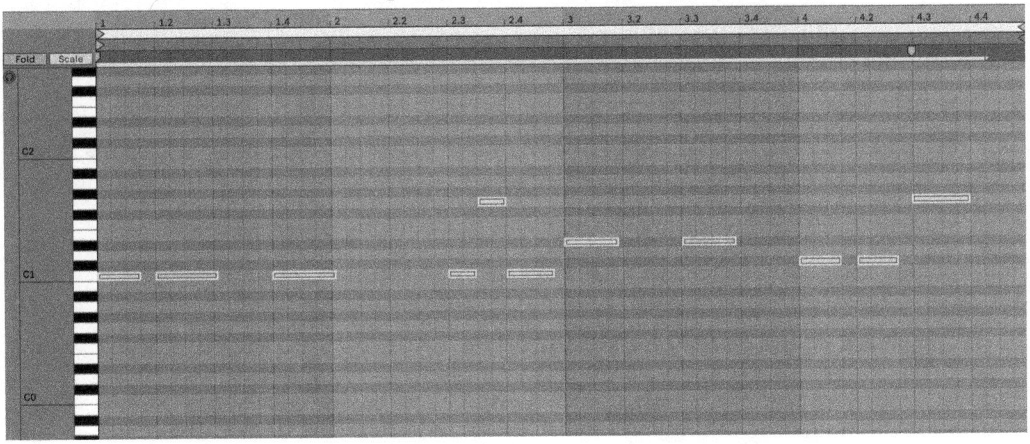

Figure 5.31 – The Clean Reese track's staccato clip before inverting notes

In the duplicated clip, I selected the notes and then hit the **Invert** button (*Figure 5.32*).

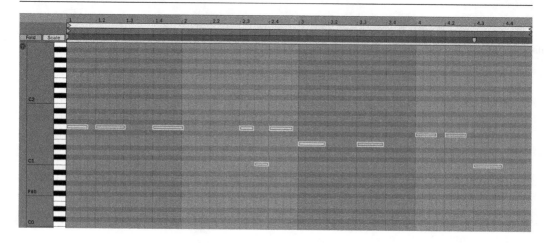

Figure 5.32 – The Clean Reese track's duplicated staccato clip after inverting notes

Both **Reverse** and **Invert** are helpful tools to help you create a variation of your MIDI patterns.

- **Legato** (*Figure 5.30*): This feature will lengthen or shorten notes so that they will just be long enough to reach the beginning of the next note in the sequence.

  For example, let's say you just recorded some bass notes and there are gaps between the notes. You would want to extend the notes so that they "meet on the grid" but don't overlap. This can be done, of course, by adjusting each note's length manually, but instead, you can just select all the notes, hit the **Legato** button, and then the notes will "meet on the grid" with no gaps between them, and no overlapping either.

- **The Duplicate button** (*Figure 5.30*): When you hit this button, Live will double the notes within the clip. So, for example, if you are looking to quickly double your one-bar loop to two bars, then just hit this button instead of trying to move the notes manually, which can be time-consuming.

Now that we have covered the MIDI transform tools that can provide you with a quick and seamless editing workflow, in the next section, we are going to discover multi-clip editing in Live 11!

An introduction to multi-clip editing

We can also edit notes of multiple MIDI clips at the same time, within the MIDI Editor.

In *Figure 5.33*, I selected the **legato** clip from the **Clean Reese** track, the clip from the **E-Piano** track, and the **k c hh m** clip from the **808 Fairweather** track that holds hi-hat notes by holding down the *Cmd* button and clicking on the desired clips.

Figure 5.33 – Multiple clips selected for multi-clip editing

You can see in the MIDI Editor that there are three clips selected, which are written in the Clip Detail View, and you can also see the loop braces of the three clips at the top of the MIDI Editor, which can be adjusted individually by clicking on the one that we want to adjust.

All the notes we are displaying can now be moved and edited together, even though they are clips from various tracks.

We can also choose to work with **Focus** mode, which will allow us to select a single clip for editing while we are still viewing multiple clips.

In *Figure 5.34*, you can see that I selected in the Loop Bar the **k c hh m** clip, which holds some hi-hat notes. By hitting the **Focus** button, I can still see the other clip's notes, but I cannot edit them because I'm only "focusing" on the selected ones.

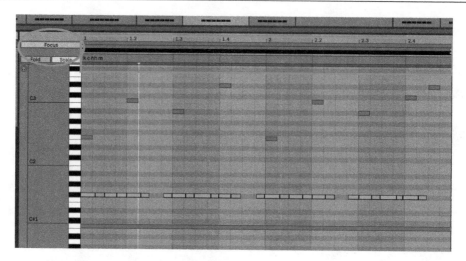

Figure 5.34 – The Focus button and the focused clip in the MIDI Editor

This is a super useful function if you have instruments programmed in a way that they "talk to each other" within an arrangement, they are layered, or you are comparing notes of clips within the same track, so you can edit them simultaneously while viewing them alongside each other.

In *Figure 5.35*, you can see that I **deactivated** some notes of this hi-hat sequence.

This can be done by selecting notes and then hitting *0* on your computer keyboard, or choosing the **Deactivate Notes** option from the context menu after *Ctrl + click* (*right-click* for Windows) on the selected notes.

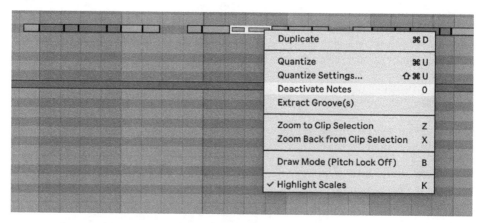

Figure 5.35 – Deactivated notes and further notes selected to be deactivated from the contextual menu

This is a great editing technique to use, as we didn't actually delete the notes; we just made them inactive, so they are still there but will not play back.

If you change your mind later, you can *Ctrl + click* (*right-click* for Windows) on the selected deactivated notes and choose **Activate Notes**.

> **Note**
>
> You can select up to eight clips to be viewed together in the MIDI Editor for multi-clip editing.
>
> These clips can be selected from the same track or from across various tracks in the Session View, or from eight different tracks in the Arrangement View.

We have arrived at the end of the editing functions in Live in this chapter. In the next section, we are going to take a look at Live's MIDI effects.

Exploring Live's MIDI effects

There are a great number of MIDI effects that we can access in the browser:

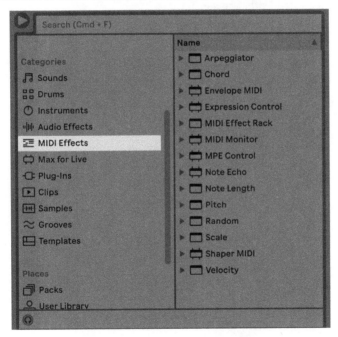

Figure 5.36 – MIDI effects in the browser

> **Note**
>
> Some of the MIDI effects in *Figure 5.36* are from **Packs** and **Max for Live** devices. If you are an owner of a Live Suite license, you can download these from **Packs** under **Places** in the browser.

MIDI effects will only work on MIDI tracks, since they will be manipulating the MIDI data before it hits the inserted instrument on the track, which will convert this MIDI data into an audio signal.

We can simply drag and drop MIDI effects onto MIDI tracks. They will be inserted before the instrument that the MIDI notes are triggering.

We can load multiple MIDI effects onto a track, and we can also load the same MIDI effects onto the same track multiple times.

Let's dive in now and take a look at what these MIDI effects can do!

Arpeggiator

The **Arpeggiator** device will create a repeating pattern of notes.

For example, if you have one note sequenced, the arpeggiator will just keep repeating this one note; however, if you hold down on your MIDI controller (or program in) two or more notes, you will have a very interesting result created by the arpeggiator.

Please note

MIDI effects won't change the original notes in the MIDI Editor, so you will not be able to see the notes created by the MIDI effects; you will only hear the result.

If you want to capture the result of the MIDI effects, you need to record it to a new MIDI track. This can be done by using the method that we used earlier in this chapter when we learned about *note chance* (*Figure 5.15*).

Let's try out the **Arpeggiator** device:

1. If you navigate to the **Aaghra Keys** track and click on the clip called **synth** on this track, you will see the chords containing two notes in the MIDI Editor.

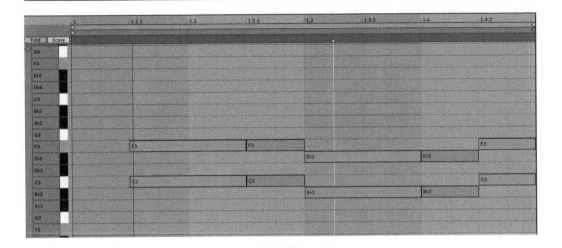

Figure 5.37 – Chords of the Aaghra Keys track

2.   Now, you can enable the **Arpeggiator** device inserted onto this track already:

Figure 5.38 – The Arpeggiator, its settings, and the Bypass button

You will hear the result, the arpeggiated notes; however, you will still see the same continuous notes in the MIDI Editor.

3.   In *Figure 5.39*, you can see the arpeggiated notes of the chords of *Figure 5.37* recorded onto a new MIDI track called **9 MIDI**.

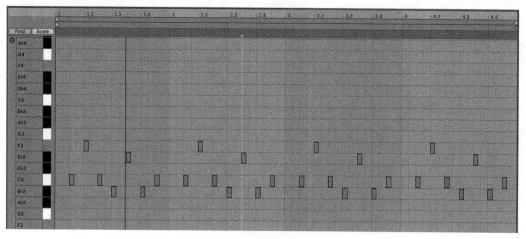

Figure 5.39 – The resulting arpeggiated notes recorded onto a new MIDI track

The Arpeggiator is a great MIDI effect that can be used to come up with more rhythmic melodic elements, and it can also be really nice to use as an extra instrument layer.

For example, if you have a chord progression triggering a pad sound, you can have the same chords copied over to, for example, a piano track. This piano track would also have the Arpeggiator on it. This will result in two instruments playing the same notes, but the instruments are different; furthermore, one is playing continuous notes, and the other is playing the same notes but in an arpeggiated manner.

Chord

The **Chord** MIDI effect will create chords from the incoming MIDI notes. Each incoming MIDI note can have up to six additional notes added to it.

Figure 5.40 – The Chord device

Note Length

Note Length will alter the length of incoming notes. It can also be set up in a way that it will trigger notes of a *MIDI off* message (for example, when you release a note on your MIDI controller) instead of a *MIDI on* message (pressing a note down).

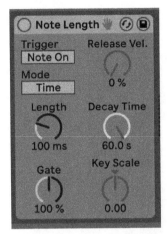

Figure 5.41 – The Note Length device

Pitch

The **Pitch** device will simply transpose incoming MIDI notes.

Figure 5.42 – The Pitch device

Random

Random will introduce some surprises into your sequences (*Figure 5.43*). It will randomize which inputted notes will actually play back. Once this device is set up and you experiment with it, you can achieve some super fun results with it.

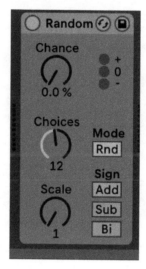

Figure 5.43 – The Random device

Scale

Personally, I find the **Scale** device quite an exciting effect. It can be a useful tool if you are not very confident with music theory (*Figure 5.44*).

You can select a specific scale type and a root note, and then any incoming MIDI notes that aren't part of the chosen scale will be "snapped" to the closest note that is part of the chosen scale. Pretty cool, huh?

> **Important note**
>
> Once again, let me remind you what we learned earlier about MIDI effects not changing your MIDI notes in the MIDI Editor; you will only hear the result until you delete or bypass the MIDI effect on the track. If you want to have the resulting notes captured within Live and see them represented in the MIDI Editor, then you will need to record the output of the track with the **Scale** device applied to it to a new MIDI track.

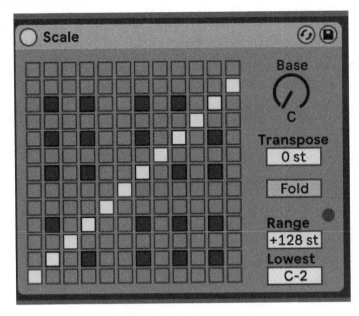

Figure 5.44 – The Scale device

Velocity

The **Velocity** device affects incoming velocity values based on various settings. These alterations can be controlled precisely or in a more random manner.

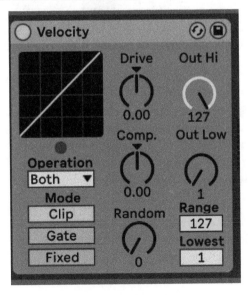

Figure 5.45 – The Velocity device

We are getting near the end of this chapter; however, before we wrap it up, I wanted to show you how we can stack up various MIDI effects to let Live generate some cool sequences for us.

If you navigate to the track called **MIDI FXs**, you will see that I sequenced one single note of **F3** into a clip in the Session View (*Figure 5.46*).

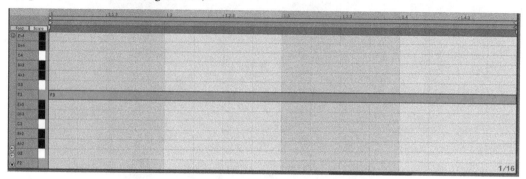

Figure 5.46 – A single note of F3 sequenced in the Session View on the MIDI FXs track

If you navigate to the device view of the track, you will see the single chain of MIDI effects that I added to the track, which consists of the **Chord**, **Arpeggiator**, **Random**, **Velocity**, and **Scale** devices (*Figure 5.47*).

Figure 5.47 – A chain of MIDI effects on the MIDI FXs track

You can set these devices to your taste; the point is that with the help of these MIDI effect devices, we are generating an interesting sequence out of one single note. The **Chord** device will create a chord from a single note, which then gets fed into the **Arpeggiator** device to create an arpeggiated sequence, which then will be randomized by the **Random** device. After that, the velocity gets altered by the **Velocity** device, and the **Scale** device will ensure that we are only hearing notes from the generated sequence that are part of the chosen scale we set up.

Of course, the order of these devices is really important; as you can see, the generated notes on one device are fed into the next device. Experiment with the devices, and you will usually come up with something really cool and creative in no time!

Summary

We have reached the end of this chapter.

First, we learned how we can apply MIDI editing functions, and explored some new Live 11 features such as note velocity and probability randomization.

We had an extended look at the Groove Pool and how to work with grooves in Live, which is super important knowledge for any producers, no matter what genre of music they are creating.

We looked at MIDI transform tools that can speed up our workflow, as well as allow us to modify our patterns more creatively, using the **Invert** and **Reverse** functions.

Finally, we learned how much difference multi-clip editing can make and what MIDI effects Live has available for us.

In the next chapter, we are going to dive in and discover how we can extensively use take lanes and comping as well as track linking, which are all new and exciting Live 11 features.

Part 2:
Creative Music
Production Techniques
with Ableton Live 11

By successfully navigating through Part 2 of this book, you will sharpen your music production skills and deepen your understanding of the capabilities of Live 11. You will have the ability to incorporate Live 11's new and enhanced effects into your existing workflow, manage effect chains and processing more efficiently, and build intricate Device Racks. The book will also cover the powerful Audio to MIDI conversion tools, allowing you to quickly translate and generate ideas. Moreover, you will delve into Live's automation and modulation features, and learn about techniques to streamline project organization and enhance your workflow. To round it all off, you will be introduced to one of Live 11's latest additions, MIDI Polyphonic Expression, giving you the power to create dynamic and evolving sounds and textures.

This part comprises the following chapters:

- *Chapter 6, Comping and Track Linking*
- *Chapter 7, Discovering Some of Live 11's Creative Audio Effects*
- *Chapter 8, Exploring Device Racks in Live 11*
- *Chapter 9, Audio to MIDI Conversion, Slicing to MIDI, and the Simpler Device*
- *Chapter 10, Utilizing Arrangement and Organization Techniques in Our Ableton Live Project*
- *Chapter 11, Implementing Automation and Modulation*
- *Chapter 12, Getting Started with MPE in Ableton Live 11*

6

Comping and Track Linking

There are two new functions that arrived with the Live 11 update, track linking and Take Lanes and comping, which we already started to have a look at in *Chapter 2, Recording Audio in Ableton Live 11*. These features are available in **Arrangement View** only and can be applied to both audio and MIDI! These techniques will not only offer you quicker editing in Live but can also be applied in creative ways too.

In this chapter, we are going to cover the following topics:

- Track linking
- Take Lanes and comping
- Creative comping

Technical requirements

In order to follow along with this chapter, you will need the following:

- A computer with at least 8 GB of RAM at least and an Intel Core i5 processor
- A pair of headphones
- A copy of Live 11 Suite
- The **Chapter 6** Ableton Live project

Track linking in Live 11

For someone who is coming from using Pro Tools, for example, track linking is a golden feature.

No matter whether you have multiple layers of vocals and harmonies, different tracks that are working together within the same tune in the timeline, or you took the time to multi-track record drums with multiple microphones and all of them need to be edited together, this feature will cut a great amount of time spent on editing materials:

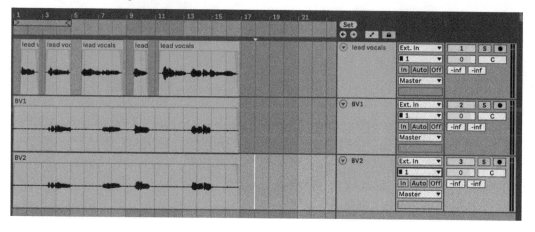

Figure 6.1 – Two backing vocal tracks following the lead vocals

In the example here (see *Figure 6.1*), we can see that we have two backing vocal tracks recorded. They are working together with the lead vocals, so I would apply similar editing to them. Before, this would have been done by either selecting both clips and holding down *Shift* while editing or editing them separately.

Now, we are going to link the tracks together:

1. Select the tracks that you would like to have linked together (have them in a link group).
2. *Ctrl + click* (*right-click* on Windows) on the selected tracks and choose **Link Tracks** (see *Figure 6.2*):

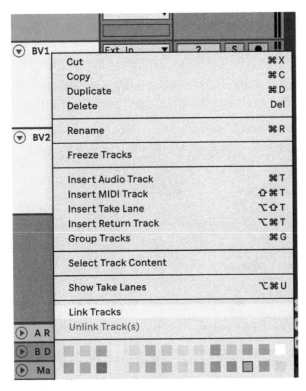

Figure 6.2 – The Link Tracks option in the context menu

Now, you will see the linked track indicator in the corner of the linked tracks (see *Figure 6.3*):

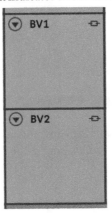

Figure 6.3 – The linked track indicator on linked tracks

If you decided to record additional layers before starting editing, you can add the freshly edited tracks to these linked tracks too. Just select the linked track indicator on the linked tracks, also select the new tracks that you'd like to add to the already linked tracks, and perform the same steps as before for track linking.

(If you'd like to remove one or more tracks from this link group, just select the track header of the track or tracks, *Ctrl + click* (*right-click* on Windows), and choose **Unlink Track(s)**).

Now, we can perform editing on multiple tracks at once (see *Figure 6.4* and *Figure 6.5*):

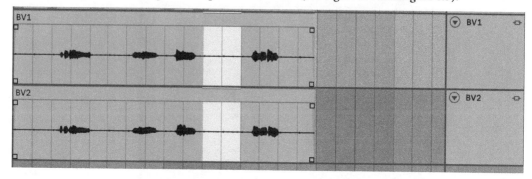

Figure 6.4 – Making a selection across linked tracks

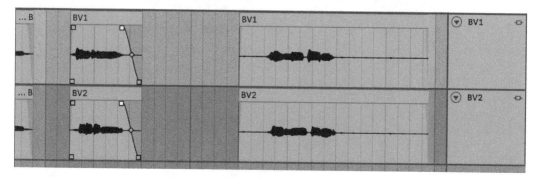

Figure 6.5 – Adjusting fades across linked tracks

Besides making selections, splitting or trimming clips, and adding or adjusting fades (as we looked at previously), you will also be able to do the following to the linked tracks at once:

- Consolidating.

- Warping, transposing, or adjusting clip gain (operations performed in the Clip View) (see *Figure 6.6*):

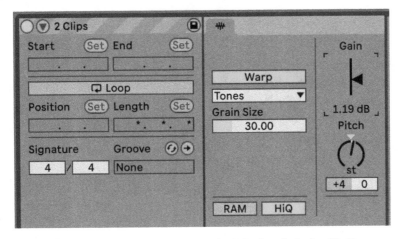

Figure 6.6 – Adjusting parameters to the linked tracks in the Clip View

Tip

It is important to note that these linked track editing operations will work best if the clips that you are trying to edit all at once have the same clip length across the linked tracks!

- Arming and disarming tracks. This is particularly handy for multi-track recording. Maybe you are recording guitars and you'd like to capture the amp with a microphone and also record the clear direct signal on different tracks, or you are recording drums (see *Figure 6.7*):

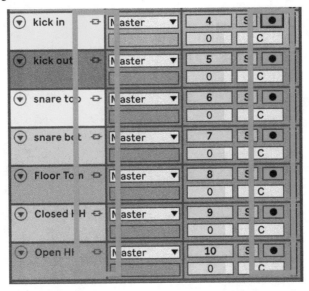

Figure 6.7 – Tracks are linked and armed for multi-track drum recording

- Comping operations, enabling and disabling audition mode on Take Lanes, and renaming, inserting, and deleting Take Lanes.

Now we have introduced the previously mentioned comping features, let's dive into comping with Live 11, to gain a deeper understanding of all this. For this step-by-step example, I used audio tracks. However, track linking works exactly the same way with MIDI tracks.

Comping in Live 11

Another fantastic new feature arrived with the Live 11 update. If you have used a different DAW before, you most probably came across the comping feature in your DAW before.

We have already looked at how to use Take Lanes and record into them in *Chapter 2, Recording Audio in Ableton Live 11*. Now, we are going to open that project that we recorded and comp those takes.

I have renamed the clips in the Take Lanes and re-colored them, which you can do by *Ctrl + click* (*right-click* for Windows) on the clip and choosing these options from the context menu (see *Figure 6.8*):

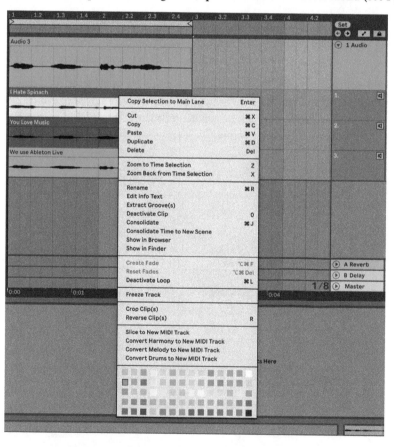

Figure 6.8 – Take Lanes are re-colored and renamed

You can give this process a bit more thought when you are recording vocals or instruments, also in terms of how you are naming the Take Lanes themselves.

> **Tip**
> You can use color coding to indicate the quality of the Take Lanes, so, for example, the not-so-great ones can be orange and the ones that have quite a few mistakes in them can be red, so this traffic light coloring will make it easy for you to navigate your Take Lanes when coming back to it later and comping.

I have also renamed the track itself **MAIN COMP** and numbered the Take Lanes (see *Figure 6.9*).

Now, we are going to pick parts of each take to comp the main take.

In order to audition (as in, hear) each take, we can use the Audition buttons (see *Figure 6.9*):

Figure 6.9 – The Audition buttons on the renamed track and Take Lanes

Let's begin comping!

1. Audition Take Lane 1.
2. Enable the Pencil Tool by pressing *B* or using the button in the control bar.
3. With the Pencil Tool, paint over the area in Take 1 that says "**I.**"

    Notice that the area that you painted over in the Take Lane with the Pencil Tool has just moved up to the main take.

4. Move to the second take and audition it.

5. Disable the Pencil Tool and simply select the part of this take that says "**Love**."

6. Now, press *Return* or *Enter*.

    Again, the selected area moved up to the main take!

7. Next, make sure you select the remaining clip within the main take (see *Figure 6.10*):

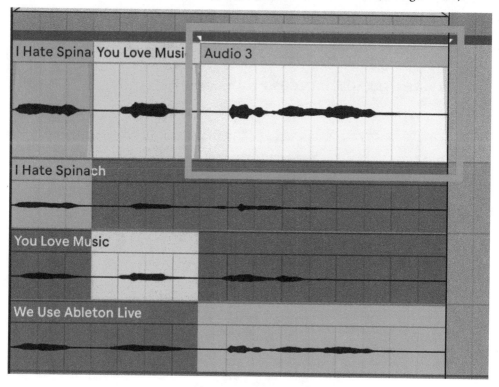

Figure 6.10 – The remaining clip selected in the main comp area

8. Now, loop this area on the timeline.

9. Press play and you should hear this clip play back over and over again.

10. Use the *Shift + Cmnd + up/down arrow* (*Shift + Ctrl + up/down arrow* for Windows) key command to cycle through the takes while you are also listening to them.

11. Select the last take that says "**Ableton Live**."

12. Now, if you disable looping on the timeline and you listen to your entire **MAIN COMP** track, you should hear "I Love Ableton Live," which is the comped combination of all the takes we have recorded onto this track (see *Figure 6.11*):

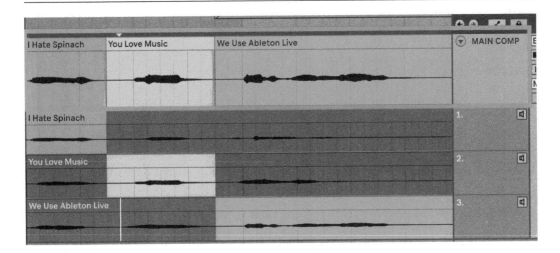

Figure 6.11 – The main comped track

You can hide the Take Lanes if you think you are done for now and open them again if you'd like to make further tweaks to the comp later.

Just simply *Ctrl + click* (*right-click* for Windows) on the track and untick the **Show Take Lanes** option in the context menu, or use the *Cmd + Option + U* (*Ctrl + Shift + U* for Windows) key command.

This is surely a feature that will come in very handy when working with musicians in order to capture multiple takes of their performances and comp together the best bits of each take. However, there are other scenarios when comping can come in handy!

Creative comping in Live 11

For this example, we are going to create a drum break out of multiple drum breaks to come up with something unique and interesting in no time:

1. Create a new audio track.

2. *Ctrl + click* (*right-click* on Windows) on the track header and choose **Insert New Take Lane** in the context menu or use the *Shift + Option + T* (*Shift + Alt + T* for Windows) key command.

3. Repeat this until you have inserted four Take Lanes.

4. Now, fill these Take Lanes with drum loops (make sure all of these drum loops are warped correctly).

5. Re-color the different drum loops on the Take Lanes (see *Figure 6.12*):

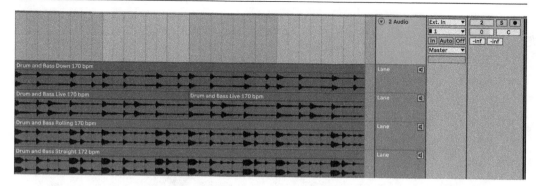

Figure 6.12 – Re-colored clips in the Take Lanes

6.   Loop the area on these clips on the timeline and begin playback.

Notice that there will be nothing playing back from this track at this point, as we haven't selected any clips yet to go into the main take.

7.   Enable the Pencil Tool and start painting over different areas within the different Take Lanes to combine these clips in the main take.

Now, you should have something similar to what follows (see *Figure 6.13*):

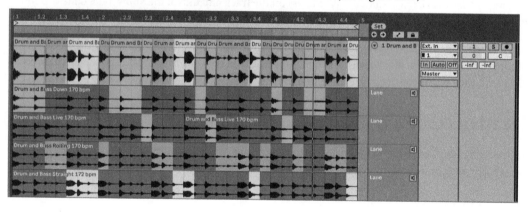

Figure 6.13 – Comped drum breaks

This technique can be used on many other instruments as well, for example, bass lines and different pitched vocals – your creativity here can fly free!

For these step-by-step examples, again, I used audio tracks. However, the concept and the way that it works are exactly the same when applied to MIDI tracks.

Summary

Track linking and comping are both extremely important features to help speed up your workflow. Furthermore, as we have seen, comping is also a great tool to transform parts into something new and be applied more creatively.

In the next chapter, we will start looking at how we can add some spicy processing to the elements in our tracks by looking at some of Live 11's exciting audio effects!

7
Discovering Some of Live 11's Creative Audio Effects

In the previous chapter, we learned how we can use Take Lanes and comping in various ways to speed up our workflow and boost creativity. We also looked at the Track Linking feature, which enables us to record and edit multiple tracks simultaneously.

In this chapter, we will take a look at some of Live's creative effects, which were released with the Live 11 software update.

We will also discover the difference between using effects inserted directly onto a track versus those inserted onto a return track.

Furthermore, we are going to explore various sidechaining techniques with multiple devices that Live has to offer.

We are going to cover the following topics in this chapter:

- Hybrid Reverb
- Other new and updated effect devices in Live 11
- Understanding the differences between insert effect chains and return tracks
- Looking into sidechaining techniques

Technical requirements

In order to follow along with this chapter, you will need the following:

- A computer with at least 8 GB of RAM and at least an Intel Core i5 processor
- A pair of headphones
- A copy of Live 11 Suite
- The **Chapter 7** Ableton Live Project

First, we are going to discover Hybrid Reverb and what makes it an outstanding reverb device that can be an amazing tool for sound design or to add a lusher texture and depth to your sounds.

Hybrid Reverb

As you probably already know, reverb is all around us at all times. When any sound occurs in any space, the sound sends sound waves out in all directions. These sound waves bounce around and reflect off different objects and surfaces we have in our space until the reflections die off. Just think about it; in a soundproofed, smaller, empty studio, if you clap your hands, you will hear very little reverb, if any. However, in a church, or even in your bathroom, you would hear quite a lot of reverb, which will vary based on the size of the space, the surfaces, and the objects around you.

Both reverb and delays are generally great devices to add depth and make our sounds more interesting.

Figure 7.1 – The Hybrid Reverb device

When we record any audio in an acoustically treated, controlled studio environment, we are aiming to record the signal as "dry" as possible, without any reverb or reflections. This will give us the opportunity to later decide what "space" we would like to put our sounds into. We can use devices to manipulate the dry sound to our taste.

Hybrid Reverb allows you to combine algorithmic and convolution reverb.

Algorithmic reverb means it is artificially created and mathematical algorithms are used to simulate the reverb.

On the other hand, convolution reverb uses impulse responses that have been physically recorded. Convolution reverb generally sounds more realistic and smooth; however, it can put more pressure on the computer's CPU.

Live 11's Hybrid Reverb device allows you to use either convolution or algorithmic reverb, or route them both in **Serial** (feeding into each other) or parallel. We can blend the two types of reverbs together with the **Blend** control:

Figure 7.2 – Blending convolution and algorithmic reverbs

On the convolution side, you can choose from different impulse responses using the **Convolution IR** dropdowns.

You will notice that as you change the impulse response, the waveform of the impulse response will be displayed in the middle of the device.

> **Important note**
>
> Where this can get really creative is that you can use random samples as impulse responses, just by simply dragging and dropping the sample onto the device.
>
> For example, you could try to use a Cowbell sample as an impulse response to create a metallic-sounding reverberation that has a fairly clear pitch. You can also browse the internet and find impulse responses that you can download to experiment with.

You cannot go wrong with any of the offered convolution impulse responses or reverb algorithms; however, if you are looking to apply some more creative processing during your sound design process and create not only some lush-sounding textures and depth but also some more interesting sounds, experiment with the **Textures** category under **Convolution IR** dropdowns.

Also, under the **Algorithms** dropdown, the **Shimmer** option can bring loads of shine and new texture to a sound, which you can also manipulate by pitching it.

You can take a look at how I used these options in the provided project (the **Chapter 7** project). If you select the **Bell Reso Noise** track within the **HYBRID REVERB** group, you will see that I used the **Chains** impulse response from the **Textures** category.

I also used the **Shimmer** algorithm and pitched down the shimmer by -12 semitones (*Figure 7.3*).

Figure 7.3 – Hybrid Reverb applied to the Bell Reso Noise track

If you bypass the device, you will immediately hear how much more texture and depth the device is bringing to the sound.

Another great feature of Hybrid Reverb is the onboard **EQ**, which allows you to, for example, filter out the low end of the sound so you don't end up mudding up your mix with reverb on lower frequencies (*Figure 7.4*).

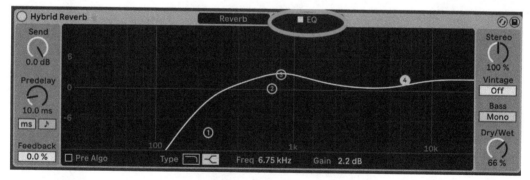

Figure 7.4 – The EQ section of Hybrid Reverb

Last but not least, let's talk about the **Freeze** function (*Figure 7.5*).

Figure 7.5 – The Freeze function

Here, we can freeze the algorithmic reverb's decay time infinitely and let it sustain endlessly with or without the input signal feeding into this infinitely sustained reverb tail – which can be decided by enabling or disabling the arrow button. It can be a good idea to capture the outcome of this process by, for example, recording it to a new track.

To do this, you can simply follow these steps:

1. Create a new audio track.

2. Make sure, in the I/O section, that this track is picking up the signal from the appropriate track (in this case, the **Bell Reso Noise** track) and the track is routed with Post FX to ensure that the signal is recorded after it has passed through the Hybrid Reverb FX (*Figure 7.6*).

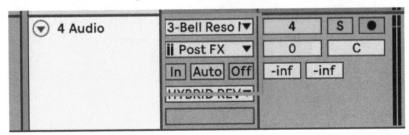

Figure 7.6 – The Bell Reso Noise track is routed to be recorded onto the new 4 audio track

3. Once it is done, hit record in either the **Arrangement** or **Session** view (which we learned about in *Chapter 2, Recording Audio in Ableton Live 11*), and engage the **Freeze** functions on the Hybrid Reverb device on the **Bell Reso Noise** track while you are recording the output of this track.

The recorded audio can be further edited, processed, and used as an element of a track. This is a great technique to come up with beautiful drone sounds, for example.

Now that we have explored Hybrid Reverb, let's move on and have a look at some other new devices!

Other new and updated effect devices in Live 11

Upon the release of Live 11, there was a wealth of new and updated devices.

Let's discover these, starting with one of my personal favorites, Spectral Resonator.

Spectral Resonator

Spectral Resonator uses resonance and overtones to manipulate the tonal characteristics of the signal that it is applied to.

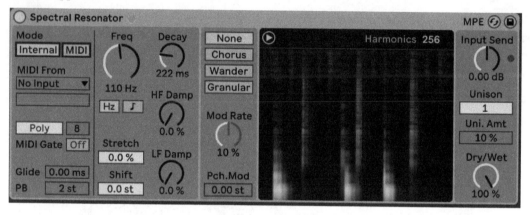

Figure 7.7 – The Spectral Resonator device

Spectral Resonator uses a spectrogram to display the affected frequencies. Let's look at some of the settings of the device:

- The **Harmonics** setting at the top right of the spectrogram creates a kind of filtering effect, by applying more or less harmonics to change the "brightness" of the sound.

- We can also add **modulation** by selecting from **Chorus**, **Wander**, or **Granular**.

- We can also change the fundamental frequency/pitch of the resonator by using the **Freq** knob.

- We can adjust the **Decay** knob and damp high and low frequencies within the partials by adjusting **HF Damp** and **LF Damp**.

- The **Mode** section is where things can get even more interesting! In **Internal** mode, the device is tuned to the value defined by the **Freq** knob; however, in **MIDI** mode, the device is tuned to an incoming MIDI signal that we can assign.

Using MIDI mode can create some super interesting results. Let's take this for a test drive:

1. In the provided project for this chapter, you will find a track called **drums** within the **SPECTRAL RESONATOR** group. It contains a clip that you can take a listen to. You will also find, in the same group, a track called **piano**, which also contains a clip of chords. We will use these piano chords to tune the Spectral Resonator device to it.

    On this **drums** track, I already inserted Spectral Resonator.

2. Switch to **MIDI** mode and choose the **piano** track as the MIDI sidechain source (*Figure 7.8*). We will look into sidechaining in depth later in this chapter!

3. You can also define whether you'd like to take the piano signal **Pre or Post FX or Post Mixer**. This means you can choose whether you'd like any effects applied to the piano track to be considered when it is fed into the Spectral Resonator device or not. Similarly, you can decide whether you'd like the mixer settings of the **piano** track to be considered before reaching Spectral Resonator. In this case, I chose to ignore all the effects on the piano track and use **Pre FX** (*Figure 7.8*).

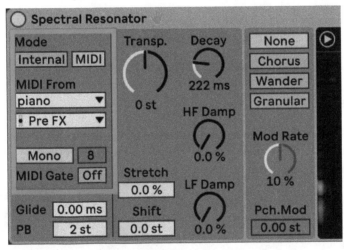

Figure 7.8 – Spectral resonator in MIDI mode, sidechained to the piano track

You will straight away hear the resonator pitch following the melody of the incoming MIDI signal.

However, since it is still in **Mono** mode, we only hear one pitch at a time, not the full chords.

4. If you switch the mode to **Poly**, then you will allow polyphonic information to come through the MIDI sidechain and will start hearing the chords through the sidechain trigger affecting the Spectral Resonator straight away.

5. You can also apply extra transposition by using the **Transp.** knob, and finetune the amount of effect applied by using the **Dry/Wet** control at the bottom right of the device (*Figure 7.9*).

6. You can thicken the sound further by applying extra voices using the **Unison** slide and the **Uni. Amt** slide (*Figure 7.9*).

Figure 7.9 – Unison and Dry/Wet controls

7. You can create more movement and an interesting effect by automating, for example, the **Dry/Wet** control, as well as the **Transp.** control and **Decay**.

We will be looking at automation in Live soon, in *Chapter 11*.

Spectral Time

Spectral Time applies time freezing and spectral delay effects to manipulate the sound. This is an excellent device to re-synthesize sounds and create beautiful, evolving textures.

Figure 7.10 – Spectral Time device

Similar to Spectral Resonator, it uses a spectrogram to display how the frequencies are affected over time.

Spectral Time has two main sections: **Freezer** and **Delay**. These sections can be used independently, or **Freezer** can feed into the **Delay** section. Let's have a look at these settings in detail:

- In the **Freezer** section, you can choose from **Manual** or **Retrigger** mode. These either allow you to manually toggle the **Freeze** button on and off or the effect can be frozen automatically at every transient (**Onset**) or regular intervals (**Sync**) of milliseconds or beat divisions.

- In the **Delay** section, you can find regular delay parameters, as well as some more interesting settings, such as **Tilt**, **Spray**, and **Mask**. Here, you can create delayed copies of the spectral information created by the device:

  - **Tilt** changes the delay time for different frequencies. Higher values will affect high frequencies more, while lower values will affect low frequencies.

  - **Spray** spreads out the delay time for different frequencies in a random manner.

  - **Mask** limits the effect of **Tilt** and **Spray** either for higher or lower frequencies depending on whether we set positive or negative values.

On the right side of the device, we can also reverse the effects' (**Freezer** and **Delay**) order by using the **Frz > Dly** and **Dly > Frz** buttons (*Figure 7.11*).

Figure 7.11 – Controls to reverse the effects' order

Both Spectral Resonator and Spectral Time were unexpected but very welcome surprises when Live 11 was released, putting even more creative tools in the hands of a modern music producer.

Chorus-Ensemble

This isn't a brand-new device in Live 11; rather, the old Chorus device got a facelift.

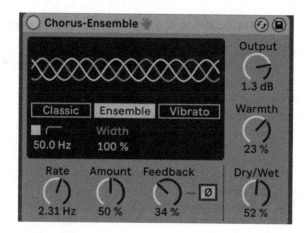

Figure 7.12 – Chorus-Ensemble device

Now, we have **Ensemble** mode, which provides three, instead of two, delayed voices, which enables you to create thicker and wider sounds.

It also has the **Warmth** knob, which provides some filtering and distortion for a "warmer" sound.

It is a great device to add some chorus effects for vocals, for example, but it can also be very useful in the sound design process for synth and bass sounds too. It is always a good idea to roll off the low end for a cleaner mix, which can be done by using the settings below the **Classic** button.

We can also add a vibrato effect to our sound, by switching to **Vibrato** mode.

Phaser-Flanger

Phaser-Flanger is also not fully new to Live 11. This device combines the old Phaser and Flanger devices in one place. It has a better interface than before; therefore, it is a more powerful device.

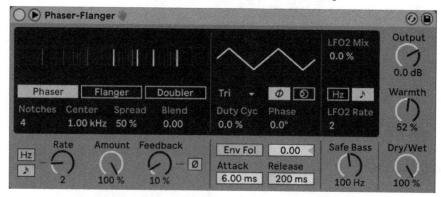

Figure 7.13 – Phaser-Flanger device

We have three modes in Phaser-Flanger:

- One of the greatest new additions to this device is the **Doubler** mode.

  This mode creates the effect of a double-recorded sound by adding a time-modulated delayed signal to the sound. This is often something that would be achieved with vocals by recording the same line twice and stacking the recordings together. This effect device can emulate the double-recorded effect artificially pretty well.

- **Flanger** mode will add a consistently changing filtering effect, again by adding a time-modulated delayed signal.

- **Phaser** mode has a pretty wide range of frequency modulation options that will create notch filters by feeding back a phase-shifted version of the signal.

This is a great device to experiment with for sound design purposes, and also to create some interesting parts within the arrangement by automating the parameters of the device.

Now that we have covered some amazing effects in Live, let's dive into the differences between using effects as insert effects versus send effects.

Understanding the differences between Insert Effect Chains and Return Tracks

How we manage our effects in Live will not only impact our speed and how efficient our workflow is but also the CPU usage of our computer.

Effects can be used on a track in serial, meaning you put effects after each other, forming a single effect chain on the track.

This means the first effect's output will feed into the effect after it, and so on.

However, what if you would like to apply, for example, reverb to a vocal track and a delay without the reverberated signal feeding into the delay device, so the two effects are used in parallel, not affecting each other?

Well, that's when you could use return tracks and use the effects as "send effects."

Let's have a look at this.

In *Figure 7.14*, you can see that I inserted a **Reverb** and **Delay** device onto the vocal track called **INSERT** in the project.

This is the first scenario that I described previously. The output of the **Reverb** device is feeding into the **Delay** device. This means the reverberated signal will have delay applied to it. This also means that even if you swap the devices over, you will not be able to get a clean delay without reverb as they are still set up in serial and inserted onto the track directly.

This also means that in order to control the dry/wet signal (the unaffected signal and the effect's balance), you will always need to click on the track and display the effect chain.

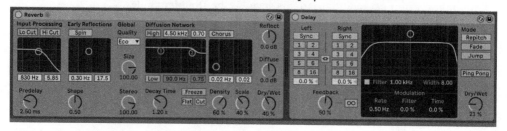

Figure 7.14 – Reverb and Delay devices set up as insert effects in serial, forming a single chain on the track

There is nothing wrong with this scenario if this is the effect that you are after, which is a bit of reverberated delay.

However, if you'd like to separate the two effects, you need to use **Sends** and **Return Tracks**.

In *Figure 7.15*, you can see that there are two Return Tracks set up. Return **A** has a **reverb** device inserted onto it, and Return **B** has a **delay** device.

Figure 7.15 – Return Tracks set up

You can also see that now, in Live, every single track has a corresponding Send **A** and Send **B** displayed in the **Sends** Section (*Figure 7.16*).

Figure 7.16 – Corresponding Sends to Return Tracks

These sends will now allow you to send any tracks to the corresponding Return Tracks.

The tracks themselves will be the dry signal and the Return Tracks will output *only* the inserted effects' output (100% wet). So, to control the dry/wet ratio, you will just need to adjust the Sends. The more signal you send into the return tracks, the more "wet" they will be, and vice versa.

> **Note**
> However, to gain this separation and control, you must always make sure that effects inserted onto Return Tracks are 100% wet! (See *Figure 7.17*.)

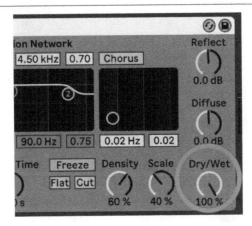

Figure 7.17 – Effects inserted onto the Return Tracks must be set to 100% wet

Besides effect separation, there are other uses for using effects as **send effects**.

In my project, I got the vocals doubled up (recorded twice). One layer is the original take, called **SEND 1**, and the other one is the same vocal line but pitched down by 7 semitones, called **SEND 2**. When you are working with backing vocals, harmonies, or any other stacked layers of the same instruments that you would like to "put in the same place/room," meaning have the same kind of reverb on them, there is no point in putting the same reverb device with the same settings onto the single tracks. Doing so will make it harder to adjust the control of the effects independently when you need to simultaneously change settings on the reverb for all tracks, and also will use more CPU power.

Instead, you would send each track to the same Return Track, which has the effect inserted onto it that you would like your tracks to share.

For example, in my project, the original vocals (**SEND1**) and the pitched harmony layer (**SEND2**) are both sent to the same reverb and the same delay devices on the return tracks (*Figure 7.18*).

Figure 7.18 – Both vocal layers are sent to the same reverb and
delay devices on the Return Tracks, via the Sends

> **Note**
> Live Suite allows you to have up to 12 return tracks set up in a project. Therefore, if you have effects that you are only going to use on one or two tracks, you should go ahead and insert those effects directly into the tracks, as there isn't much point in wasting your return tracks on those occasions. Instead, only use effects on return tracks that you are sure you would like to use in multiple tracks in your project.

You can also apply a different technique for parallel processing, but on a per-track basis, which we will be exploring in *Chapter 8, Exploring Device Racks in Live 11*.

In a nutshell, effects that are specific to tracks or need to affect the whole signal (wouldn't be controlled by the **Dry/Wet** control) should mainly be used as insert effects, and you could use effects that you might share among multiple tracks within your project, time based, or controlled by the Dry/Wet control, as send effects, inserting them onto a return track.

Now that we have covered some crucial workflow techniques, let's get a bit more creative and take a look at the devices in Live that you can use for sidechaining.

Looking into sidechaining techniques

Sidechaining lets you use one track to trigger an effect on another. You must have heard, for example, a "pumping sound" on a synth, where the volume of the track drops each time the kick drum hits. That is done with sidechain compression. There are other effects in Live that allow sidechaining too, and we will discover them in this section of the chapter.

Let's start with sidechain compression.

Sidechaining with compressors

As you probably already know, compressors help to even out the dynamics of a sound, by reducing louder peaks and moving them closer to the quieter parts of the signal.

When applying sidechain compression, the compressor will reduce the volume of the sound each time the sidechain trigger (the other sound) plays.

To examine this effect, in this example, I set up a compressor on the track called **SYNTH**:

1. I enabled the **Sidechain** section by using the toggle to the right button (*Figure 7.19*).

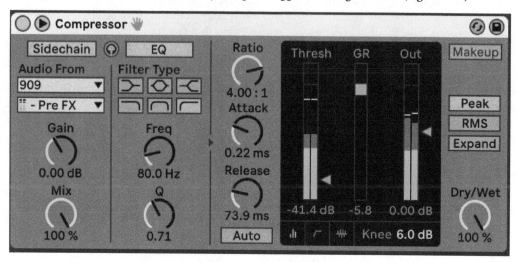

Figure 7.19 – Sidechain section set up within the compressor

2. I also set up a track called **909**, which is playing back some drums; this track will be the sidechain trigger.

3. In the **Audio From** section, I chose the **909** track, and underneath it, I made sure to only pick up the kick drum chain pre-effects (so if there were any effects on the kick drum chain, those wouldn't be taken into consideration for sidechaining). See *Figure 7.20*.

    Also, choosing only the kick drum as the sidechain trigger will ensure that the other drum hits are not affecting the compressor.

Figure 7.20 – Choosing the kick drum chain from the Drum Rack as the sidechain trigger

Now you can hear that there is a noticeable pumping effect going on, as the kick drum is setting off the compressor each time it plays.

4. You can further finetune this "pumping effect" by adjusting the compressor settings further via the **Thresh**, **Ratio**, **Attack**, **Release**, and **Out** settings.

The **EQ** section allows you to equalize the incoming signal (the sidechain trigger). This can be useful if you are working with a drum loop (audio, not MIDI), so you don't have access to the different drum sounds independently. In this case, if you'd still like to have the kick drum of the audio loop to be the sidechain trigger, you can just filter out the other drum elements with **EQ**.

The **headphone button** between the **Sidechain** and **EQ** buttons enables you to listen to the sidechain trigger.

Setting the compressor to **Peak** or **RMS** mode will have an effect on the compressor's reactivity, as **Peak** mode is more sensitive to peaks, and therefore reacts fast, while **RMS** mode requires the signal to exceed the thresholds for a longer period of time; therefore, the compressor will react slower.

Sidechain compression was originally invented to get around frequency masking problems, especially between the kick and the bass. Kick drums and bass lines tend to share a great number of frequencies, and because of that, the bass line can mask the kick drum in the mix. Sidechain compression solves this problem by making the bass line duck down each time the kick drum hits, so the kick can come through in the mix.

Nowadays, sidechain compression is used in much wider and more creative ways, for example, on synths and vocals, to achieve certain genre-specific effects, as well as its traditional function for problem-solving, of course.

Another compressor, called **Glue Compressor**, also has a sidechain section, and it works exactly the same way as it does with the compressor we already looked at (*Figure 7.21*).

Figure 7.21 – Glue Compressor

The differences are more present between the two compressors themselves.

Glue Compressor was modeled after an SSL bus compressor, and it's a great device to glue elements of the mix together, often used on groups of instruments, rather than single tracks.

Sidechaining with the Gate device

While a compressor will reduce the signal level, once the signal exceeds the threshold, a Gate will reduce the volume of a signal once the signal falls below the threshold.

Gates can be used, for example, to remove unwanted background noise from vocal takes.

Again, it has more creative uses in modern music production. Let's have a look at one of those.

The **Sidechain** section of this device works exactly the same way as it does with the compressors. The difference is just in the result of the effect (*Figure 7.22*).

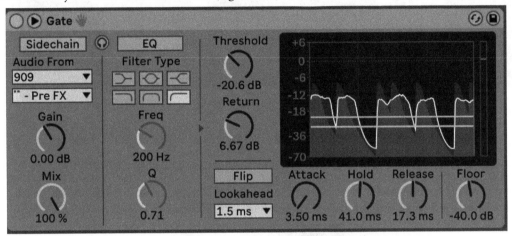

Figure 7.22 – Gate device sidechained to the kickdrum of the 909 Drum Rack track

With the compressor, each time the sidechain trigger plays (the kick drum), the compressor reduces the volume of the synth, creating this ducking effect.

Doing the same sidechain routing and procedure will result in our synth's volume dropping down each time the sidechain trigger (the kick drum) doesn't play, and the gate will allow the sound to play when the sidechain trigger plays.

So, essentially, we are getting the exact opposite effect of sidechain compression.

This technique can create some interesting rhythmical effects of melodic elements in our track.

Sidechaining with Auto Filter

The **Auto Filter** device allows us to apply classic filtering to certain frequencies of our sound.

Sidechaining with **Auto Filter** can introduce some lush modulated movement of the filter to the chosen sound.

Again, the **Sidechain** section works exactly the same way on this device as it did in the previous examples (*Figure 7.23*).

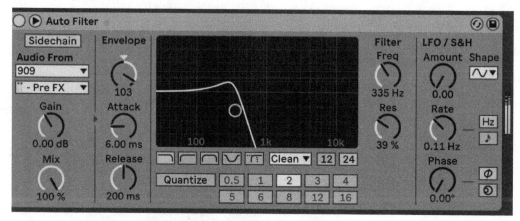

Figure 7.23 – Auto Filter device sidechained to the kick drum of the 909 Drum Rack track

I set my example up on the **SYNTH** track, and again, I sidechained the kick drum of the **909** track to it.

I also applied some low-pass filtering to the synth sound within Auto Filter.

Nothing really happens with the sidechain until you increase the **Envelope** value (*Figure 7.24*), which controls how much of an effect the sidechain signal has on the frequency.

Figure 7.24 – Envelope setting on the Auto Filter device

Let's discuss something interesting.

What if you have your drums set up, but your drum sequence is quite complex or *fast*, which you don't find pleasing in order to achieve the sidechaining effect that you are looking for?

It is a common practice in certain genres for the kick drum to play a different rhythm from what is being used as a sidechain trigger. In fact, the sidechain trigger might play entirely differently from any of your drum sounds.

You do not have to use any of your active tracks in your composition as a sidechain trigger.

Instead, you can set up something called a "Ghost Sidechain Trigger."

I'll show you what I mean in the following section.

Using a Ghost Sidechain Trigger

In this scenario, I have a fairly complex and fast drum sequence on the **909** track (*Figure 7.25*).

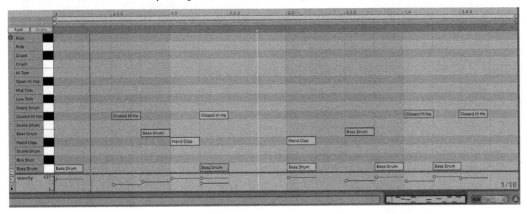

Figure 7.25 – More complex drum pattern. Not really suitable to use as a sidechain trigger in this case

I don't find this suitable to use as a sidechain trigger.

Therefore, I duplicated the **909** track, so it has the same Drum Rack on it, but I renamed the track **GHOST SIDECHAIN** and re-sequenced the pattern in the clip with a sequence that I would like to use as the sidechain trigger. I also muted this track, as it will not be part of my track sonically; I only would like these notes to act as sidechain triggers (*Figure 7.26*).

Figure 7.26 – Ghost Sidechain track set up with a new sequence, muted to act as a sidechain trigger

Then, I inserted a compressor on the **SYNTH** track, and in the **Sidechain** section, I chose the **GHOST SIDECHAIN** track as the sidechain trigger (*Figure 7.27*).

Figure 7.27 – Compressor's Sidechain section fed by the GHOST SIDECHAIN track

Voilà, now we have a track dedicated to acting as the sidechain trigger for our compressor.

This is a great technique to have full control over and spike your creativity when using sidechaining effects. Using a ghost sidechain track will also enable you to manage the sidechain effect better within your arrangement, without affecting your composition and your musical notations.

And with this, we have reached the end of this chapter.

Summary

In this chapter, we had a look at some of the awesome new and updated effect devices that arrived with the Live 11 software update to spark our creativity and discover new possibilities.

We also explored the differences between using effects inserted directly onto tracks in serial or using effects with Return Tracks for parallel processing, which is super important for a more efficient mixing workflow, as well as managing our CPU usage.

Last but not least, we also had a look at what sidechaining is and how we can use this technique with various devices to achieve different effects, as well as learning how to have more control over our sidechaining by using a ghost sidechain track.

In the next chapter, we will further explore parallel processing on a track basis and learn more interesting and complex techniques by discovering Racks and the new improvements to them that Live 11 brought.

8

Exploring Device Racks in Live 11

In the previous chapter, we were learning about some of the brand-new and updated audio effects in Live 11.

We also looked at sidechaining techniques, and we discussed the differences between using effects as "insert effects" (effect inserted directly onto the tracks) and "send effects" (effect inserted onto a return track and then sending tracks to this return track).

We explored the benefits of using parallel processing with the return tracks.

In this chapter, we will further explore parallel processing but, instead, on a track basis via device racks.

We will be looking at Instrument, Effect, and Drum Racks, and take a look at the Rack improvements that were made with the Live 11 software update.

In this chapter, we are going to cover the following topics:

- An introduction to Device Racks in Live
- Instrument Racks
- Effect Racks
- Drum Racks

Technical requirements

In order to follow along with this chapter, you will need the following:

- A computer with at least 8 GB of RAM and an Intel Core i5 processor
- A pair of headphones
- A copy of Live 11 Suite
- The **Chapter 8** Ableton Live project

Let's start off by gaining a deeper understanding of the use of Device Racks in Live.

An introduction to Device Racks in Live

By creating Device Racks, you can build your own complex devices that contain effects and instruments.

You can create multilayered instruments, apply signal splitting and parallel processing, to name just a few of the uses of Device Racks.

If you think about it, when you have, for example, a MIDI track, you insert a MIDI effect on it, an instrument, and stack up some audio effects to follow the instrument. You are creating one chain of devices, just like how you would in other **DAWs (Digital Audio Workstations)**.

However, if you are, for example, working on an Instrument Rack, you are able to create multiple device chains playing in parallel, meaning you can have several instruments stacked up on the same track. All these instrument chains can also have their own effect processing, and then the output of all these chains gets summarized as the output of the Instrument Rack.

Drum Racks work a little differently, but we will be having a closer look at them later in this chapter.

Device Racks are truly innovative and have many benefits and uses for creative production, sound design, mixing, and performance techniques.

Device Racks also give you the opportunity to bypass all the devices within a Rack at once. This is super useful if you want to make a comparison between the processed and unprocessed signals. You just need to group all the effect devices you'd like to **bypass** together into a Rack.

To do that, follow these steps:

1. Select all the effect devices by holding *Shift* and selecting the first and last device.

2. *Ctrl + click* (*right-click* on Windows) on one of the selected device's names.

3. Select **Group** from the contextual menu (or hit *Cmd + G* (*Ctrl + G* for Windows)).

Now, you will have all the devices in one Effect Rack (*Figure 8.1*).

Figure 8.1 – The effect devices grouped into an Effect Rack, which now has a bypass button

In the next section, in order to get to know the layout and elements of Device Racks, we are going to build a few of them from scratch.

Let's get started and first have a look at Instrument Racks!

Exploring Instrument Racks

In this section, we will build a few Instrument Racks for different scenarios and uses!

First up, let's design a multi-layered instrument! Follow these steps with me:

1. Head to the browser, navigate to **Instruments**, and drag and drop **Instrument Rack** onto an empty MIDI track (*Figure 8.2*).

2. Now, you will see the Rack in the device area at the bottom.

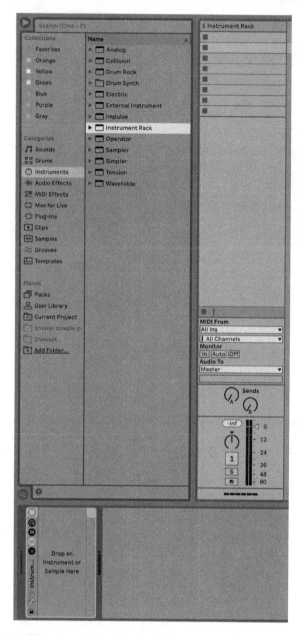

Figure 8.2 – The empty Instrument Rack dropped onto an empty MIDI track

3.   The Instrument Rack at the bottom of the screen in the device area is already instructing you to **Drop an Instrument or Sample Here**.

You can go back into the browser and pick a pad sound from **Sounds**, under **Categories** in the browser. Drag and drop it onto the Instrument Rack.

4. Now, make sure you display the chain list by pressing the **Show/Hide** button:

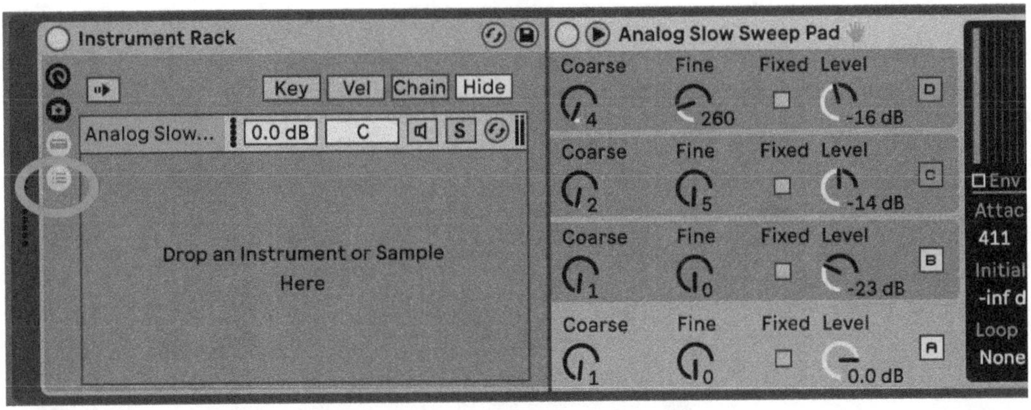

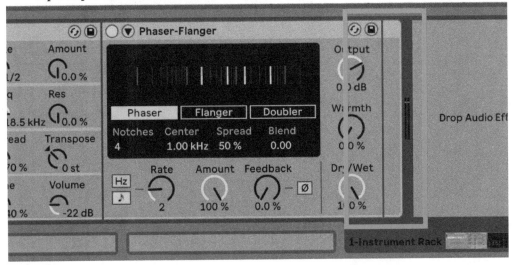

Figure 8.3 – Using the chain list Show/Hide button to display the chain list

5. Above the chain list button, you can see that the **Show/Hide Devices** button is also engaged, which is what's allowing you to also see the devices on the chains.

For now, we have one chain created, so this MIDI track is behaving exactly how it would behave without any racks, as we are building one single device chain at the moment.

After the device that is playing your pad sound (in my case, it is the Operator), you can insert an audio effect. I will use **Phaser-Flanger** and drop it straight onto the chain in **Instrument Rack**.

Now, you will see that the effect was inserted after the instrument but within the Rack. It is super important that the effect isn't outside of the rack!

Figure 8.4 – The audio effect inserted onto the chain, within the rack

6. Head back to the chain list where you dropped the instrument before, go to the browser, choose another **Pad** sound, and again drop it onto the chain list.

7. Now, you will see two different chains:

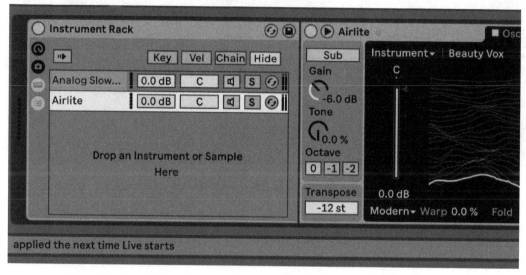

Figure 8.5 – Two different instruments on two different chains within the chain list

8. You can already start triggering the MIDI track that we are building the Rack on, and you will hear that you are playing both instruments at the same time!

9. On the chain list, next to the names of the sounds, you can see that there is a **volume control slide**, where you can mix the two chains together, and a **pan slide**, where you can pan the two chains independently. You can also **mute** and **solo** the chains, as well as use the **hot swap** button to change the preset quickly (*Figure 8.5*).

10. You can also get access to these controls within the mixer in the Session View (*Figure 8.6*).

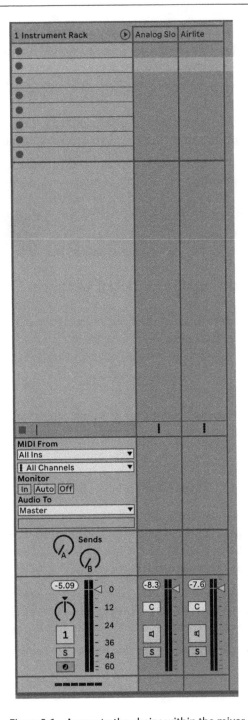

Figure8.6 – Access to the chains within the mixer

11. To the second chain, called **Airlite**, I inserted an **Auto Filter** audio effect, which I use to roll off some of the high frequencies. (Again, it is super important that the Auto Filter gets inserted directly onto the appropriate chain; otherwise, if the effect lands outside of the rack, the effect will be manipulating the output of the Instrument Rack, meaning both of the chains instead of just the **Airlite** chain.)

12. To spice things up even more, we are going to insert a third instrument in the Instrument Rack's chain list, creating a third chain and a third layer to our layered sound. I picked a piano sound.

13. Let's insert an arpeggiator onto the third piano chain only (*Figure 8.7*).

Figure 8.7 – Arpeggiator inserted onto the third piano chain

You can see in the preceding screenshot that the piano sound I picked in the browser is also made out of a Rack, and it already has effects inserted after the instrument on its chain, which we can start manipulating straight away or; we can swap them for different effects that we might prefer more .

> **Note**
>
> This is something truly beautiful and provides endless possibilities in Live. As you now know, you can actually use Racks inside Racks, and that means that you can create amazingly complex and detailed sounds with Racks!

At the top of the chain list, we can find the following buttons: **Key**, **Chain**, **Vel**, and **Hide**:

- The **Key** button will display the **Key Zone Editor**, which allows us to split the chains across key zones. These zones are areas of a piano roll which can be also represented by a MIDI keyboard. So, essentially, you could use one MIDI keyboard while performing to trigger three different instruments that are living on three different chains.

  In my example (*Figure 8.8*), I have the first pad triggered by the keys of C2 up until C3. Between C2 and C3, both the first and second chains are triggered; between C4 and C5, the second and third chains are triggered; and above C5, only the third chain is triggered.

  I also faded between the chains by dragging the bar above the zones.

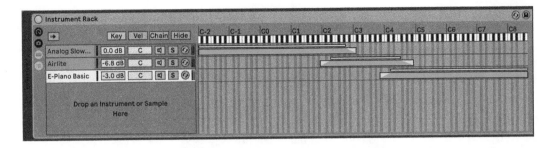

Figure 8.8 – Chains are split in the Key Zone Editor

With this technique, you are limiting the pitches that each chain can play – for example, the first chain will never play any notes higher than C2.

If you are looking to split the chains on your keyboard without limiting the pitch that can be played by each chain, then you can use the **Chain Select Editor**.

- The Chain Select Editor can be displayed by pressing the **Chain** button.

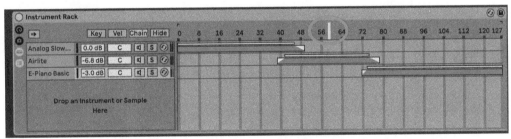

Figure 8.9 – Chains are distributed in the Chain Select Editor

In the preceding screenshot, you can see how I distributed the chains. The small blue bar circled in red is the **Chain Selector**. You can move the **Chain Selector** to play back the appropriate chain or chains. Here, also you can fade between the chains, especially when they have certain areas where they overlap for a smoother transition.

If you are trying out the **Chain Selector**, make sure you first reset the changes we made in the Key Zone Editor, so the chains can access all the key zones.)

The Chain Selector is something that you probably want to map to a Macro, to have better access to it. There'll be more on that a bit later.

This is a gift for live performance, as you can have a set worth of instruments you would like to play live within your set in one Instrument Rack, instead of having them on separate MIDI tracks and changing between them while performing. Instead, you can just move the Chain Selector as you move on to the next track in your set.

- The **Vel** button displays the **Velocity Zone Editor**, which shows the velocity values from left to right.

Here, you can assign chains to particular velocity values, which will trigger the appropriate chain when they are played (*Figure 8.10*).

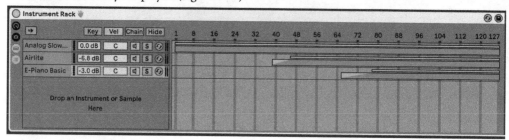

Figure 8.10 – Chains split by velocity values in the Velocity Zone Editor

- **Hide** will hide the information that the **Key**, **Vel**, and **Chain** buttons display.

In the example I am building in the **Chapter 8** Ableton Live project, I have reset the Velocity and Key Zones and only kept the Chain Zone settings.

Now, let's move on to look at Macros!

Macros

You can press the **Show/Hide Macro Controls** button on the left side of the Rack (*Figure 8.11*).

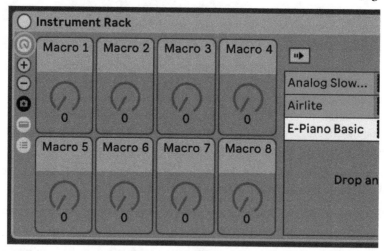

Figure 8.11 – The Show/Hide Macro Controls button

Note that now you can see some new + and - buttons underneath the **Show/Hide Macro Controls** button. These buttons enable you to display fewer or more Macro Controls. You can have up to 16 Macro Controls since the release of Live 11.

Macros can control the internal parameters of the Rack, meaning you can map any parameters present on any of the chains to a Macro Control.

Let's set up a few of them:

1. Navigate to the first chain where I inserted the Phaser-Flanger.

2. On the Phaser-Flanger, *Ctrl + click* (*right-click on Windwos*) on the **Dry/Wet** control and choose the appropriate Macro from the contextual menu that you'd like to map this parameter to. I chose **Macro 1**.

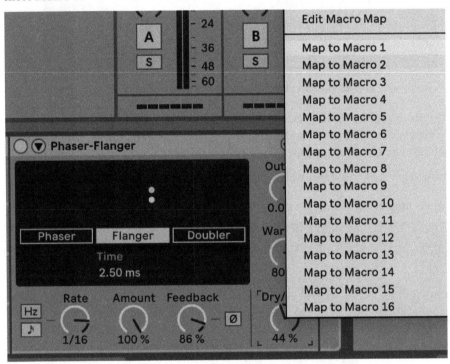

Figure 8.12 – Mapping the Phaser-Flanger's Dry/Wet control to Macro 1

Now, if you look at the Macro Controls, you will see Macro 1 named as **Dry/Wet**. If you move this Macro, the parameter that you mapped to it (Phaser-Flangers's **Dry/Wet** control) will move accordingly.

Rename and recolor this Macro Control by *Ctrl + clicking* (*right-clicking* on Windows) on the Macro Control and choosing the appropriate color and **Rename** function (*Figure 8.13*).

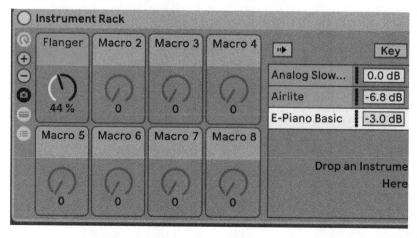

Figure 8.13 – The Macro Control renamed and recolored

In the preceding screenshot, you can see that I recolored the chains themselves too, as I will be mapping various Macros across the various chains. This way, I can see better which Macro Control belongs to which parameter on which chain.

Now, we are going to look at another way we can map parameters to Macro Controls:

1. Press the **Map** button on the top of the Rack (*Figure 8.14*).

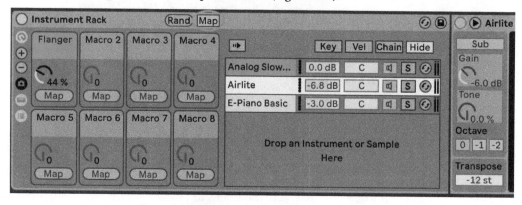

Figure 8.14 – The Map button at the top of the Rack

Note that every parameter that can be mapped to Macro Controls turned green across all the chains and devices.

2. Now, navigate to the second chain and then go to the **Auto Filter** effect that we inserted onto this chain earlier in this chapter.

3. Press on the **Frequency** parameter; you can see that it has a bracket around it now. This means that it is selected (*Figure 8.15*).

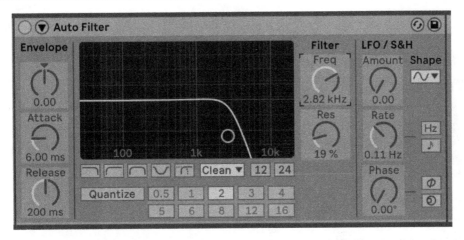

Figure 8.15 – The Frequency parameter is selected to be mapped to a Macro Control

4. Now, go back to the Macro Controls and press the **Map** button on the Macro Control where you'd like to map the **Frequency** parameter of the **Auto Filter** effect. I chose **Macro 2** (*Figure 8.16*).

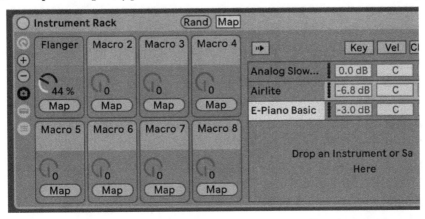

Figure 8.16 – The Map button on the Macro Controls to map the parameter selected for them

5. Now, do the same again, but this time, map the **Resonance** parameter of the Auto Filter to **Macro 3**. Alternatively, we can try something else.

6. We can actually map multiple parameters to the same Macro Controls. In this example, I will map the **Resonance** parameter of the Auto Filter to **Macro 2**, where I already mapped the **Frequency** parameter of the Auto Filter.

7. At this point, as I turn **Macro 2** (where both parameters are mapped) to the right, both parameters will increase in value.

8. However, I'd like the resonance to decrease in value, while the frequency increases by the same degree.

To do this, all we need to do is press the **Map** button again at the top of the Rack. You will then see a **Macro Mappings** page popping up on the left side of the screen.

Here, we can adjust further controls to our Macros.

9. If I *Ctrl + click* (*right-click* on Windows) on **Resonance** in this list, I can choose the **Invert Range** option to create the behavior I previously described (*Figure 8.17*).

Link	Tap	120.00		4 / 4		1 Bar

Macro Mappings

Macro	▲	Path	Name	Min	Max
Flanger		Analog Slow Swe...	Dry/Wet	0.0 %	100 %
Macro 2		Airlite | Auto Filter	Frequency	26.0 Hz	19.9 kHz
Macro 2		Airlite | Auto Filter	Resonance	125 %	0.0 %
				Invert Range	

Figure 8.17 – Inverting the range of parameters on the Macro Mappings page

In the preceding screenshot, you can see that we can also set **Min** and **Max** values for the Macro Controls and the parameters that they are controlling.

Let's say you'd never want **Resonance** to exceed 80%; however, when you are performing and you have limited sight of your computer screen, it can be difficult to precisely control parameters, so you could easily exceed the 80% **Resonance** value by accident.

10. Now that I have my additional mapping done, I will go ahead and color this new Macro purple to match the color of the chain that the device I mapped actually belongs to. I will also rename the Macro (*Figure 8.18*).

11. I also mapped the rate of the arpeggiator on the third chain to a Macro Control, renamed it, and recolored it (*Figure 8.18*).

12. I also mapped the Chain Selector to a Macro Control, so I don't always need to display the Chain Select Editor (*Figure 8.18*).

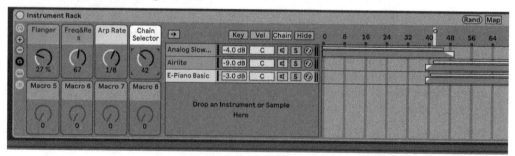

Figure 8.18 – The Macro Control of parameters across all the chains and the Chain Selector mapped to Macro 4

Macro Variations

There is something super exciting that came with the Live 11 update – **Macro Variations**. This new feature allows you to create Macro Snapshots and store them as variations, as well as allowing you to randomize the Macro Controls' values.

Sounds exciting? Let's have a look at these in action:

1. Press the little camera button (**Show/Hide Macro Variations**) on the left side of the Rack. This will display the **Macro Variations** area (*Figure 8.19*).

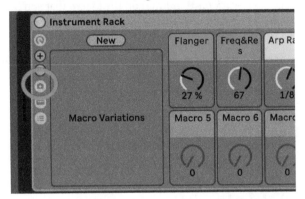

Figure 8.19 – The Show/Hide Macro Variations button

2. Press the **New** button.

   Now, you will see a variation called **Variation 1**.

3. On the side of **Variation 1**, we will press the little camera button (**Snapshot**) to save the current Macro positions into this Macro Variation.

4. *Ctrl + click* (*right-click* on Windows) on **Variation 1** and rename it **Original** (*Figure 8.20*).

Figure 8.20 – The Macro Variation snapshotted and renamed

5. Hit **New** again to create a new Macro Variation.

6. Here, you have options: you can either move the Macros to your preference to create different sound characteristics of the Rack's sound, or you can hit the **Rand** button (*Figure 8.22*) to keep on randomizing the Macro Control values until you hear something you like.

Important

If you have **chains** set up in the Rack that you would not like to be changed by Macro randomization (the Chain Selector's position would also be randomly changed, as it is mapped to a Macro now), you can *Ctrl + click* (*right-click* on Windows) on the Macro that you mapped the Chain Selector to and choose for it to be excluded from Macro Variations and Macro randomization (*Figure 8.21*).

This is a super useful feature that you can apply to any macros that you would like to manually and independently move, regardless of the Macro Variation that is launched, or that you simply don't want to be affected by the randomization command.

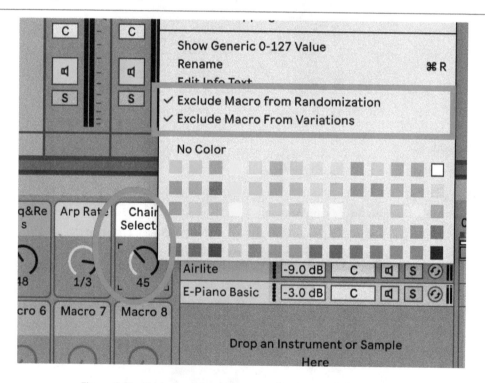

Figure 8.21 – Excluding Macros from randomization and variations

7. Once you like the result, you can use the **Snapshot** button again, to store this variation of the Macro position (*Figure 8.22*).

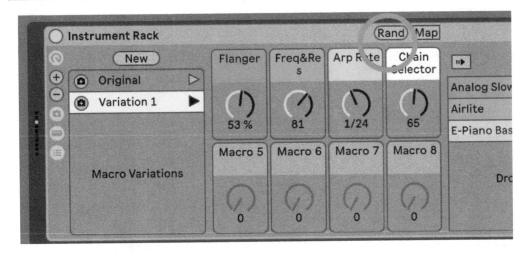

Figure 8.22 – The randomize button and the new variation with
which we stored the randomized Macro positions

8. Go ahead and rename the variation again.

9. In order to switch between the Macro Variations, you can use the **launch buttons** next to the
    name of the Macro Variations.

Now, we have arrived at the end of creating this Instrument Rack. The last thing for us to do is rename
it by *Ctrl + clicking (right-clicking on Wndows)* on its name and choosing the **Rename** option from the
contextual menu. After that, we save it to our **User Library** as our own preset.

To do that, just click on the little floppy disk button (the **Save** button) (*Figure 8.23*).

Figure 8.23 – Saving the Instrument Rack into our User Library

With that, we have finished creating our first Instrument Rack together!

Now, let's move on and create an Audio Effect Rack in the next section of this chapter.

Creating Audio Effect Racks

Loads of things will feel similar in this section; after completing the previous section with me, you should feel more comfortable with Device Racks.

As mentioned at the beginning of the chapter, one of the points of Audio Effect Racks is to group effects into a Rack to be able to save the effect chain as a preset, or to bypass all the effects inside the Rack at once by bypassing the Rack itself, which contains the effects.

We can also carry out parallel processing by having multiple device (in this case, effect) chains on the same track.

Audio Effect Racks work much like Instrument Racks. However, they don't have the Key and Velocity Zone Editors; they only have the Chain Select Editor.

In this section, we are going to create an Audio Effect Rack for vocal processing.

There is a track in the provided project called **VOCALS** that we are going to use to create our Rack.

Follow these steps:

1. Navigate to the browser and choose **Audio Effects** under **Categories**.

2. Insert the Audio Effect Rack device onto the **VOCALS** track.

3. Now, you will see the empty Audio Effect Rack in the device area.

4. Open the chain list and *Ctrl + click* (*right-click* on Windows) on the area that says **Drop Audio Effects Here**. Choose the **Create Chain** option (*Figure 8.24*).

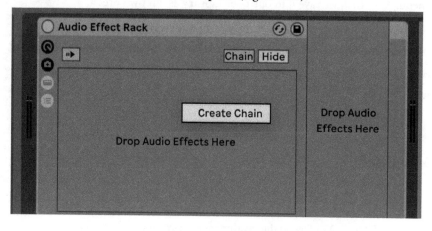

Figure 8.24 – The Create Chain option in the Audio Effect Rack

5. Create two more chains.

6.   Rename the first one Lead Vox, the second one Reverb, and the third one Delay (*Figure 8.25*).

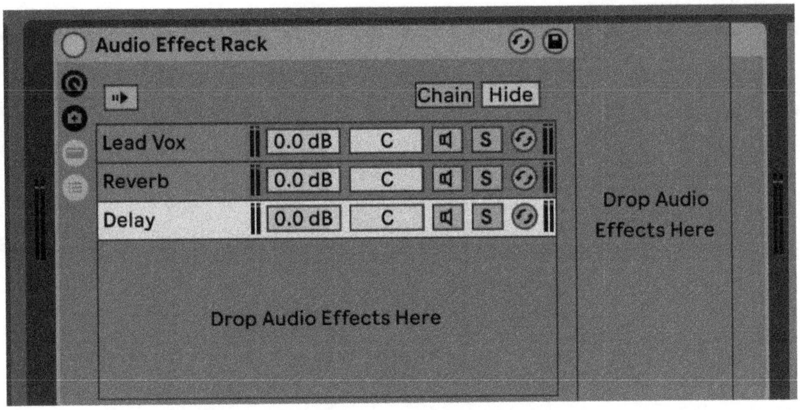

Figure 8.25 – The three chains

7.   For the first chain called **Lead Vox**, you can use the regular basic processing you apply to vocals; for me, the device chain is the following: **EQ8** (to subtract unwanted frequencies), **Compressor** in **Peak** mode (to catch the higher peaks and control the dynamics), another **EQ8** (to boost some of the frequencies), and sometimes another **Compressor**, but this time I will skip it and go straight for **Saturator** to spice the sound up a bit.

> **Note**
> While you are processing this chain, it is best to **solo** it by hitting the small **s** button on the chain within the chain list. As we have created three chains, we tripled the vocals, which means you will hear them three times from the three chains.

8.   For the second chain called **Reverb**, let's insert **Hybrid Reverb**. For now, make sure that **Hybrid Reverb** on this chain is set to 100% wet with the **Dry/Wet** control.

9.   For the third chain, let's insert the **Delay** device.

10.   Make sure that **Delay** is also set to 100% wet with the **Dry/Wet** control.

11.   Open up the **Chain Select Editor** by pressing the **Chain** button.

Now, we will see something similar to what we saw in the Instrument Rack we have already created (*Figure 8.26*).

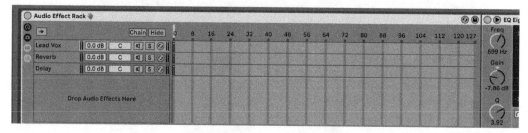

Figure 8.26 – The Chain Select Editor

You can see that the Chain Selector is currently covering all three chains, and since we set the effects on the **Reverb** and **Delay** chains to 100% wet, you can hear that there is plenty of them on the vocals. What you have right now is one chain of lead vocals with basic processing on, another chain that is *just* the reverb (since it's set to 100% wet), and another chain that is *just* the delay (as it's also set to 100% wet).

At this point, you could use the **volume slides** to mix the chains together to your preference, but we will take advantage of the **Chain Select Editor** and **Macro Controls** and set up the Chain Selector as our dry/wet controller.

Setting up the Chain Selector as our dry/wet controller

Let me show you how to do this:

1. Drag the zones of all three chains all the way out to fill the **Zone Editor** (*Figure 8.27*).

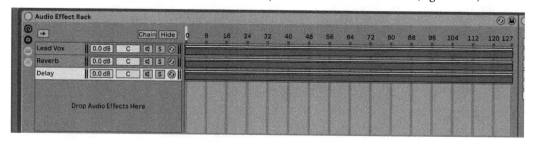

Figure 8.27 – Chain zones are dragged all the way out

2. Now, we are going to **fade** between the chains. Use the bars above the zones. Fade the **Lead Vox** chain out, and fade the **Reverb** and **Delay** chains in (*Figure 8.28*).

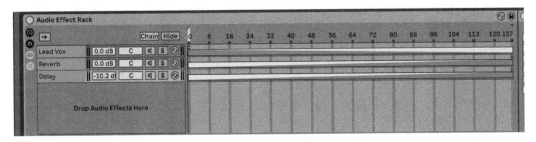

Figure 8.28 – The chain zones are faded

3. Now, with the current position of the Chain Selector bar, you will hear no reverb or delay, as their chains fade in later in the Zone Editor. However, as you start moving the Chain Selector to the right, you will hear the reverb and delay increasing. This means that, right now, you are controlling the dry/wet control between the **Lead Vox** chain and the **Reverb** and **Delay** chains with the Chain Selector.

4. You can further control the effects with the **volume slide** and the **pan slide** in the chain list.

5. In order to have easy access to the Chain Selector, which is essentially our dry/wet controller now, we are going to map it to a **Macro**, as we did already when we built our Instrument Rack. *Ctrl + click* (*right-click* on Windows) on the Chain Selector bar, and map the Chain Selector to **Macro 1** (*Figure 8.29*).

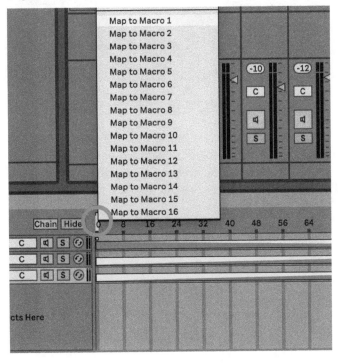

Figure 8.29 – Mapping the Chain Selector to Macro 1

6. Once you are done, you can rename the Macro Control and re-color it (I named mine **DRY/WET**).

7. To further advance this Rack, we are going to map a few more device parameters from across the chains.

8. I mapped the **Drive** control of **Saturator** on the **Lead Vox** chain, the **Size** and **Decay** controls of **Hybrid Reverb** on the **Reverb** chain, and the **Feedback** control of **Delay** on the **Delay** chain (*Figure 8.30*).

9. Of course, the more effects you are using, the more parameters you could map out, but for the effects I used, these would be the parameters that I would most likely want to control when manipulating the sound, so it makes sense to set up quick access to these parameters by mapping them to Macro Controls.

10. At last, we can go ahead and rename the Rack and save it to the **User Library** as we saw in the *Exploring Instrument Racks* section of this chapter. I called mine **Vocal Processor**. So, next time I'm dealing with vocals, I can call back this Audio Effect Rack and adjust the parameters in the rack, according to the tonal characteristics of the vocals I'm working with (*Figure 8.30*).

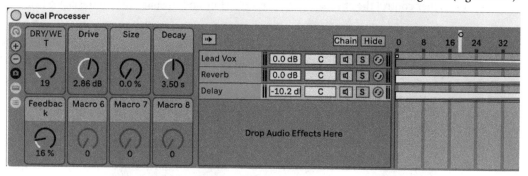

Figure 8.30 – The renamed Audio Effect Rack with the mapped Macro Controls

Creating a Rack that you can use over and over again in your workflow is a practical use of an Audio Effect Rack for *mixing* purposes. However, there are many other scenarios in which you could build Audio Effect Racks. Now that you understand how Audio Effect Racks function, you can learn more about them by checking out the presets in the browser (*Figure 8.31*).

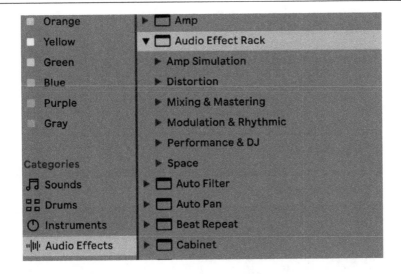

Figure 8.31 – Audio Effect Rack presets in the browser to explore

> **Tip**
>
> You could take this further and build a Rack where you set up different effect chains on your vocals for each track in your **live performance** set, so you can just bounce between the effect chains by the Chain Selector and give yourself various processing options for your voice while you are performing.
>
> You could even save **Macro Variations** for each track of your live performance set and just launch them as you move on to perform your next track (*Figure 8.32*).
>
> I included this Rack in the **Chapter 8** project, so check it out!

Figure 8.32 – The Audio Effect Rack for use in live performance

We have reached the end of our exploration of Audio Effect Racks. In the next section, we are going to take a closer look at Drum Racks!

Exploring Drum Racks

You may have found a lot of similarities in the functions, purposes, and looks of Instrument and Effect Racks, but Drum Racks work a little differently. Let's see how Drum Racks operate by building one from scratch!

Follow these steps:

1. Create a new MIDI track.

2. Head to the browser, choose **Drums** under **Categories**, and insert an empty Drum Rack on the new MIDI track (*Figure 8.33*).

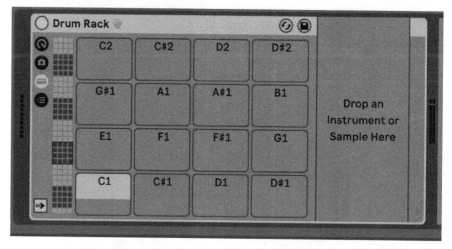

Figure 8.33 – An empty Drum Rack inserted onto the new empty MIDI track

3. Go ahead and display all the other areas and functions on the Drum Rack by using the small buttons on the left side of the Rack, as we did before with the other Device Racks we looked at. Now, you will see what the Drum Rack looks like when all the control areas are fully open (*Figure 8.34*).

Figure 8.34 – Fully displaying the Drum Rack

4. You can already see that there are familiar areas, such as the **Macro Variations** area, the Macro Controls, and the chain list. Let's take a look at the **Pad View** first, which is next to the Macros on the right.

    Each of these pads can be filled from 1 to 128, and they are assigned to MIDI notes that will trigger them. For example, if you have a MIDI keyboard, each of the keys will trigger one of these pads.

    As you can see, you can only display 16 pads in focus in the Pad View at once; however, you can decide which 16 pads (notes) to focus on by moving to the **Pad Overview** area (*Figure 8.35*).

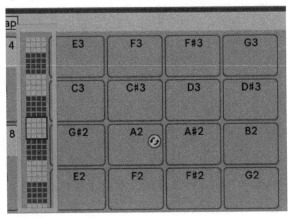

Figure 8.35 – Pad View and Pad Overview

We can fill the pads in the Pad View with **samples**, **effects**, **Device Racks**, and **audio loops**.

5. Let's fill these pads! For the first pad called **C1** (which means this pad will be triggered by the note C1), I will use a kick Drum Synth. (You can find Drum synths in the browser under **Categories | Instruments | Drum Synths**.) I simply drag and drop the kick Drum Synth device onto the pad.

6. For the rest of the pads, I will use some one-shot drum samples. (I included a folder of drum samples called DRUM SAMPLES in the **Chapter 8** project folder, which you can add to the browser for easy access, or you can use your own samples! These royalty-free samples also can be downloaded from https://www.musicradar.com/news/drums/1000-free-drum-samples.) Once you have found sounds in the browser that you'd like to work with, just simply drag and drop them onto the pads one by one.

7. Once you have filled the pads, you will notice that each sound on the pads created a relevant chain in the chain list. Now, you can also rename and recolor the chains for better navigation by *Ctrl + clicking* (*right-clicking* on Windows) on the chains and choosing the appropriate option (*Figure 8.36*).

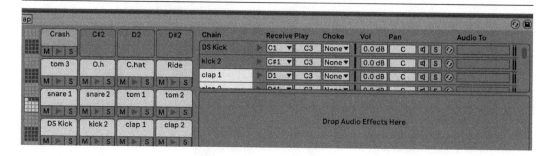

Figure 8.36 – Pads and their relevant chains in the renamed and recolored chain list

Each pad has a pad mute (**M**), a preview (play), and a pad solo (**S**) button. You can also find these options in the chain list between the **Pan** slides and **Hot-Swap** buttons.

8. You can drag and drop audio effects onto the chosen chains in the chain list or directly on the pads in the Pad View. This will allow you to mix the different drum sounds independently. I dropped **Saturator** on the kick drums in this instance (*Figure 8.37*).

Figure 8.37 – Saturator inserted into the DS Kick chain

9. On the chain list, the **Receive** dropdowns will allow you to choose what note will trigger a particular sound. This is a great place to set up some sound layering!

You can see that the first chain, **DS Kick**, is being triggered by **C1**, and **kick 2** is being triggered by **C#1**. Let's go and change **kick 2** also to **C1** under **Receive**. Now, if you trigger C1 on your MIDI controller, you will hear that you are triggering both sounds at the same time with the same note! You can also see in the Pad View that you have created a **Multi** pad (*Figure 8.38*).

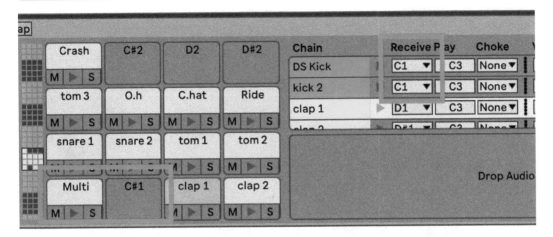

Figure 8.38 – A Multi pad created via the chain list's Receive section

> **Note**
>
> When you are trying to trigger the kick drums with the **C1** note and you can not hear any sound, or you are are triggering the wrong sound, it might be because you are using a smaller MIDI controller with less keys and pads. In this case be sure to make your MIDI controller focus on the "right key range" by going up or down octaves on your controller until you find **C1**.

10. The **Play** section will allow you to set up what note will be outputted by that particular chain. **Choke** allows us to get around notes overlapping. Let me explain this in some more detail. If you think about when a real drummer plays, they aren't able to play the open hi-hat and the closed hi-hat simultaneously. But when we are sequencing drums, there aren't such rules, as we can trigger all notes whenever we want.

    However, we can mimic this behavior by putting the open hi-hat and the closed hi-hat into the same **Choke** group. This will mean they will cut each other out, and only one can play at a time. This can also be used for long sounds that need to be choked by the kick drum – for example, to tighten up drum sequences.

    When you look at the presets of Drum Racks, this is something that is automatically set up in, for example, the 909 Kit, and if you don't know about it, you might find it weird why the hi-hats are cutting each other out. In our project, I put the **O.h** and **C.hat** pads into the same **Choke** group.

11. Next to the **Choke** section on the chain list, you will find the **Volume** and **Pan** slides of the chains. You can also gain access to these in the mixer in the Session View by pressing the **Chain Mixer Fold** button (*Figure 8.39*).

Figure 8.39 – Opening up the Drum Rack in the Session View's mixer with the Chain Mixer Fold button

12. Under the chain list, we can see the **return chain list** and the text displayed, **Drop Audio Effects Here**.

Here is the good news – if you were wondering how you could utilize return tracks with Drum Racks, the MIDI track that is holding the Drum Rack has **Send** controls on it. However, if you send the track to the **return tracks** setup in your set, you will send the entire drumkit to the effects which you have on the return tracks. In reality, you would probably exclude sending your kick drums to a reverb; however, maybe you'd like a little reverb on the hi-hats and even more on the claps and snares. In order to do this, we can use the internal routing of the Drum Rack and the return chain list.

Simply drop the effect you desire (for example, reverb), and make sure you set the device to 100% via the dry/wet controller of the reverb. (If you need to refresh your memory on how sends and returns work, refer back to *Chapter 7, Discovering Some of Live 11's Creative Audio Effects*.)

Now, you will see that you have in the return chain list a reverb (which is **return -a Reverb**), and on the chain list, you have a corresponding **Send – a** (*Figure 8.40*). (If you cannot see the sends in the chain list, make sure you select the **S** button on the left side of the Rack.)

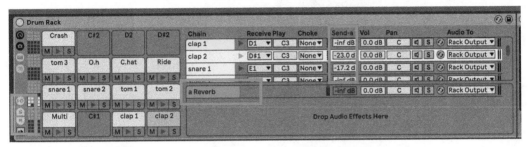

Figure 8.40 – Utilizing sends and returns within the Drum Rack via the internal routing

You are now free to send any of the chains (drum sounds) to the reverb as much as you want.

The Macro Controls and Macro Variations work exactly the same way as in the Instrument and Audio Effect Racks.

I already mapped out the **Drive** parameter of the Saturators on the kick drums, however, we are going to take these a little further!

I want to process the whole Drum Rack, map some of this processing to the Macro Controls, and then save some Macro Variations. However, if I wanted to process the whole Drum Rack, I would need to insert the effects after the Drum Rack – outside of it. However, we know that the effects must be inside the Rack in order to be able to map their parameters to the Macro Controls.

There's a simple solution to this; we will insert the effects outside of the Drum Rack (such as **Drum Buss** and **Multiband Dynamics' OTT preset**), and then group these effects and the Drum Rack itself in a new **Instrument Rack** (*Figure 8.41*)!

Figure 8.41 – The Drum Rack and additional audio effects grouped into a new Instrument Rack

If you recall, we already discovered that we can have Racks inside Racks, and this is one of the occasions when it comes in handy!

Now we have our new Instrument Rack, we can open up the Macro Controls, map the Drum Rack's Macro Controls to the Instrument Racks's Macro Controls, and then map the desired parameters of the Drum Buss and OTT (*Figure 8.42*).

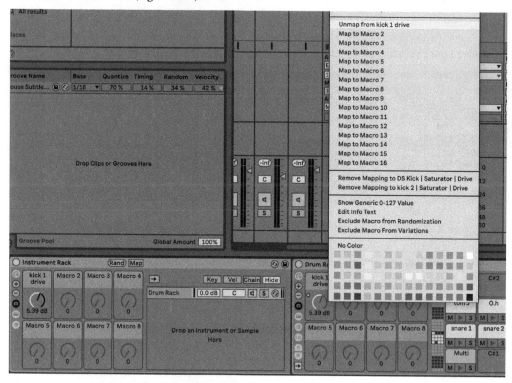

Figure 8.42 – Mapping the Drum Rack's Macros to the Instrument Rack's Macro Controls

I also mapped a few parameters of the Drum Buss device as well as the OTT preset, and then created a couple of Macro Variations, just as we learned with the previous Device Racks that we looked at earlier in the chapter (*Figure 8.43*).

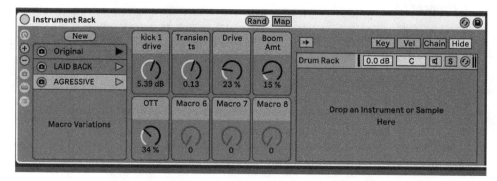

Figure 8.43 – Further Macros and Macro Variations set up

You can check this out in the **Chapter 8** project file!

Summary

We have finally reached the end of Chapter 8! Device Racks truly provide an unlimited amount of fun and creative possibilities once you understand how they function.

In this chapter, we looked at what Device Racks are generally useful for and how we can build an Instrument Rack, an Audio Effect Rack, and a Drum Rack. In the process of building these Racks, we gained a practical understanding of the layouts of Device Racks and how they work.

As I mentioned, there are endless possibilities for how Racks can be used, so my best advice after you are done with this chapter is to dive into the already existing presets, to further your knowledge and get inspired to build more of your own!

In the next chapter, you are in for some fun, as we will be looking at one of my favorite Ableton Live features – audio to MIDI conversion and the Simpler device!

Audio to MIDI Conversion, Slicing to MIDI, and the Simpler Device

In the previous chapter, we discovered the amazing world of device racks in Live. We looked at some of the ways they can be utilized for production and live performance and had a look at the improvements that the Live 11 software update brought to us.

In this chapter, we are going to check out some of my personal favorites: the audio-to-MIDI conversion feature and the Simpler device, among others.

You will learn about some wonderful creative tools that can enhance your workflow and can be especially useful when you are in a creative block or just simply finding it hard to spike a first initial idea and get started.

Furthermore, you will discover how you can quickly turn MIDI information into audio in Live, which can be helpful, for example, to commit to your ideas.

By looking at the Simpler device, you will quickly realize how efficient it is for creative sampling and sound design!

We are going to cover the following topics:

- Introduction to audio-to-MIDI conversion
- Converting melody, harmony, and drums (audio) to MIDI
- Converting MIDI into audio with Freeze and Flatten
- Slicing to MIDI
- The Simpler device

Technical requirements

In order to follow along with this chapter, you will need the following:

- A computer with at least 8 GB of RAM and at least an Intel Core i5 processor
- A pair of headphones
- A copy of Live 11 Suite
- The **Chapter 9** Ableton Live project

Let's jump right into audio-to-MIDI conversion in the next section!

Introduction to audio-to-MIDI conversion

Audio-to-MIDI conversion is one of Live's most exciting features.

Have you ever found an audio loop of chord progressions, for example, in which you absolutely loved the chords, but you didn't really like the sound of the instrument that the chords were playing?

Or have you wished that you could modify some of these chords to your taste in terms of notation?

If you answered yes, it can go two ways… one is that you have fairly advanced music theory knowledge and you can play the chords yourself and pick a different instrument to play other than what the audio loop played.

The second reality is that you are struggling to play or recognize the chords from the audio loop. In this case, you would probably leave the audio loop and find another one in which you liked the chords and the sound too, and would settle on that. You don't have to!

You can convert the audio loop into MIDI, which will enable you to edit the converted MIDI notes better to your taste, as well as change the instrument that the MIDI notes play, and add your own MIDI and audio effects. This way, you can use the audio loop as a starting point for an idea, but you can transform it so much along the way that it will be unrecognizable by the end.

Same with drums. You must have found a nice audio drum loop before in which you had limited editing options with the notation. You couldn't change the sound of the drums, but you were really in love with the groove of the loop. Again, you can convert this audio drum loop into MIDI while extracting the swing and the velocity of the loop, giving yourself the chance to modify the notes as well as the drum sounds and the effects.

The whole concept is based on pitch and rhythm detection of the audio and translating it into the equivalent MIDI information. However, Live will not always get it fully right.

The success of the conversion is also going to depend on the quality of the audio material that you are trying to convert into MIDI.

Try to use sounds that are as dry as possible – the more the effects (such as reverb, delay, and pitch manipulation effects) mask the true pitch of notes, the harder it will be for Live to detect the pitch and convert it.

You can also manipulate the conversion further by using Warp Markers. If Live didn't create a MIDI note from the audio material where you feel like there should have been a note, you can go back to the audio file, create a Warp Marker at the place where you would like the extra note to be created, and do the conversion again.

Converting melody, harmony, and drums into MIDI

In this section, we will take a look at all three audio-to-MIDI conversion options and discover how you can utilize these in the best possible way.

Convert Melody to New MIDI Track

The **Convert Melody to New MIDI Track** command is useful for converting audio that contains **monophonic** information, meaning there is only one note playing. Melody conversion will work great on material such as vocals, basslines, instrument melodies (not chords), and, once again, instruments playing monophonic information.

In this example, we will convert an audio loop of a bass line into MIDI.

We will be working in the **Arrangement View**. However, audio-to-MIDI conversion works the same way in both **Session View** and **Arrangement View**.

There are multiple ways to perform the audio-to-MIDI conversion; let's have a look at the first one:

1. You can open up the provided **Chapter 9** project.

2. Navigate to the track called **BASS LOOP.**

3. *Ctrl + click* (*right-click* for Windows) on the audio loop and choose the **Convert Melody to New MIDI Track** command.

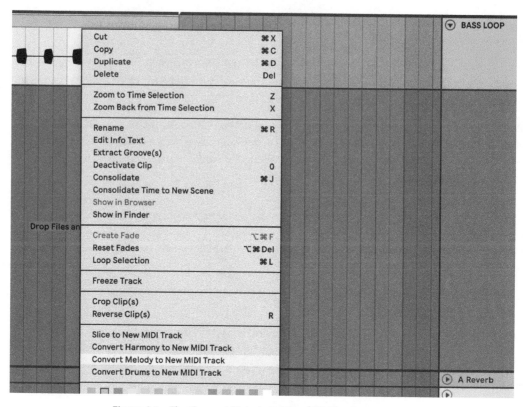

Figure 9.1 – The Convert Melody to New MIDI Track command

Now, you will see Live has created a new MIDI track called **Melody to MIDI** with a default **Instrument Rack** inserted on the track (*Figure 9.2*):

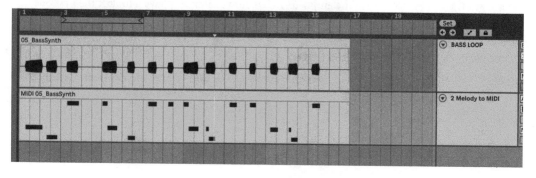

Figure 9.2 – The audio loop and the converted MIDI underneath it

From this point in time, you can go ahead and perform any editing to the MIDI notes you would like in the **MIDI editor**, change the default instrument to a bass sound of your choice, or any other sound you wish. You could use these notes, transpose them up a few octaves, and insert an instrument with a violin or piano preset and totally transform the original loop into something else.

You can also go ahead and delete the original bass loop and you will be left with your own customizable material.

Sometimes, I also grab a microphone if I have an idea and quickly record myself just singing the melody, then convert the recording of my voice into MIDI, and voila, I might have just sung my own bassline.

Convert Harmony to New MIDI Track

Harmony-to-MIDI conversion is suitable for audio material that plays back **polyphonic** information, meaning there are multiple notes and pitches to detect at once.

The **Convert Harmony to New MIDI Track** command can be useful for audio material such as piano, guitars, strings playing chords, or synth sounds that have no clear pitch information.

In our example, we will be converting a clip of piano chords while looking at another way that you can perform an audio-to-MIDI conversion:

1. Navigate in the project to the track called **PIANO LOOP**.

2. In this case, I already have a MIDI track set up with the preferred instrument playing a pad sound that I eventually would like the extracted notes of the piano loop to play back (**Analog Slow Sweep** track).

3. Now, simply drag the piano loop to the MIDI track called **Analog Slow Sweep** and you will see a pop-up window in which you can choose the type of audio-to-MIDI conversion you need.

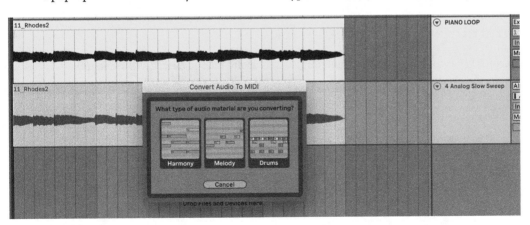

Figure 9.3 – Convert Audio to MIDI commands

4.   Pick the **Harmony** option.

5.   Now, you will see the extracted MIDI notes playing back the instrument we set up.

6.   If you open up the new MIDI clip in the MIDI editor and enable **Scale** in the **Clip View** tool (the chords are in E minor), then you will see that some of the notes were detected and placed outside of the scale. Since the information we are now working with is MIDI, you can easily move the notes or delete some of them to your taste:

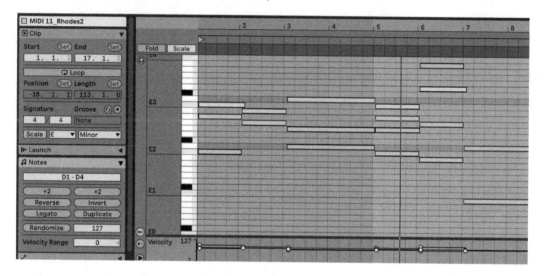

Figure 9.4 – MIDI editor with Scale enabled in Clip View

You can also bring in the **Scale** MIDI effect to keep control of the extra outside of the scale notes (we looked at the **Scale** MIDI effect device in *Chapter 5, MIDI Editing and MIDI Effects*).

Convert Drums to New MIDI Track

Drums-to-MIDI conversion, as the name suggests, is useful for converting a drum loop:

1.   Navigate to the track called **DRUM LOOP**.

2.   *Ctrl + click* (*right-click* on Windows) on the clip and choose **Convert Drums to New MIDI Track**.

3.   Now, you will see the result of the conversion:

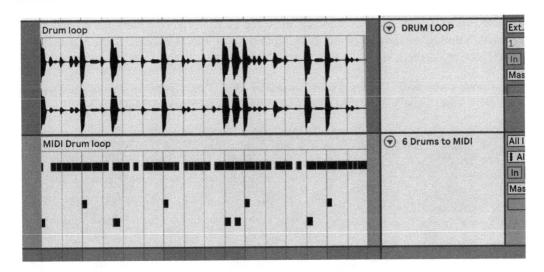

Figure 9.5 – The drum loop and the converted MIDI

4. If you bring up the **MIDI editor**, you will see that with the conversion, you have gained access to the full **groove** of the original loop, the **velocity** changes are there, and now you can go ahead and edit the notes to your taste, apply another groove from the browser, or do anything you wish.

5. You can also go ahead and change the drum rack instead of the default **606 kit** to something you like better, or you can build your own drum rack, which we learned about in *Chapter 8, Exploring Device Racks in Live 11*.

Converting MIDI into audio with Freeze and Flatten

Converting audio into MIDI is actually super easy in Live. Besides the obvious reasons why you would do this, it also gives you a chance to commit to your ideas by "printing" the MIDI track's editable notes and device parameters, forcing you to commit to your ideas.

Also, working with audio takes way less CPU power than MIDI. Therefore, it can be a way to take some stress off your CPU.

Let's have a look at how to do this:

1. In the **Chapter 9** project, navigate to the track called **E-PIANO**.

2. *Ctrl + click* (*right-click* for Windows) on the **track title** bar and choose **Freeze Track** from the contextual menu.

3. Once the track is frozen, you are not able to tweak the parameters anymore. This is already taking stress off your CPU. This step is also crucial, as you will only see the **Flatten** option if the track is already frozen.

4. Now, in order to use **Flatten** on the track (flattening tracks will convert them into a new audio track, "printing" all the processing, as well into the new waveform of the converted audio), you have two options:

    • Create a new audio track and move the MIDI clip(s) down from the frozen MIDI track (*Figure 9.6*) while holding the *Option* (*Alt* on Windows) key on your keyboard:

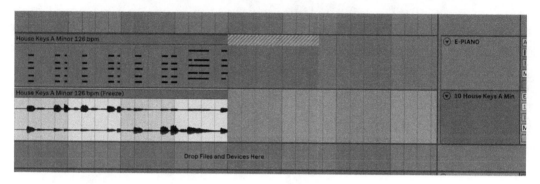

Figure 9.6 – Moving the frozen clip down to a new MIDI track while holding the Option key

Now, you will notice that you kept the original frozen track with all the MIDI notes and the tweakable parameters, but you also have the audio version of the frozen track. This way, you can keep the original track **muted** in your composition if you'd like to, and go back to that track to tweak parameters if needed after you unfreeze the track (you can unfreeze a track by using *Ctrl* + *click* (*right-click* for Windows) on the track title bar and choosing **Unfreeze Track** from the contextual menu.

You will notice that the new audio clip doesn't contain the effect tail of the MIDI track. You can drag out the new clip to display the full clip, including any effect tails (*Figure 9.7*):

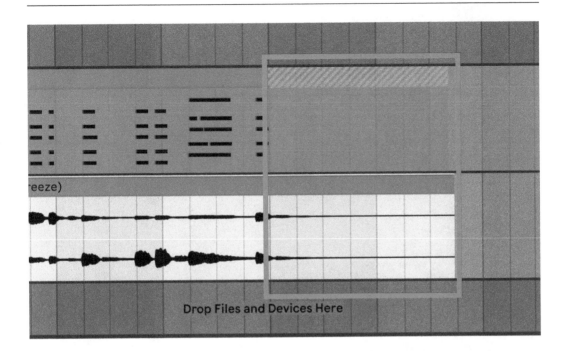

Figure 9.7 – Effect tail

- The second option is that you don't keep the original MIDI track, so the flattened audio will replace the original MIDI. To do this, simply *Ctrl + click* (*right-click* on Windows) again on the track title bar of the frozen MIDI track and choose **Flatten Track** from the contextual menu.

Now that we have looked at three audio-to-MIDI and MIDI-to-audio conversion options, let's take a look at another one, **Slice to New MIDI Track**.

Slice to New MIDI Track

The **Slice to New MIDI Track** command will allow you to slice (or chop up) audio and trigger the slices with MIDI notes.

This way, you can re-sequence audio material, and play the slices like an instrument.

To do this, see the following:

1. Navigate in the project to the track called **SLICE**.
2. Make sure the audio is warped correctly.
3. *Ctrl + click* (*right-click* on Windows) on the audio clip and choose **Slice to New MIDI track** from the contextual menu.

4. You will see a pop-up window:

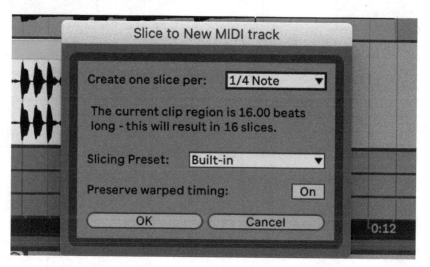

Figure 9.8 – Slice to New MIDI track pop-up window

The first dropdown (**Create one slice per:**) will allow you to choose how you want to slice the audio (by what value). I chose **Transient**, so Live will create a slice by each transient of the clip.

> **Tip**
>
> When I work with more complex audio material and I'd like to manipulate this slicing further, I tend to choose **Create one slice per: Warp Marker**. Before I got to this option, I would go into the sample editor for the original audio clip and create the Warp Markers where I would like to create the slices later.

The second dropdown enables you to choose a **Slicing Preset** option. Here, Live offers you some slicing presets with some great effects. For now, just choose **Built-in**.

5. Once you have clicked **OK**, you will see thatLive creates a new MIDI track with a MIDI clip that contains the original sequence of the drum loop:

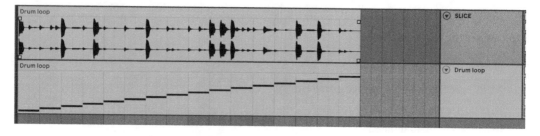

Figure 9.9 – The original audio loop and the sliced-up material on a new MIDI track

6. Now, let's have a look at where the slices are stored. If you bring up **Device View** for the new MIDI track created, you will see that all the slices live in a new **Drum Rack**, and each pad contains one slice that can be triggered by the appropriate MIDI notes (you can revisit how drum racks work in *Chapter 8*):

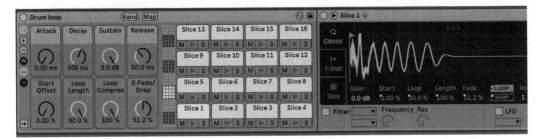

Figure 9.10 – Slices stored in our Drum Rack

7. As the final step, you can go ahead and re-sequence the slices to your taste.

As we can see in *Figure 9.10*, the slices are stored in **Drum Rack**, and on the pads, the device that hosts the slices is the **Simpler device**, so it is time to take a closer look at it.

The Simpler device

The Simpler device is one of the best devices, in my opinion, that Live has to offer!

It is a MIDI instrument with a simple sampler and subtractive synth features. What makes it special is that you can slice and dice loops easily and play audio files back as an instrument with just a few clicks, so it is definitely one to get creative with.

Let's take a look at it:

1. You can find the Simpler devicein in the browser under the **Instruments** category.

2. Once you have loaded the empty Simpler device, you can insert an audio sample where it says **Drop Sample Here**.

3. You can also bring this device up by dropping an audio file into a new empty MIDI track's device area. This will place the audio automatically in the Simpler device.

   I have already loaded a Simpler device with a sample in it onto the track called **SIMPLER** in the **Chapter 9** project.

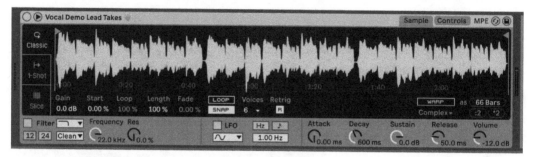

Figure 9.11 – The Simpler device with a vocal loop loaded in it, displaying the Sample area

The Simpler device has three playback modes: **Classic**, **1-Shot**, and **Slice**.

Figure 9.12 – The three playback modes

4.   We can also display the **Sample** area (*Figure 9.11*) and the **Controls** area (*Figure 9.13*):

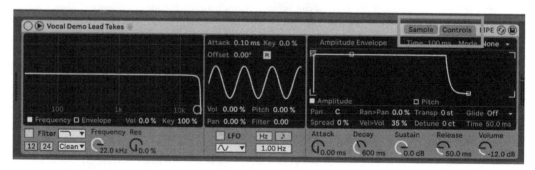

Figure 9.13 – The Controls area in the Simpler device

- The **Sample** area allows us to choose from the three playback modes and edit the sample that we would like to sequence

- The **Controls** area allows us to display further the filter, modulation, and envelope settings, with basic subtractive synth features

Let's check out the main features and the three playback modes and when you would want to use them!

5. First of all, if you now trigger this sample in the Simpler device with your MIDI controller, you will notice that the lower the pitch, the slower the sample plays back, and the higher the pitch, the faster it becomes.

6. This is standard sampler behavior, but luckily, you can stretch the sample inside the Simpler device because there is an internal **warp** option! You can click on the **WARP** button, and choose the appropriate Warp Mode for the material you're working with!

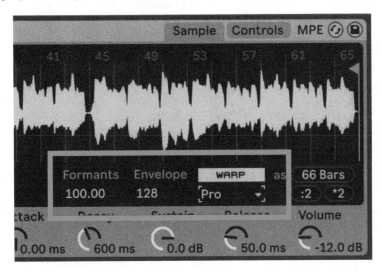

Figure 9.14 – Internal warping in the Simpler device

You can revisit how warping works in *Chapter 3, Editing Audio and Warping*.

7. Now, you will notice that if you start playing the sample again, the audio is stretched in the Simpler device, regardless of the pitch. You can even hold down a chord and create perfect harmony.

8. In the **Sample** display, you can use the small arrows to trim off parts of the sample that you wouldn't like to play back. If you *Ctrl + click* (*right-click* for Windows) on the **Sample** display after you made your selection, from the context menu you can use **Crop Sample** accordingly (among other options), which will reduce some of the stress on your CPU, as there is less audio for the device to process.

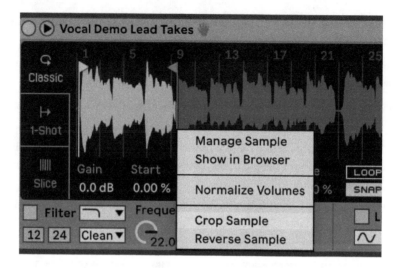

Figure 9.15 – Crop Sample in the Simpler device

9. Once you have selected the sample range and cropped the sample, it is time to look at the three playback modes:

    - **Classic**: This mode allows for **polyphonic** playback and looping partials of the sample. This is the mode that is super-useful for sound design, for example, as you can loop a small portion of the sample, which can give you some sort of granular synthesis effect.

    - **1-Shot**: This mode is useful for playing back one-shot drum samples, for example, or shorter phrases, as it will play back the entire sample regardless of how long you have your finger on the note. You can disable this behavior, however, by clicking on the **Gate** button. This will only play back the sample for as long as you hold your finger on the note.

    As such, this mode only allows **monophonic** playback.

    - **Slice**: Now, here is where things get even more exciting!

    You can slice up a sample with this mode. Obviously, it is best suited for working with longer phrases. As soon as you use this mode, you will already see some slices created for you. In this case, Simpler automatically uses **Slice By | Transient**. On the **Sensitivity** slide, you can create fewer or more slices (*Figure 9.16*):

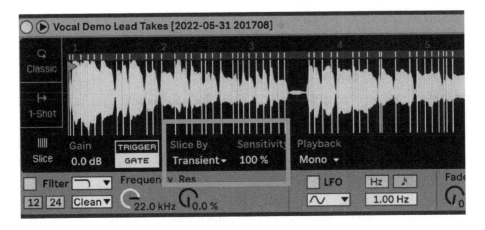

Figure 9.16 – Simpler's Slice By settings

10. If you click **Transient** under the **Slice By** text, you can change the dropdown to the following:

- **Beat**: Slices created by beat divisions

- **Region**: Slices created by time division and the sample will be sliced into equal parts

- **Manual**: You can use the **Sample** display to create your own slices by double-clicking on the area where you'd like to create a slice

11. You can also use the small triangle button to expand the **Sample** display:

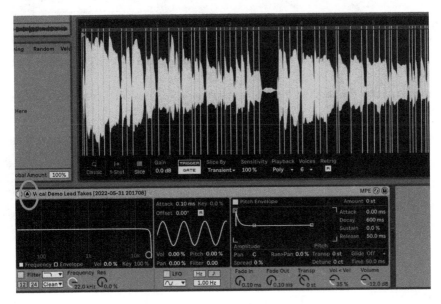

Figure 9.17 – The Sample display expanded

12. In Slice mode, you can decide whether you want the slices to be played back as monophonic or not by selecting the desired mode under **Playback** (next to **Sensitivity**) (*Figure 9.18*).

13. Once you have set up the desired slices, you can go ahead and sequence them and come up with something super-creative.

14. Furthermore, you can head to the control area and fine-tune some filtering, modulation, and envelope settings.

    You will quickly notice that any settings you are applying – detuning, modulation, and so on – will be applied to all the slices equally. Especially with vocal chops, it can be nice to apply different settings to the slices independently.

15. It is actually possible to do so – all you need to do is *Ctrl + click* (*right-click* on Windows) on the **Sample** display and either choose **Slice to Drum Rack** or **Slice to New MIDI Track**:

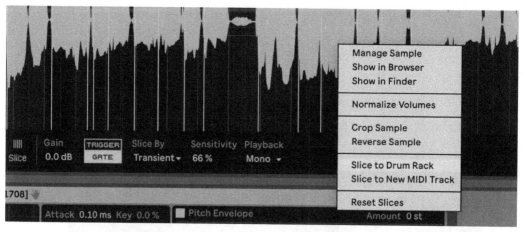

Figure 9.18 – Transferring slices into your Drum Rack using Slice to Drum Rack or Slice to New MIDI Track

Both options will transfer the slices into a drum rack (*Figure 9.19*), in which each slice will live on a pad inside the rack:

Figure 9.19 – Slices transferred into a Drum Rack piece, each slice living in its own Simpler device

This means each slice will also be living in its own Simpler device, where you can independently apply any settings we looked at before to the slices. The difference between **Slice to Drum Rack** and **Slice to New MIDI Track** is that **Slice to Drum Rack** will replace the original MIDI track on which you have been working, while **Slice to New MIDI Track** will create a new MIDI track with the slices placed into a drum rack and keep the original track at hand, too.

Once you have applied any of the commands and the slices are in the drum rack, you will notice a MIDI clip with the original sequence will have been automatically created (*Figure 9.20*):

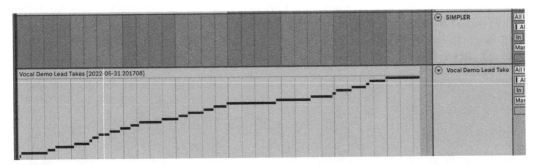

Figure 9.20 – MIDI clip with the original sequence after using the Slice to New MIDI Track command

You can use this clip to rearrange the slices, or you can delete it and create your own sequence from scratch.

Simpler inspiration material

I created a new sequence, **transposed** a couple of the slices in the control area of Simpler (*Figure 9.21*), and also renamed this track **Sliced**. You can check it out in the **Chapter 9** project:

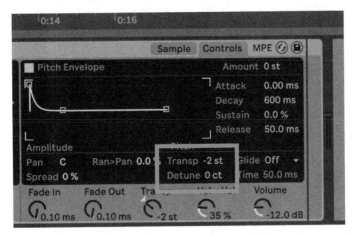

Figure 9.21 – Detuning and transposing samples in Simpler via the control area

You could also consider applying different effect processing to the slices independently and taking advantage of all the features available in **Drum Rack** that you already learned about in the previous chapter.

I also created a vocal pad instrument (**Simpler vox pad**) track in the project with the technique I explained earlier in this chapter while using the **Classic** playback mode in Simpler by looping a small part of the sample and then processing it in the control area.

You can also check that out in the **Chapter 9** project for inspiration.

With this **Simpler vox pad** track, you will notice that there is a **Tuner** device after Simpler (*Figure 9.22*). This is to make sure that the looped sample part is tuned to C (via **Transpose** and **Detune** in the control area of the Simpler device) when you are holding down the C note on your MIDI controller so that you can stay in key.

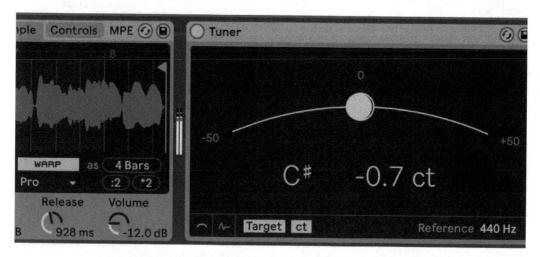

Figure 9.22 – The Tuner device inserted after the Simpler device

As we can see, the Simpler device gives us plenty of options to spike our creative juice and improve our basic sampling options through sound design.

Summary

And with that, we have reached the end of this chapter.

I hope this chapter gets your creative juices flowing!

We looked at how we can use audio-to-MIDI conversion to extract MIDI data out of audio material and customize it to our taste so that we can build on it, which is sometimes just what we need when we don't seem to be able to get started creatively.

We also looked at how to turn MIDI data into audio by using the **Freeze** and **Flatten** functions.

We also explored how we can slice audio to MIDI to be able to trigger the audio slices with MIDI data, as well as exploring the Simpler device, not just to slice and dice but also to have a look at the sound design possibilities that this "simple" but powerful device can provide us with.

In the next chapter, we will dive into arrangement techniques and project organization!

10

Utilizing Arrangement and Organization Techniques in our Ableton Live Project

In the previous chapter, we learned how to utilize audio-to-MIDI conversion, convert MIDI to audio, slice audio to MIDI, and discovered how to use the Simpler device. All these features are amazing for sparking your creativity and helping you to get started.

In this chapter, we will look at some crucial workflow techniques for arranging in Live. We will explore how we can move clips and scenes from the Session View into the Arrangement View and how we can utilize Locators and organize our session for better navigation.

As an active producer, you probably already know the building blocks of an arrangement for certain genres and the importance of a good arrangement.

Even if the produced parts and all the musical ideas are awesome, they will still need a properly executed arrangement in order to tell the story and take the listener on a journey with your music.

A good arrangement will have plenty of variations within the track, but it must also be balanced with carefully thought-through repetition.

The key is balancing the expected and the unexpected. Energy level changes are also super important as they create contrast between the parts within the track.

Without going into too many details about the theories of composition and genre studies, we will focus on the technical aspects of arranging your song in Live and discovering what tools are available for you in the software.

In this chapter, we will cover the following key topics:

- Preparing to arrange – session organization techniques
- From the Session View to the Arrangement View
- Editing your arrangement
- Locators and info text
- Track grouping

Technical requirements

In order to follow along with this chapter, you will need the following:

- A computer with at least 8 GB of RAM and an Intel Core i5 processor
- A pair of headphones
- A copy of Live 11 Suite
- The **Chapter 10** Ableton Live project

Preparing to arrange – session organization techniques

It is very important to be able to navigate the project to organize it.

You can use the **Chapter 10** project to follow along with me:

1. Open the project.

   You will find a bunch of tracks with clips organized into scenes, which will form sections of our arrangement (*Figure 10.1*).

   (You can recap how to navigate and organize clips and scenes in Session View in *Chapter 1, Taking a Quick Tour of Ableton Live 11*.)

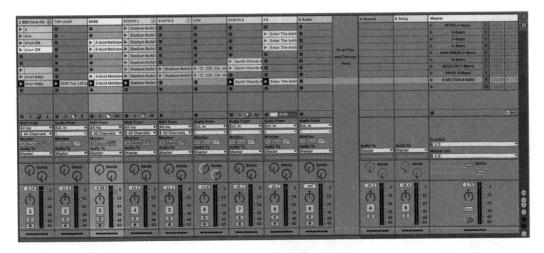

Figure 10.1 – The Chapter 10 project

2. Let's make sure that all the tracks are renamed to our taste, unused tracks are deleted, tracks and clips are color-coded, and similar tracks are moved to be next to each other (for example, the three synth tracks).

3. Start with renaming and recoloring the tracks. To do this, *Ctrl + click* (*right-click* on Windows)on the track title bar and choose the appropriate options from the contextual menu (*Figure 10.2*).

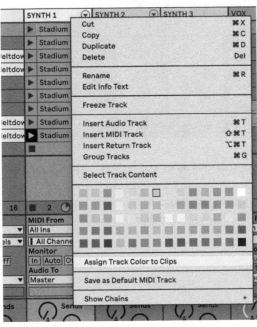

Figure 10.2 – Contextual menu with Rename, color options, and Assign Track Color to Clips functions

Also, you can assign the same color to the clips that you chose for the track itself by choosing the **Assign Track Color to Clips** option (*Figure 10.2*).

You should also rename clips according to what's in them. So, for example, if you transposed the chords in one of the clips, that clip could have a different color and be named accordingly to indicate the variation in the sequence.

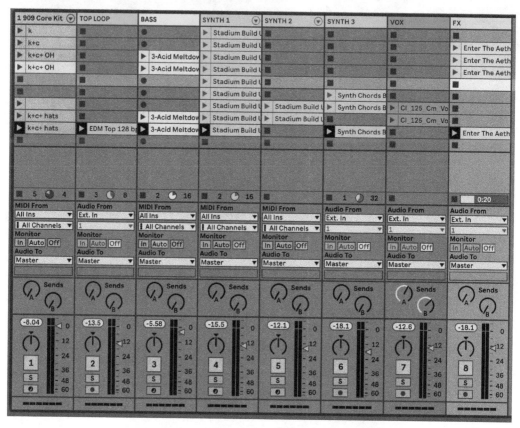

Figure 10.3 – Renamed and recolored tracks and clips

4.   Once this is done, make sure you also name the scenes according to the arrangement you are planning to execute. I also like to type in how many bars I would like that scene to be played.

Figure 10.4 – Renamed scenes

Once Session View is organized, we are ready to move into the Arrangement View!

From Session View to the Arrangement View

We already learned that we can copy-paste clips from the Session View to the Arrangement View.

But what is actually more exciting is that we can record the arrangement on the fly!

This is why organizing the Session View properly is so important, as it means we can just press record and launch the scenes and record our first sketch for the arrangement.

First, you shouldn't feel the pressure to compose an entire track in the Session View, record it, and be done. It is a common practice to lay down the main ideas (a couple of tracks), the backbone of a track, quickly in the Session View, then move into the Arrangement View to finish the composition. You can still add additional instruments, edits, and transition sounds, as naturally, having the track idea laid down on the timeline will give you new ideas on how to proceed further with your track until it is finished.

To record your arrangement on the fly, do the following:

1. Make sure that no clips and scenes are launched in the Session View. (You can do this by clicking the *Stop All Clips* button.)

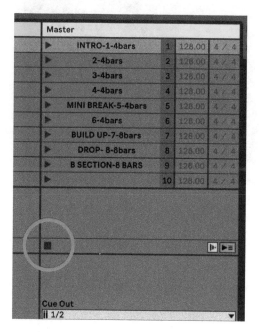

Figure 10.5 – The Stop All Clips button

2. Make sure you have at least **1 Bar Count-In** set up by pressing the *Metronome Settings* button (*Figure 10.6*).

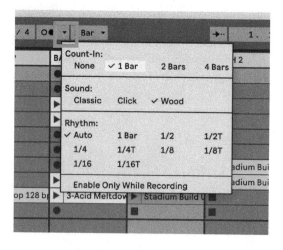

Figure 10.6 – The Metronome Settings button and the Count-In settings

3. Before we hit the **Arrangement Record** button, let's head to the Arrangement View and make sure that there is no time selected or looped on the timeline.

4. Now we can hit the **Arrangement Record** button, and while the count-in is ticking off, we can launch our first scene!

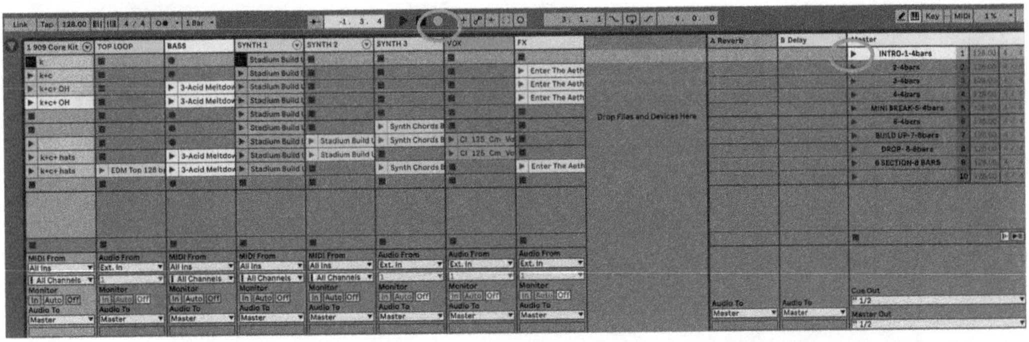

Figure 10.7 – Pressing the Arrangement Record button and launching the first scene

5. Let it play for as long as you would like it to be in your arrangement, then launch the next scene until you are through all the scenes you have set up.

6. You can switch to the Arrangement View while you are recording to check what is going on.

Figure 10.8 – Recording the Session View's content into the Arrangement View on the fly

7. Once you are done and have stopped recording, you will notice that if you press play, you will start playing back the last scene in the Session View, as the scene is still launched and the arrangement is not prioritized.

8. You can press the **Back to Arrangement** button in order to activate the playback of the Arrangement View (*Figure 10.9*).

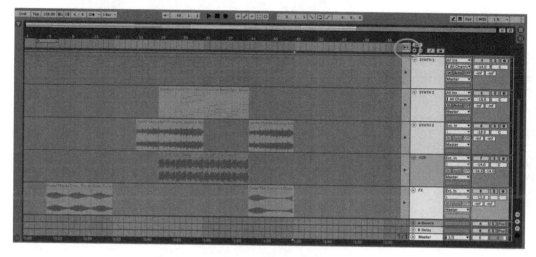

Figure 10.9 – The Back to Arrangement button

And with that, we just recorded our arrangement on the fly from the Session View.

Of course, there could be occasions when you aren't starting your track in the Session View, but you are instead composing straight into the Arrangement View and creating the main parts of your song there.

There is nothing wrong with that, and if that is the case, then in the next section of this chapter, you will find out how you can create a full arrangement out of your existing parts by employing various commands in the Arrangement View.

Editing your arrangement

We already looked at how we can trim, split, fade, move, duplicate, and consolidate clips in the Arrangement View in *Chapter 3, Editing Audio and Warping*. Most of these also apply to MIDI clips.

In this section, we will explore the Cut/Copy, Paste, and Duplicate Time commands and Insert Silence!

Cut, Copy, Paste, and Duplicate Time commands

Let's start with the Cut, Copy, Paste, and Duplicate Time commands:

1. The first thing that needs to be done is to make a selection in the timeline. It can be a bunch of clips, or just one, as we will be working with the chunk of time that the clip(s) occupy (not just the one clip) and affect the overall arrangement!

2. Once the clip(s) are selected, as in my example (*Figure 10.10*), we can visit the **Edit** menu (*Figure 10.11*).

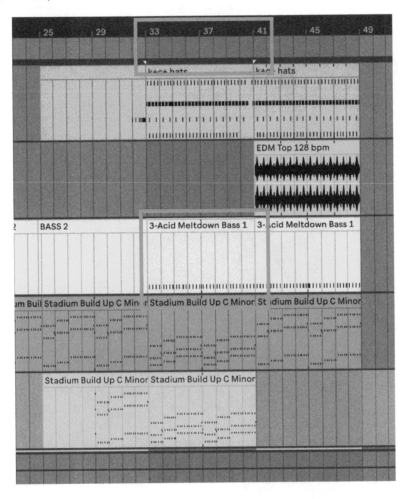

Figure 10.10 – Clip/Time is selected to perform the Time command

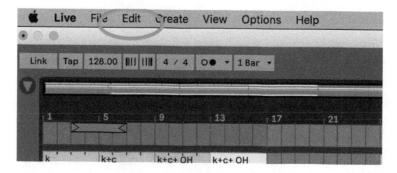

Figure 10.11 – The Edit menu

3.   In the **Edit** menu, we can now see the **Time** commands (*Figure 10.12*).

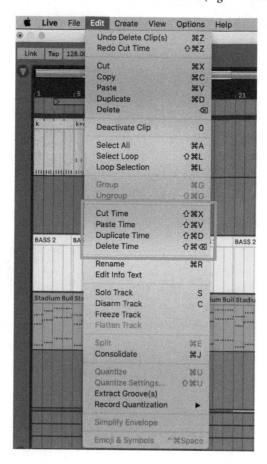

Figure 10.12 – The Time commands in the Edit menu

Next to the commands, you can also see the shortcuts written; learning these will significantly speed up your workflow!

4. As the commands suggest, here you will be able to cut, paste, duplicate, and delete all the active clips under the selected time on the timeline. Let's look at **Duplicate Time** as an example. Let's click on it and see the result in *Figure 10.13*.

Now you will see that in our initial arrangement when we selected our time by selecting a clip in this example (*Figure 10.10*), the selection was from bar **33** until bar **41**. After performing the **Duplicate Time** command, we can now see all the clips under the selected time have been duplicated and now occupy space until bar **49** (*Figure 10.13*).

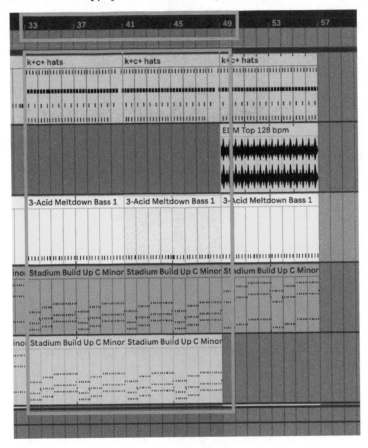

Figure 10.13 – Duplicated Time and the corresponding clips

Inserting silence

Sometimes we might want to insert some **silence** into our song to fill it up with transition sounds, record or compose a whole new section, or simply just create more impact in the arrangement by having a small silent part in the song.

To insert silence, take the following steps:

1.   Make a selection on the timeline again.

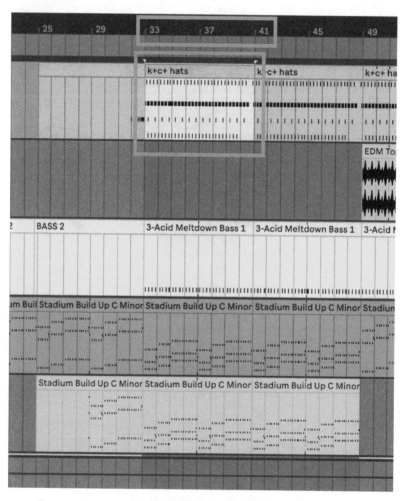

Figure 10.14 – Timeline selection to replace this section with silence

2. Now we will navigate to the **Create** menu. Here, choose **Insert Silence** (*Figure 10.15*).

Figure 10.15 – The Insert Silence command

3. Now, you will see that the selection we made before is replaced by silence on our timeline and all the clips are shifted to the right (*Figure 10.16*).

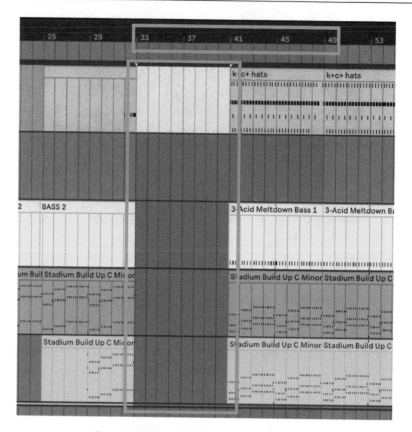

Figure 10.16 – Inserted silence in the timeline

These **Time** commands combined with clip editing will enable you to define and finetune your arrangement in no time and provide you with a fluid workflow.

Once you have worked on the sections of your arrangement in the timeline, it is important that you mark these sections with **locators** so you can actually see the *mapping* of the elements of your arrangement and identify any sections that might need more variation or development.

In the next section, we will have a look at how to work with these locators.

Locators and Info Text

Locators in Live are not just useful to help you navigate your arrangement better, but they are also equipped with **launch buttons** that respond to the **Global Quantization** settings. This can be super useful to test out how your arrangement would sound if you changed the order of some of your sections by having the sections launched by the locator's launch button on time/in sync with your song tempo, thanks to the Global Quantization settings.

Let's have a look at how to set them up:

1. The locators will appear in the Scrub Area.

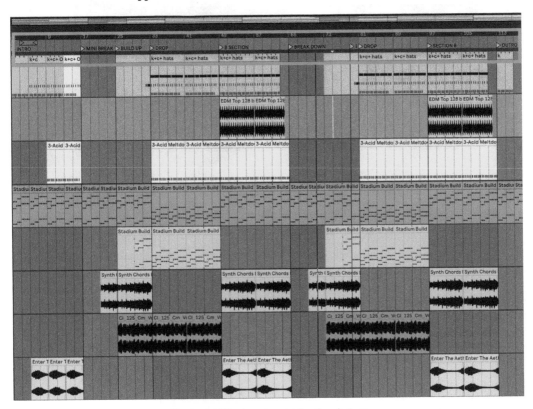

Figure 10.17 – Locators in the Scrub Area

2. To set one up, you can *Ctrl + click* (*right-click* on Windows) where you'd like to set the locator in the Scrub Area and choose **Add Locator** (*Figure 10.18*).

3. Alternatively, you can use the **Set** button. This can also work during playback.

Figure 10.18 – Setting up locators

4. In order to rename a locator, just simply *Ctrl + click* (*right-click* on Windows) on the locator and choose the appropriate option from the contextual menu.

5. The two arrows under the **Set** button allow you to jump between the next and previous locators (*Figure 10.18*).

Something that can also be very useful is adding notes/info text to the locators. This is amazing when you are still deeply in the production process, and you are identifying what else you need to add or work on in certain sections.

To set these up, follow these steps:

1. *Ctrl + click* (*right-click* on Windows) on the locator.

2. Choose the **Edit Info Text** option from the contextual menu (*Figure 10.19*).

Figure 10.19 – Adding Edit Info Text to a locator

3. Now you will see that in the **Info View** area at the bottom left of the screen, you can add text to the locator.

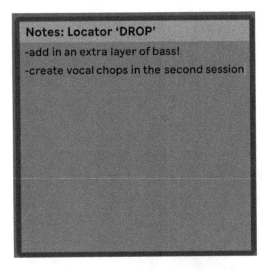

Figure 10.20 – The Edit Info Text area

From now on, any time you hover your mouse over the locator, the text will appear at the bottom left of the screen.

This is also very helpful when you are *collaborating* with someone where you are sending each other the projects, so you can leave notes for your collaborator!

Track grouping

Track grouping is important for organizing your tracks for a more fluid arrangement, but it is also super important for mixing purposes as once tracks are grouped they can all be processed together. This is common practice to group tracks with similar dynamic and tonal characteristics.

Let's see how to group tracks:

1. Select multiple tracks while holding down the *Shift* key. In this example, I am looking to group all the synth tracks (*Figure 10.21*).

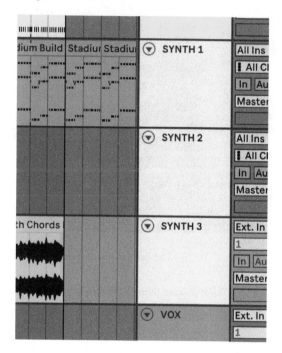

Figure 10.21 – Selected tracks for grouping

2. Now you can *Ctrl + click* (*right-click* on Windows) on one of the selected tracks and choose **Group Tracks** from the contextual menu or use *Cmd + G* (*Ctrl + G* for Windows).

3. Now, you will see the tracks are grouped. You can solo and mute all the grouped tracks and also adjust sends, volume, and panning.

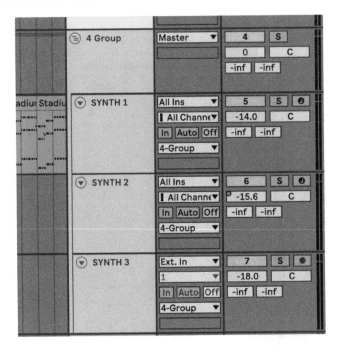

Figure 10.22 – Grouped tracks

4. You can, of course, rename and recolor this group appropriately to your taste. This will work exactly the same way in the Session and Arrangement Views.

5. You can also show and hide the tracks that are a member of the group by pressing the **Unfold Track** button (*Figure 10.23*).

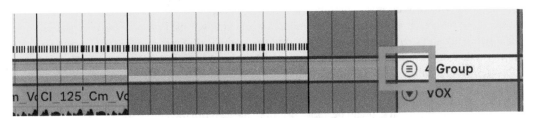

Figure 10.23 – The Unfold Track button

You can drag and drop tracks outside of the group at any time if you decide one of the tracks shouldn't be in the group. You can also ungroup all tracks by *Ctrl + click* (*right-click* on Windows) on the group track and choosing **Ungroup Tracks** (or use the keyboard shortcut: *Cmd + Shift + G* (*Ctrl + Shift + G* for Windows)).

You can also have **groups in groups** for further processing options.

This can be done by either selecting two groups and grouping them or selecting multiple tracks within the group and grouping them.

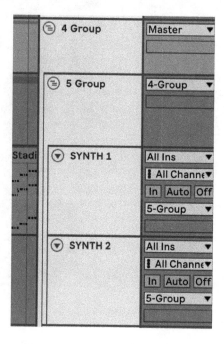

Figure 10.24 – Grouped tracks inside a track group

> **Tip**
> Having groups inside groups is something that I personally regularly use, for example, with vocal layers. I tend to group all the harmonies and all the backing vocals. I process the two groups independently and then group these groups and the lead vocal(s) into a main vocal group so I can further process them to make them *stick* better together, especially with compression. This is, of course, more related to **mixing** than arrangement.

When we are arranging a track, it can be super useful to have an organized session in order to have a fast and efficient workflow. After a while, it becomes second nature to organize our project as we go along with the production.

Summary

And with that, we have arrived at the end of this chapter.

We looked at how we can prepare our project for arrangement, and how we can record our clips and scenes on the fly from the Session View into the Arrangement View.

We also discovered some useful **Time** commands to edit our arrangement and looked at how to use locators and group tracks together, which will not only help us with arranging and session management but also give us some useful possibilities for mixing.

In the next chapter, we will explore how we can use automation and modulation to enhance our arrangement and musical parts.

11

Implementing Automation and Modulation

Automation is a change of parameters over time, which is programmed into your **Digital Audio Workstation (DAW)**.

There are multiple reasons why you might want to implement automation. It can be used for corrective reasons, such as automating the volume of your tracks in the project for mixing purposes, and for loads of creative purposes, for example, automating device parameters, such as a Dry/Wet control of reverb at the end of the vocal phrase.

Automation also can enhance the dynamics of your arrangement, help with transitioning from section to section, and provide some interest for certain instruments.

In this chapter, we will discover how we can work with automation in both the Session and Arrangement Views.

We are going to cover the following key topics in this chapter:

- Tempo and time signature changes
- Recording automation in the Arrangement View
- Recording automation in the Session View
- Drawing and editing automation
- Clip envelopes

Technical requirements

In order to follow along with this chapter, you will need the following:

- A computer with at least 8 GB of RAM and an Intel Core i5 processor
- A pair of headphones
- A copy of Live 11 Suite
- The **Chapter 11** Ableton Live project

Tempo and time signature changes

In this section, we are going to discover how we can automate the session tempo as well as how to implement time signature changes.

Implementing tempo changes

This can be useful if you would like a section of your song to speed up or slow down at some point. It can provide some real contrast to your song, or can be useful you are recording various tracks into the same project with different song tempos.

Let's check out how we can implement tempo changes into our project by automating the song tempo!

1. Open the **Chapter 11** project (I already applied some automation and modulation for inspiration in this project, so feel free to work around these or delete them).

2. Navigate to the Arrangement View.

3. Navigate to the **Master** track.

4. To be able to automate any parameters, we need to enable **Automation Mode**, by pressing the **Automation Mode** button or using the hotkey *A*.

Figure 11.1 – The Automation Mode button

We have two ways to select a parameter for automation in Live:

1. Use the choosers on the tracks. In this case, on the **Master** track, select **Mixer** from the first chooser (the **Device** chooser) and **Song Tempo** from the second chooser (the **Automation Control** chooser).

Figure 11.2 – Selecting a parameter for automation

2. Or you can simply click on the parameter in Live (after you enabled Automation Mode) that you would like to automate (in this case, click on the **Tempo** within the **Control** section), and you will see the envelope is automatically displayed of the chosen parameter on the track.

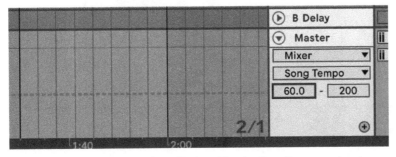

Figure 11.3 – Automation lane displayed for the Song Tempo parameter

In the **BUILD UP** section of the song, we are going to slow the track down (drop the tempo down to 100 BPM) gradually and then increase it using the **DROP** section.

3. We can see the automation lane and the breakpoint envelope (the red line displayed by the automation lane) for **Song Tempo**; we are going to create a **breakpoint** by double-clicking on the envelope at bar **25** (the beginning of the **BUILD UP** section). This breakpoint can be moved with the mouse, and you will see the value next to the breakpoint even as you move it. That value is the song tempo.

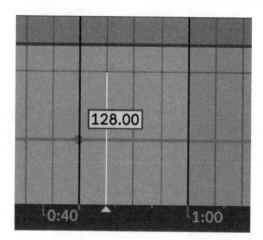

Figure 11.4 – Automation breakpoint at bar 25, displaying the current tempo

4. Now, we are going to create another breakpoint at bar **29** and bar **33**.

5. Move the breakpoint at bar **29** to the value of **100** (100 BPM) and then the third breakpoint at bar **33** back to **128** (*Figure 11.5*).

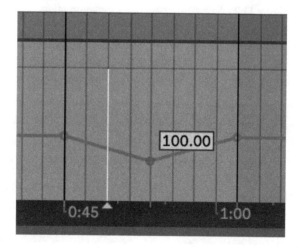

Figure 11.5 – Song Tempo automation written

6. Now, if you play back this section, you will hear the implemented tempo change.

On the **Master** track, the numbers **60-200** underneath the Automation Control chooser indicate the current minimum and maximum **Tempo Range** between which you can automate.

Now let's go and see how we can also change time signatures.

Implementing time signature changes

This is not something that can be automated; however, it feels appropriate to cover it together with tempo changes.

Sometimes you might want to produce a track where the time signature changes for a section of the song. It can be really nice for **instrument** solo sections – just as an example.

In order to change the time signature of your song (and, accordingly, the grid as well), all you need to do is the following:

1. Head to the scrub area (where your locators reside).

2. *Ctrl + clicking* (*right-clicking* on Windows) on the location where you'd like to have the time signature changed.

3. Choose **Insert Time Signature Change**.

4. Type in the desired time signature values. Now you will see the time signature change implemented.

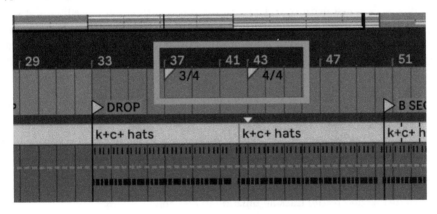

Figure 11.6 – Time signature changes implemented

You can also *move* the location of the time signature changes by simply grabbing and moving them in the scrub area.

You can also *delete* time signature changes by *Ctrl + clicking* (*right-clicking* on Windows) on the time signature and choosing the appropriate option.

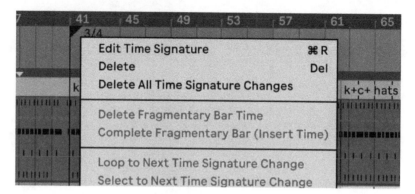

Figure 11.7 – Deleting time signature changes

> **Note**
>
> Needless to say, if you have a guitar solo that was recorded over the metronome with the time signature of 4/4, then just because you change the session's time signature to 3/4, it won't suddenly change your recording as the material was already recorded in 4/4. Only the grid and the metronome will follow the 3/4 time signature; the existing parts will need to be re-recorded and programmed following the new time signature.

Now that we have covered the crucial tempo and time signature changes within your project, we will jump in to see how we can automate further parameters.

Recording automation in the Arrangement View

We already learned how, in the previous section, to select a parameter for automation. In this section, we will take that further and record track automation in real time!

Take the following steps with me:

1. We could automate mixer parameters, such as panning, volume fader, or even sends, as we learned that nearly all parameters in Live can be automated. However, for this example, we are going to automate a device parameter.

2. Insert an **Auto Filter** effect onto the **SYNTH 1** track.

3. Make sure that Automation Mode is enabled.

4. We also need to enable the **Automation Arm** button, as we are going to **record** automation.

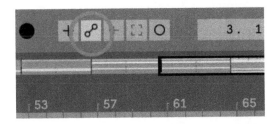

Figure 11.8 – The Automation Arm button

5. We are going to automate the frequency cutoff of the **Auto Filter** device we have just inserted and click on the **Frequency** parameter on **Auto Filter,** so the parameter appears with its automation lane and automation envelope (the value represented by the parameter at any given moment) on the track.

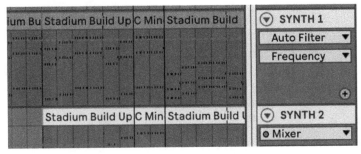

Figure 11.9 – Automation lane for the Frequency parameter of the Auto Filter device on the SYNTH 1 track

6. Now hit the **Arrangement Record** button and start moving the **Frequency** parameter of the **Auto Filter** device with the mouse. You will see the automation of the parameter that you are recording.

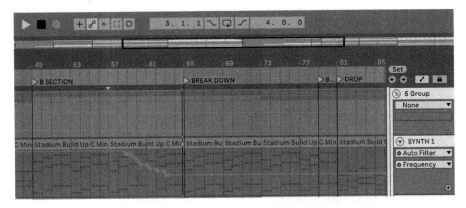

Figure 11.10 – Automation being recorded

Attention

Make sure when you record automation in the Arrangement View that the track that you are working with is *not* armed unless you also have the **Overdub** button (*Figure 11.11*) enabled. If the track is armed and there is no **Overdub** button enabled, then Live will expect new incoming MIDI notes, so your automation will be recorded, but not over the already existing MIDI notes – you will overwrite the existing MIDI notes with silence.

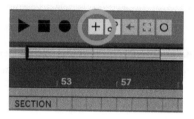

Figure 11.11 – The Overdub button

What is really cool is that you can make this experience even more tactile by mapping the parameter that you would like to automate to an encoder on your MIDI controller so you can physically move the encoder, which will move the mapped parameter while you are recording its automation. There's more on mapping parameters to MIDI controllers in *Chapter 14, Exploring MIDI Mapping, External Instruments, and MIDI CCs*.

Of course, you can automate multiple parameters within the same track by simply clicking on another parameter, resulting in the automation lane on the track being displayed for the desired parameter. The already existing automation lane will not be displayed anymore, although it is still there, and you can always switch to display a previously recorded automation by choosing to select it from the Device and Automation Control choosers (*Figure 11.12*).

Controls that are automated have a red dot next to them.

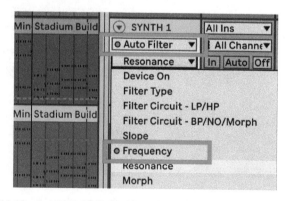

Figure 11.12 – Automated devices/parameters and the indicating red dots

Similarly, on devices and mixer controls, whatever is automated will have a red dot indicating this (*Figure 11.13*).

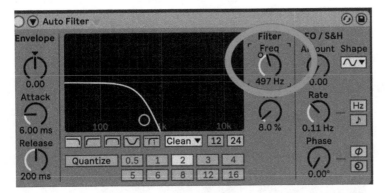

Figure 11.13 – Automated parameter with its red dot indicator

However, you can display multiple automation lanes on the same track, by adding a new automation lane using the + button (the **Add Automation Lane** button) at the bottom right of the **Track Title** section (*Figure 11.14*).

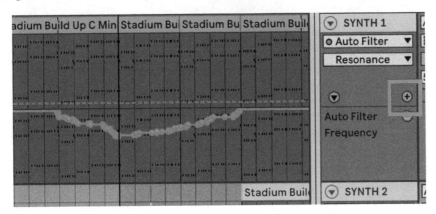

Figure 11.14 – The Add Automation Lane button

Disabling, re-enabling, and deleting automation

It is important to note that if you manually move any parameters you have already automated, then the automation will be disabled, and this will be indicated by the automation lane and the indicator becoming gray instead of red (*Figure 11.15*).

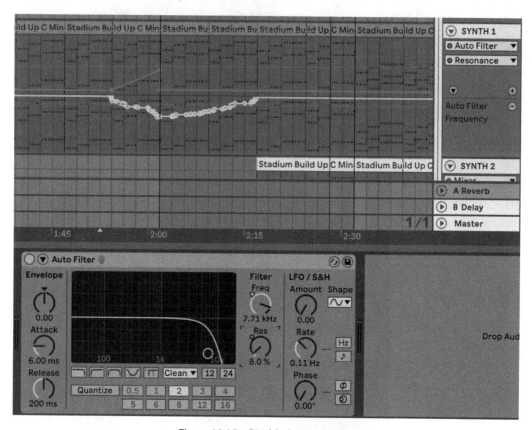

Figure 11.15 – Disabled automation

In this case, the automation is still there but is currently bypassed.

In order to re-enable automation, you can do the following:

1. *Ctrl + clicking* (*right-clicking* on Windows) on the disabled automated parameter and choose **Re-Enable Automation** from the contextual menu.

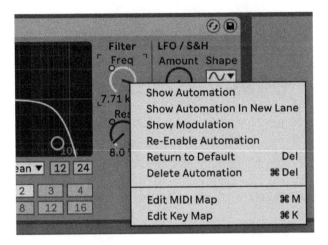

Figure 11.16 – Re-enabling automation

> **Tip:**
> Here is a useful tip for you! When you would like to automate track volume, I recommend that instead of automating the actual track's volume (via the volume fader), insert the Utility audio effect device onto the track and automate the device's Gain control. This is because if you automate your volume fader for creative purposes, once you are mixing down the track and you would like to change the overall volume of the track (via the volume fader) as soon as you adjust the volume fader, you will disable the volume automation that you have implemented. If you automate the Utility audio effect device's Gain control you will be able to freely change the overall level of the track via the volume fader, without disabling the implemented Utility's Gain automation.

2. In this same contextual menu, you can also select **Delete Automation**. You can also delete automation by *Ctrl + clicking* (*right-clicking* on Windows) on the **Track Title** section or automation lane and choosing **Clear Envelope** (delete the currently displayed automation envelope), **Clear All Envelopes** (if we have multiple device parameters automated within the same track), or **Clear All Envelopes for Auto Filter** (to delete all **Auto Filter** parameter automations).

    We can also delete selected breakpoints from the breakpoint envelopes by *Ctrl + clicking* (*right-clicking* on Windows) on the selected breakpoints and choosing **Delete** or **Clear Envelope**.

3. You can use the **Re-enable Automation** button.

    This is super useful if you have multiple automation disabled across multiple devices on multiple tracks, as this button will re-enable *all* the disabled automations across the set.

Figure 11.17 – The Re-enable Automation button

In the next section, we will look at how we can record automation in the Session View.

Recording automation in the Session View

Recording automation in the Session View is similar to how we recorded automation in the Arrangement View.

The main difference is that the automation is written into the particular clip's automation envelope that we are working with, not onto the timeline.

Let's have a look at how this works:

1. Drop an **Auto Filter** onto the **909 Core Kit** track.

2. Enable the **Automation Arm** button.

3. Arm this **909 Core Kit** track.

4. Select the clip that you would like to record the automation to – in this case this will be the yellow clip called **k+c+OH** (don't launch this clip though).

5. We are going to decrease the cutoff **Frequency** parameter of the **Auto Filter** device toward the end of the clip. Now hit the **Session Record** button and move the **Frequency** parameter.

6. The automation was recorded. To display it, double-click on the clip and hit the **Envelopes** tab at the **Tool** tabs, which you can find in the Clip View.

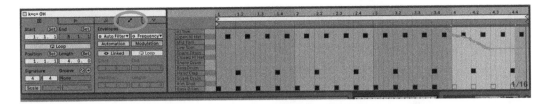

Figure 11.18 – Automation recorded into the clip's Automation
envelope, which can be found under the Envelopes tab

We can change Live's behavior when recording automation in the Session View. The current behavior is that automation will be recorded in **Armed Tracks.** This can be switched to **All Tracks** (it doesn't matter whether the track is armed or not) in **Preferences** under the **Record Warp Launch** tab.

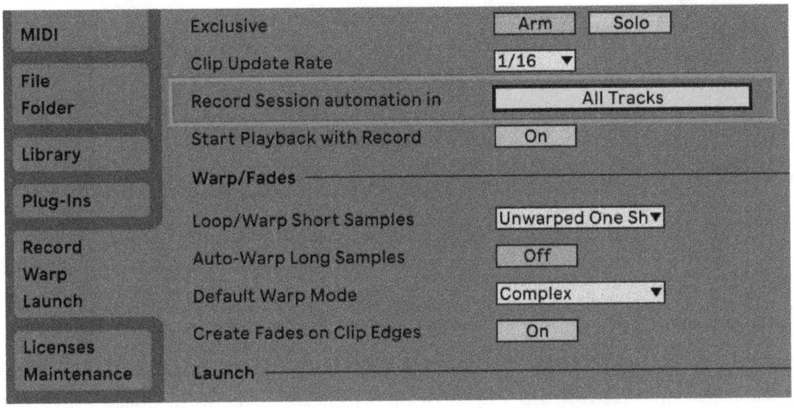

Figure 11.19 – Recording session automation preference settings

Similarly to the Arrangement View, there are **Device and Control choosers** for the clip envelope to choose from automatable devices and their parameters.

We can record multiple automation for various parameters in the Session View; however, we can only display one at a time.

To **delete** and **re-enable automation,** we can *Ctrl + click* (*right-click* on Windows) on the automated parameter (on the actual device) as we learned in the previous section (if the clip is launched) or use the **Re-enable Automation** button at the Control Bar again. We can delete the automation from the envelope by *Ctrl + click* (*right-click* on Windows) on one of the breakpoints and choosing **Clear Envelope** from the contextual menu or **Clear All Envelopes** if we recorded multiple/various parameter automations.

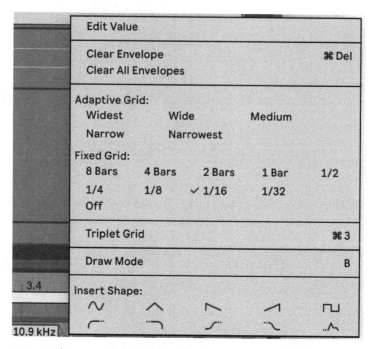

Figure 11.20 – Deleting automation envelopes using Clear Envelope or Clear All Envelopes

> **Note**
>
> Once we move or record clips from the Session View into the Arrangement View they will become a track-based automation and will show up on the timeline in the automation envelope (if Automation Mode is on).

In the next section, we will explore how we can draw and edit automation in Live.

Drawing and editing automation

As usual, recording something in real time can give a more human feel, which isn't any different for automation. However, some parameters require very precise values and movements to be mimicked; therefore, drawing the automation manually with the mouse might be a better option in this case.

Of course, you can also just record the automation and then edit it later.

Let's find out how to do all these things!

As we already briefly discussed, there are two locations where automation can live:

- The clip envelope
- The track-based automation envelope

Drawing and editing automation works the same in both locations/views (the Session and Arrangement Views); besides some of the features that relate to the timeline, they only apply in the Arrangement View, such as the Lock Envelope feature, which relates to the timeline.

Drawing automation

We already looked at how to manually create breakpoints at the beginning of this chapter while automating the **Song Tempo** (after enabling Automation Mode and choosing the parameter we would like to automate) by double-clicking on the breakpoint envelope (the red line indicating the current value of a parameter displayed by the automation lane) and then moving the breakpoints to create the desired "movement".

This time we will look at another way to manually add breakpoints by using **Draw Mode**.

With Draw Mode, you can literally draw in envelopes.

To do this, enable Draw Mode in the Control Bar (or hit *B* on your computer keyboard) (*Figure 11.21*).

Figure 11.21 – The Draw Mode button

While drawing, it will create this "step-based" shape, as wide as the current grid is (*Figure 11.22*).

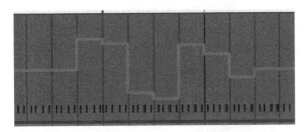

Figure 11.22 – Draw Mode influenced by the grid

You can change this behavior and "bypass" the grid for freehand drawing by holding down *Cmd* (*Alt* for Windows) while drawing (or suspend the grid altogether by hitting *Cmd + 4* (*Ctrl + 4* for Windows) (*Figure 11.23*).

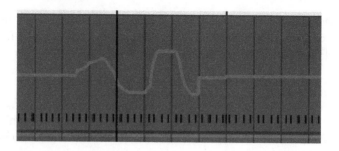

Figure 11.23 – Draw Mode while holding down the Cmd key – without grid snapping

Now let's move on and see how we can edit the already existing automation that we either recorded or drew in.

Editing automation

Time for a quick note!

> **Note**
>
> For these to work, it is important that we do not have Draw Mode enabled!

Let's see a few facts about how we can work with breakpoints:

- We can double-click on them again to delete them (or we can make a selection and hit *Delete* or *Ctrl + click* (*right-click* on Windows) on the breakpoint and choose **Delete**).

- We can move the breakpoints with **finer increments** by holding down *Shift* while moving the breakpoint(s).

- We can add **exact values** to breakpoints by *Ctrl + click* (*right-click* on Windows) on the breakpoint, choosing **Edit Value**, and then typing the desired value in the value box next to the breakpoint.

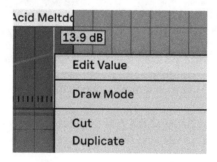

Figure 11.24 – The Edit Value option in the contextual menu

- We can **curve** the straight lines between breakpoints by holding down the *Option* (*Alt* for Windows) key while moving the line between the breakpoints.

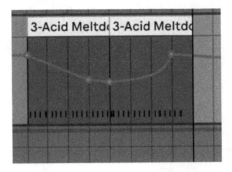

Figure 11.25 – Curved lane on the right

- Like deleting, we can also *move multiple breakpoints* within a selection. Simply make a selection and move any of the breakpoints within the selection.

- Breakpoints will snap to the grid. To place a *breakpoint between grids*, simply hold down the *Cmd* (*Alt* for Windows) key while moving the breakpoint.

- To move breakpoints in finer resolution, simply hold down the *Shift* key while moving.

- To *stretch and skew* a selection of breakpoints, you can make the selection of breakpoints and then you will see handles appear at the outer edges of the selection. You can move these handles to stretch and skew.

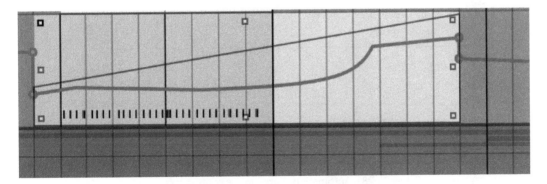

Figure 11.26 – Stretching and skewing

- You have probably noticed that when you are recording automation in real time, there are many breakpoints created during this process. This can be challenging to edit. For that reason, we can simplify envelopes so we end up with fewer breakpoints for a more efficient editing workflow.

In *Figure 11.27*, you will see the originally recorded automation and the highlighted area, which looked the same before the **Simplify Envelope** command was applied. To apply this command, simply select all the breakpoints that you would like to simplify, then *Ctrl + click* (*right-click* on Windows) and choose **Simplify Envelope** from the context menu.

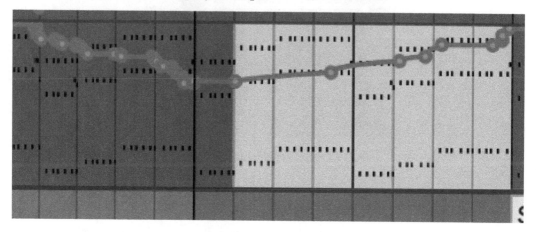

Figure 11.27 – Simplified envelope within the selected area

- We can apply **automation shapes**, which can be helpful to quickly create complex shapes. To do this, simply make a selection, then *Ctrl + click* (*right-click* on Windows) and choose a shape from the context menu.

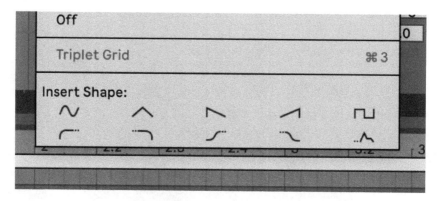

Figure 11.28 – Automation shapes in the context menu

We can apply the **Copy**, **Paste**, and **Duplicate** commands from the contextual menu to the selected automation breakpoints or apply the basic copy, paste, and duplicate shortcuts (*Cmd + C* (*Ctrl + C* for Windows), *Cmd + V* (*Ctrl + V* for Windows), and *Cmd + D* (*Ctrl + D* for Windows)) after making the selection to the desired breakpoints.

Locking envelopes in the Arrangement View

When we move a clip on the timeline from one place to another in the Arrangement View, it will also move its automation with itself. Sometimes you might not want this behavior, so in that case, you can lock the automation to the timeline.

To do this, just hit the **Lock Envelopes** button (*Figure 11.29* and *Figure 11.30*).

Figure 11.29 – The Lock Envelopes button

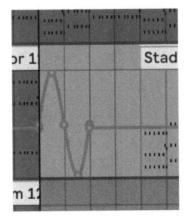

Figure 11.30 – Locked envelope on the timeline with no clip attached to it

We already briefly looked at clip envelopes when we learned how to record automation in the Session View a few sections earlier in this chapter; now let's go and look at clip envelopes in a bit more detail.

Clip envelopes

In Live, all clips have clip envelopes. These envelopes can control anything from **MIDI controller data** to **automation** and **modulation**. Clip envelopes can be set to control the mixer, the clip itself (for example, transposition and gain), and device parameters.

As we know now, in the Arrangement View, automation is stored in track-based envelopes (they show up on the timeline). The Session View automation will be stored within clip envelopes. You can access these through the **Envelopes** tab in the Clip View.

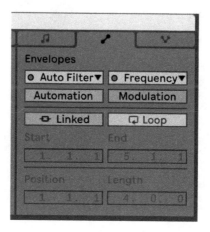

Figure 11.31 – The Envelopes tab in the Clip View

> **Note**
> You can apply all the drawing and editing features within the clip envelopes in the Session View (besides, of course, the locking clip envelopes function, as that's related to the Arrangement View's timeline.)

While discovering earlier in this chapter how to record automation in the Session View, we also established that automation stored in clip envelopes in the Session View will be converted into track-based automation envelopes once we move the clips into the Arrangement View.

On the **Envelopes** tab, you will find the **Device chooser** (left) and the **Control chooser**.

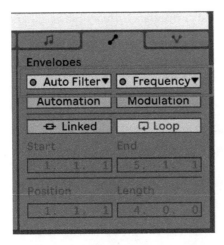

Figure 11.32 – The Device and Control choosers

Within the Device chooser, we can choose the category that we would like to work with. Here we will find devices, device racks we have inserted onto the track, and **Mixer**. Also, we can find **MIDI Ctrl** (MIDI controller data) for MIDI tracks, and **Clip** (sample control) can also be chosen for audio tracks.

Within the Control chooser, we can select the parameters we would like to control within the item we picked within the Device chooser.

We can edit, draw, and view recorded automation within **Envelope Editor** (*Figure 11.33*).

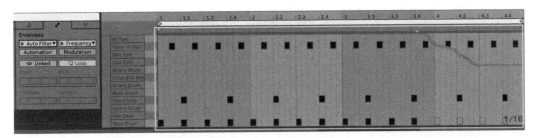

Figure 11.33 – Envelope Editor is highlighted with a green frame

Let's take a brief deeper look at clip envelopes!

Automation versus modulation

As you probably noticed, mixer and device clip envelopes can be either **automated** or **modulated**.

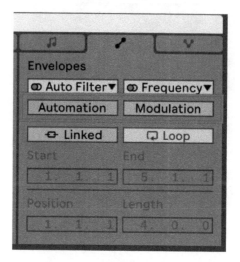

Figure 11.34 – Toggle buttons between automation and modulation

Modulation envelopes work slightly differently from automation envelopes. Automation envelopes show an absolute value of control at the given point in time, whereas modulation envelopes can only influence these shown values. This means device and mixer controls can be controlled by automation and modulation at the same time. Automation envelopes show up red, while modulation envelopes show up blue (*Figure 11.35*):

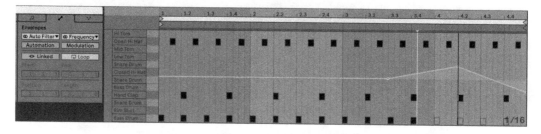

Figure 11.35 – Modulation envelope for the Auto Filter and Frequency parameters, influencing the absolute value determined by automation

Notice that underneath the Device and Control Choosers there is a button with a **Linked** value.

We will come back to this function and a bit more on clip envelopes later in *Chapter 15, Playing Live,* under the *Setting up dummy clips* section.

Summary

We have just arrived at the end of this chapter. In it, we looked at how we can record, draw, edit, and automate in both the Session and Arrangement Views.

We also further investigated clip envelopes, which are the "storage" of automation in the Session View. While we did that, we discovered the difference between automation and modulation within clip envelopes.

We reviewed the use of automation, and how it can be a tool to enhance our sounds with a bit more movement and interest, as well as our arrangement, as automation can help a lot with transitioning from section to section in our songs.

In the next chapter, we will enter the amazing world of **MIDI Polyphonic Expression (MPE)** in Ableton Live 11.

12

Getting Started with MPE in Ableton Live 11

In the previous chapter, we had a look at how we can utilize automation and modulation in Live in order to add some more movement, expression, and interest to some of the elements of our track and enhance our arrangement.

In this chapter, we are going to discover another fantastic tool that will allow us to create further movement and more expressive sounds.

Live 11 introduced us to the easily accessible and exciting world of MPE, and in this chapter, we are going to take a look at how we can easily get started on using MPE for our music.

In this chapter, we are going to cover the following topics:

- An introduction to MPE
- MPE in Wavetable and editing MPE data
- MPE control
- Expression control
- MPE with a controller

Technical requirements

In order to follow along with this chapter, you will need the following:

- A computer with at least 8 GB of RAM and an Intel Core i5 processor
- A pair of headphones
- A copy of Live 11 Suite
- The **Chapter 12** Ableton Live project

An introduction to MPE

MPE stands for **MIDI Polyphonic Expression**, and it allows you to add more feelings and movement to your music. We can add bends, slides, and pressure to each individual note we play (even if the notes are forming a chord!).

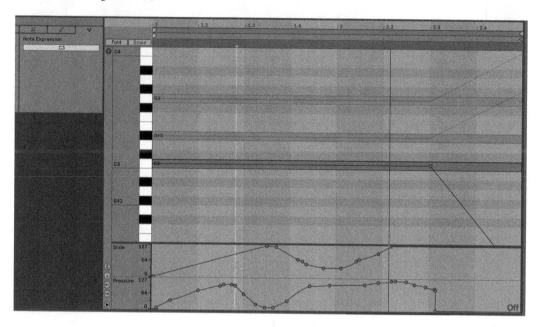

Figure 12.1 – Using MPE in Live 11

What does this mean exactly?

Let's say you have a chord recorded and would like to change the pitch of the chord toward the end of the notes. For this, you can easily write the pitch change into an automation or modulation envelope (either by automating the device's pitch parameter that is playing back the chords, or using modulation through clip envelopes). However, when you do this, the pitch change will be applied to all the notes within the chord/clip. What if you wanted to pitch down the root note of the chord but pitch up the top note? Well, that is one of the things that MPE allows you to do. With MPE, we can control multiple parameters of a single note rather than a whole clip.

We can assign MPE modulation to device parameters (on any MPE-compatible devices), meaning, for example, that you can assign pressure to modulate the filter cut-off of the MPE-compatible device.

MPE can be used with an MPE hardware controller, but if you don't have any of these controllers, that is not a problem, as you can manually draw MPE modulation within Live.

We will be looking at both cases – using MPE with and without a controller. We will begin by exploring the topic without any controllers, using only our computer, and at the end of the chapter, we will talk about MPE hardware controllers.

Live provides a bunch of devices that are MPE-compatible, for example, **Arpeggiator**, **Sampler**, and **Wavetable**. There are also MPE presets available in Live for each of these devices.

In the next section of this chapter, we will be looking at using MPE with the Wavetable device in particular, as it is an instrument device that is super fun to use and also easy to get started with.

Before we jump into the next section, now you briefly know what is MPE about, let's actually put the aforementioned example into practice and add different pitch modulations to each note of a chord!

To do this, follow these steps:

1. Open up the **Chapter 12** project.
2. Navigate to the track called **PAD** and launch the clip already sequenced in it. You will hear a chord playing and displaying when you double-click on the clip.
3. In order to be able to display **MPE data**, we need to click on the **Note Expression** tab within the Clip View (*Figure 12.2*).

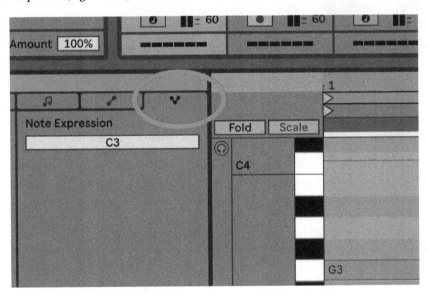

Figure 12.2 – The Note Expression tab in the Clip View

Now, underneath the **Note Expression** tab, you can see **Note Expression** written and, underneath it, **C3**. This is because I am currently selecting note C3 in the Piano Roll to work with (*Figure 12.3*).

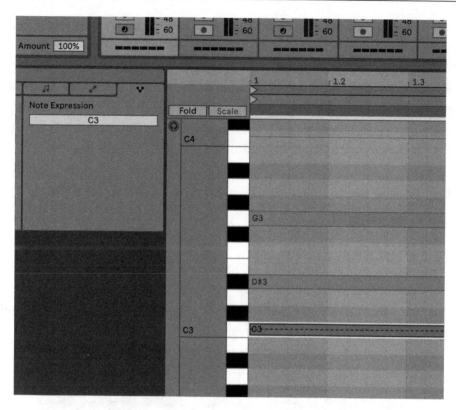

Figure 12.3 – Note Expression and the selected note in the Piano Roll, C3

In the previous example at the start of this section, I discussed pitching down the root note of the chord, which is actually C3, so as long as **C3** is selected, we are good to go:

1. Now, have a closer look at the selected C3 note! You will see that there is a line in the middle of the note in the MIDI note editor. That is the envelope where we can create breakpoints in order to modulate the pitch. Hover your mouse over it and create a breakpoint at bar 2.3, then create another breakpoint at the end of the note, and pull down the second breakpoint by 12 semitones. (Remember – if you are struggling to stop your mouse at the exact value, you can create a breakpoint, then *Ctrl + click* (*right-click* on Windows) at the breakpoint, and choose **Edit Value** to type in the exact value that you are after – in this case, **-12**.See *Figure 12.4.*)

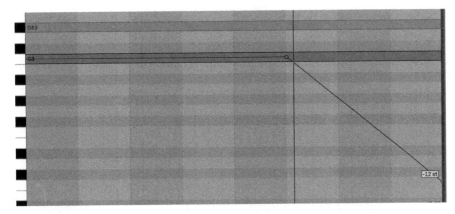

Figure 12.4 – Created break points to modulate the pitch toward the end of the note by -12 semitone.

2. Next, let's pitch up the other two notes (D#3 and G3). Select the next note (**D#3**) and apply the pitch modulation using the same procedure as before, but this time, by the value of **+5 st**.

3. After that, select the last note (**G3**) and do the same as you did with the previous note. The result should look like *Figure 12.5*.

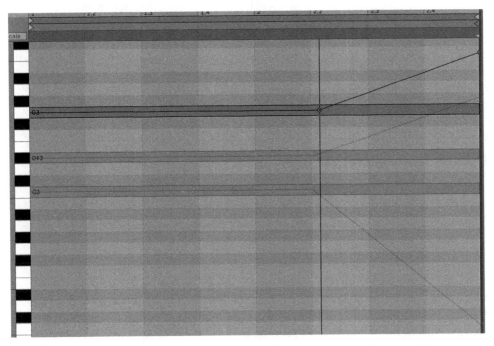

Figure 12.5 – All notes of the chords have individual pitch modulation applied

Now, press the **Play** button and enjoy the interesting result in context within **Group 1**, with some drums and a bass line.

Now, we are ready to dive in further. Let's have a look at MPE in the Wavetable device and see how we can edit MPE data.

Using MPE with the Wavetable device

In this section, we are going to explore MPE with the Wavetable device. However, the concept is the same with other MPE-compatible devices:

1. In the **Chapter 12** project, navigate to the track called **Wavetable**, and hit the **S** button in the mixer to solo the track.

2. If you launched the clip on the Wavetable track, you will hear the same chord that we worked on before.

3. Now, navigate to the device area of this track at the bottom, where you will see the Wavetable device.

4. If you click on the **MPE** button at the top-right side of the device, that will display the **MPE Modulation Matrix** (*Figure 12.6*).

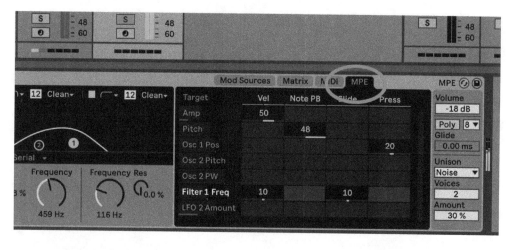

Figure 12.6 – The MPE tab and MPE Modulation Matrix in Wavetable

In this area, we can assign modulation for MPE inputs. If we had an MPE hardware controller, we would be able to send different types of MIDI messages to this synth (such as horizontal, vertical, and pressure – that is, the option to apply pressure to the keys and slide your fingers up and down and to the sides), all specific to each key/note. However, we aren't using a controller here, so we will mimic these movements by drawing them in manually to the appropriate place a little later. However, we still need to assign what those MIDI messages, or "movements," will be modulating within the Wavetable device.

Double-click on all the existing values (the green numbers within the Matrix) to remove anything that was already assigned (*Figure 12.7*).

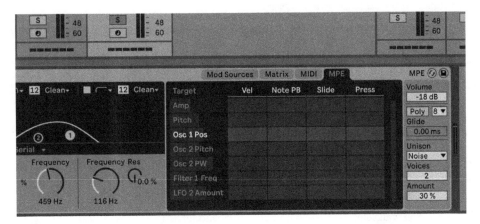

Figure 12.7 – The cleared-out MPE Modulation Matrix

Now, we are going to assign some simple target parameters in order to understand how this all works:

1. Go to the cell of **Filter 1 Freq** under the **Press** (pressure) area and slide the value up to the value of **44**, so that the filter cut-off will open up nice and wide, as shown in *Figure 12.8*. (You can adjust this parameter later to your preference if needed.

2. Now, navigate to the cell that belongs to **Osc 2 Pitch** (oscillator 2's pitch) under **Slide**, and slide the value up to **12** (*Figure 12.8*).

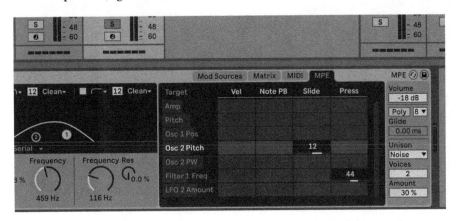

Figure 12.8 – Slide and pressure assigned to modulate Osc 2's pitch and Filter 1 frequency

Now, if you had an MPE controller in this scenario, when you played a key/note and started applying more pressure to it, the filter cut-off would react to it, and as you would be sliding your finger on the same key, the pitch would change.

However, since we aren't using a controller here, let's see how we can still apply these changes.

Note

When you are working with an already existing preset in Wavetable, as soon as you display the MPE Modulation Matrix, there are already parameters available to be controlled by MPE input data. However, if there is another parameter that you would like to modulate with MPE that is not displayed in the matrix, you can simply click on the parameter of the Wavetable device, and it will show up in the MPE Modulation Matrix. For example, if you want to control the **res** (frequency resonance) of **Osc 1**, you can simply click on the **Res** parameter to bring it to the matrix.

Of course, you could sign multiple parameters to be modulated by the MPE MIDI inputs (**Slide**, **Pressure**, etc.) to create even more expression and interest.

3. *Double-click* on the clip of the Wavetable track we have been working on (or press *Shift + Tab* to change the Device View to the Clip View).

4. Among the **Tool** tabs, select the **Note Expression** tab within the Clip Detail View.

5. Click on the **Show/Hide All Expression Editors** button (*Figure 12.9*).

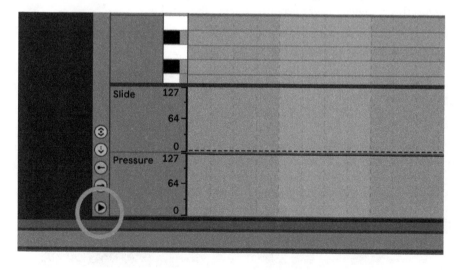

Figure 12.9 – The Show/Hide All Expression Editors button

Now, you should see the Slide and Pressure Editors. If they don't automatically show up, you can use the **Show/Hide** buttons, which you can see in *Figure 12.10*.

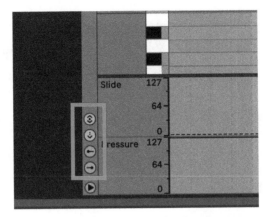

Figure 12.10 – The Show/Hide Editor buttons

From the top to bottom of the preceding screenshot, the buttons are the following: **Show/Hide Slide Editor**, **Show/Hide Pressure Editor**, **Show/Hide Velocity Editor**, and **Show/Hide Release Velocity Editor**.

Previously, we assigned **Pressure** to modulate Filter 1's frequency, and **Slide** to modulate Oscillator 2's pitch within the Wavetable device. This means as we start drawing/creating breakpoints on these envelopes, they will start moving the aforementioned parameters on a note by note basis.

Let's try it out:

1. Select the **D#3** note in the MIDI Editor, and similar to what we did with the pitch at the beginning of this chapter, create a breakpoint at bar 2.3 and another one at the end of the clip, moving all the way up to the second breakpoint (*Figure 12.11*).

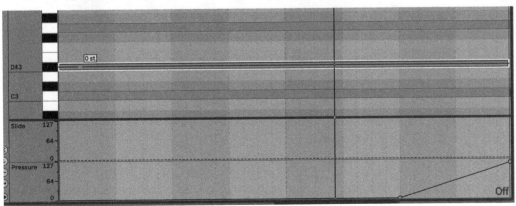

Figure 12.11 – Pressure MPE modulation applied to the D#3 note

2. Select the **G3** note, and now, create a different kind of curve. Let's try to use the **Pencil Tool** with it by pressing **B** (*Figure 12.12*).

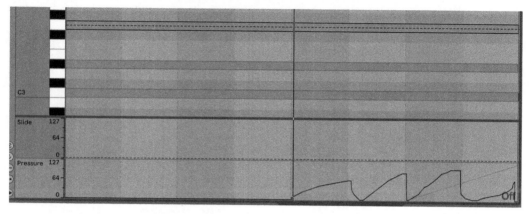

Figure 12.12 – Pressure MPE modulation applied to the G3 note and drawn with the Pencil Tool

3. Finally, create breakpoints to modulate the pitch of Oscillator 2 via the **Slide** envelope of the G3 note (*Figure 12.13*).

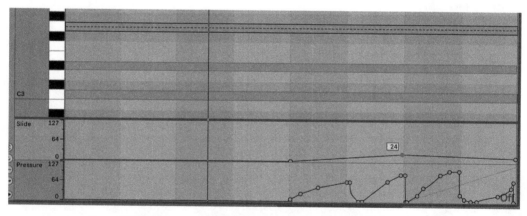

Figure 12.13 – Pressure and Slide MPE modulation applied to the G3 note

4. Now, press play and enjoy the result.

This simple example should give you a good idea of how you can get started with using MPE, even if you do not own an MPE hardware controller.

If you own an MPE controller, then all the recorded MPE modulation will show up and will be available to edit in the same place (Note Expression Editors) that we have been creating breakpoints and drawing the envelopes.

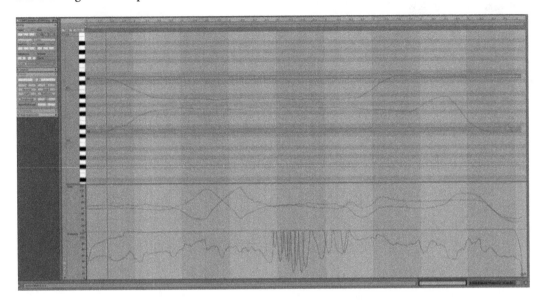

Figure 12.14 – MPE Editor with MPE data recorded with an MPE controller

Besides the other native MPE-compatible devices in Live, there are other popular third-party, MPE-compatible VST plugins available that can be used in Live, such as Pigments by Arturia, Diva by u-he, and Serum by Xfer Records.

In the next couple of sections, let's jump in and have a look at how we can take our MPE fun even further by looking at a few MIDI effects, which can be super useful to create even more expression with MPE.

MPE Control

MPE Control is a **Max for Live** MIDI effect, which we will talk about in the next chapter! For now, let's just see what this device does.

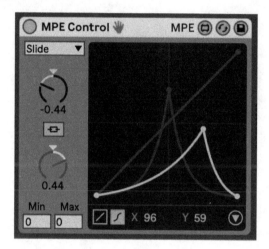

Figure 12.15 – The MPE Control MIDI effect

MPE Control will enable you to shape the incoming MPE modulation signals (**Pressure**, **Slide**, etc.). This can provide some really fun, additional controlled movement to the modulation.

This is a super fun device to use when you are recording with an MPE hardware controller; however, you can still try it out even if you do not own one.

Follow these steps:

1. In the **Chapter 12** project, navigate to the **Wavetable** track, where we have already set up and applied some MPE.

2. Load **MPE Control** from the browser. You can find it under the **MIDI Effects** tab.

3. Once it's on the track, we are going to go ahead and choose the MPE modulation source (**Pressure**, **Slide**, or **Pitch**) (*Figure 12.16*).

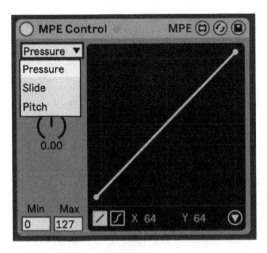

Figure 12.16 – MPE modulation sources

4. If you remember, we assigned **Pressure** and **Slide** to the parameters of the Wavetable synth, and we added/drew some modulation envelopes of these within the Expression Editors. For this example, we are going to choose **Pressure**.

5. Now, you can move the linear curve (the yellow line) on the right side of the MPE modulation source chooser. Make sure you are playing back the clip we have been working with so that you can immediately hear how the curve movement is affecting the parameters to which the **Pressure** MPE modulation is assigned.

6. You can also change the linear curve to an S-shaped curve (*Figure 12.17*).

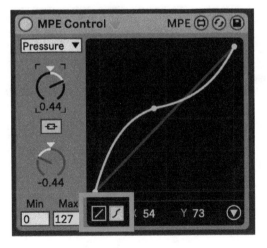

Figure 12.17 – Switching between linear and S-shaped curves

Note that this curve gives you a third breakpoint to move around, so you can create some very interesting shapes by dragging them around!

7.   You can also control the shape with these two encoders (*Figure 12.18*).

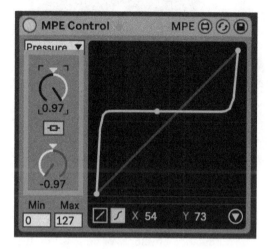

Figure 12.18 – Encoders to further shape the curve

If you disable the yellow link button between the two encoders (as shown in the previous screenshot), then you will be able to control the upper and lower curves separately.

8.   You can also control the middle breakpoint's horizontal and vertical positions by sliding up and down the two values shown in *Figure 12.19*.

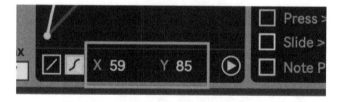

Figure 12.19 – Values to control the middle breakpoint's horizontal and vertical positions

9.   Furthermore, you can also open up the **Advanced Settings** tab, by the toggle to the right button (*Figure 12.20*).

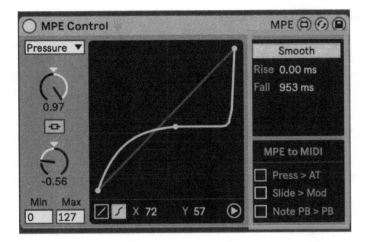

Figure 12.20 – Advanced Settings

Enabling the **Smooth** button will enable you to smooth the curve as well as further control the smoothing time for the **Rise** and **Fall** values. Additional controls also pop up if you work with **Slide** and **Pitch** within the MPE modulation sources.

You can adjust these to your own taste.

The bottom **MPE to MIDI** section can be useful if you are using an MPE hardware controller, as it can transform MPE messages into standard **MIDI CC** information (there's more on MIDI CCs in *Chapter 14*), so you can send MIDI information with the controller to instruments that aren't MPE-compatible.

MPE Control is definitely one really fun and easy-to-use device that helps the creative juices flow effortlessly.

Expression Control

The Max for Live device called **Expression Control** has actually been around for a while, and since the release of Live 11, it lives in the main MIDI effects category in the browser, as it is MPE-compatible. Even before MPE, this device was really great to push the modulation skills to the next level!

Expression Control is a very simple device that allows you to modulate parameters, which you can map yourself, so it gives you a great deal of flexibility. You can get started with it straight away with ease.

Let's take a quick tour of it!

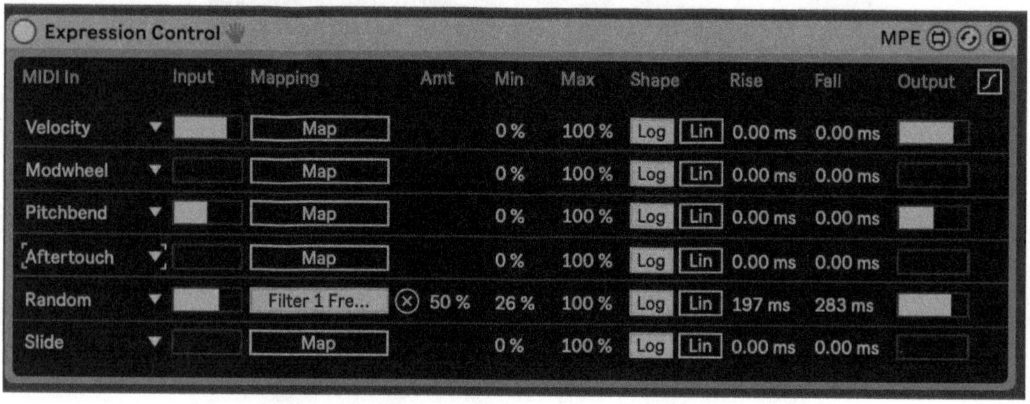

Figure 12.21 – The Expression Control MIDI effect device

You can select a MIDI parameter under **MIDI In**, which then can be mapped to a target parameter in Live with the **Map** buttons underneath **Mapping**. You can see in *Figure 12.21* that I mapped **Random** to **Filter 1 Frequency** of the Wavetable device (on the **Wavetable** track within the **Chapter 12** project).

Next to the **Mapping** tab, you can see **Amt**, which under the **Random** category means how much randomization will be applied to the modulation value. Under **Min** and **Max**, we can specify the minimum and maximum values that the modulation will move the mapped parameter between. Under **Shape**, we can choose between a logarithmic and a linear shape.

You can think about **Rise** and **Fall** as an envelope for the modulation, where **Rise** controls the attack and **Fall** controls the release of the envelope. **Output** simply displays the output level of the mappings.

As you can see, this is a great device that allows you to even reassign the pitch bend and modwheel of any ordinary MIDI controller to control a different parameter of your choice on a device.

> **Note**
>
> If you are planning to control effects with Expression Control, that can only happen monophonically!

Expression Control is great for designing sound, mapping different parameters of a synth to its MIDI parameters, as well as a really fun tool to add some interesting modulation to your sounds while you are playing.

MPE with a controller

I already mentioned at the beginning of the chapter that, ideally, you should have an MPE controller (a physical controller) to get the most out of this feature; however, as you have seen throughout this chapter, it is not fully necessary.

There are a couple of different brands making MPE controllers, which you can easily find on the internet. When you have a controller, all the different modulations created by **Slide**, **Pressure**, and so on (which we have been exploring and using by manually drawing envelopes) can be controlled physically by sliding and applying pressure with your fingers while you are playing and recording.

What is really fun is that **Ableton Push 2** can be also used to a certain extent to control MPE, as the Push has **Polyphonic Aftertouch**! (There's more about Push 2 in *Chapter 15*, *Playing Live*.) Polyphonic Aftertouch creates a MIDI message specifically to each key that can be assigned to modulate parameters specific to each key/note. (A proper MPE controller will create three different MIDI messages, horizontal, vertical, and pressure, as we already learned earlier in this chapter.)

Let's see how we can set up Push 2 to use it with MPE! Simply press **Setup** on Push 2 and set **PRESSURE** to **Poly** (*Figure 12.22*).

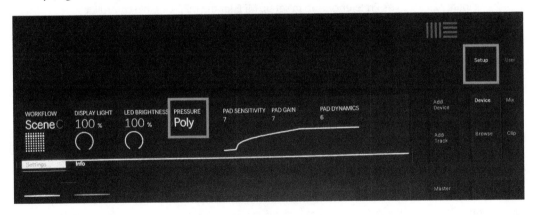

Figure 12.22 – Ableton Push 2's setup displayed on the screen

Within Live's preferences (which can be accessed through **Live | Preferences…** / **Options | Preferences…** or *Cmd +* , (*Ctrl +* , for Windows)), regardless of what MPE controller you are using, you need to make sure that under the **Link Tempo MIDI** tab, you enable MPE so that Live can receive note-based expressions from the MPE controller (*Figure 12.23*).

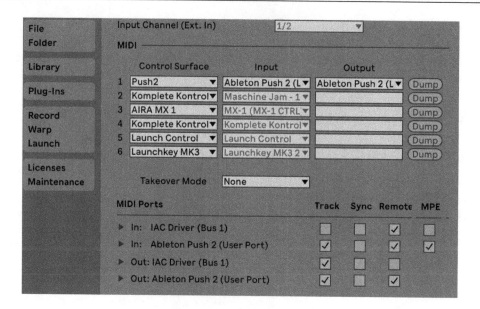

Figure 12.23 – Live's Preferences tab to set up MPE for the MPE-capable controller

It is a lot of fun to use MPE with a controller, so I do suggest getting hold of one if you have a chance to immerse yourself fully with this amazing feature!

Some of the most popular MPE controller choices are Roli Seaboard RISE 2 and the Lightpad Block. The latter is fairly cheap so could be a good choice to start experimenting in the world of MPE.

Summary

We have finally arrived at the end of Chapter 12!

In this chapter, we explored the world of MPE and how to get started with it, with or without a physical MPE controller. We took an extensive look at how we can input/draw and edit envelopes within the Expression Editors, and we gained an understanding of some of the additional Max for Live MIDI effect choices that can be used to add some more fun to the process.

By now, you should have some great ideas on how you can implement and use the best MPE to create more expressive and interesting sounds and musical parts.

In the next chapter, we are going to have a lot of fun looking at Tempo Follower, Follow Action, and Max for Live, which are all truly unique features in Ableton Live!

Part 3: Deep Dive into Ableton Live

In the final part of the book, you will gain insight into techniques that are both practical for production and relevant for live performance. The focus will gradually shift towards live performance capabilities, teaching you how to sync your session tempo with external audio signals, understand Follow Action, control Live's device parameters using external MIDI controllers, and integrate external synthesizers into your software for a more hands-on experience. The book will also delve into the world of Max for Live and show you how to incorporate video into your Live sessions, sparking new creative ideas. Additionally, we'll discover the new music-making iOS app, Ableton Note, and learn how to synchronize projects between Note and Live via Ableton Cloud. Finally, you will be introduced to various mixing techniques and learn how to apply them within Live.

This part comprises the following chapters:

- *Chapter 13, Exploring Tempo Follower, Follow Action, Max For Live, Working with Video, and Ableton Note*
- *Chapter 14, Exploring MIDI Mapping, External instrument, and MIDI CCs*
- *Chapter 15, Playing Live*
- *Chapter 16, Interesting Mixing Techniques in Live 11*
- *Chapter 17, Troubleshooting and File Management*

13

Exploring Tempo Follower, Follow Action, Max for Live, Working with Video, and Ableton Note

After looking at the amazing world of MPE that was introduced in Live 11, in this chapter, we are going to start off with another exciting new feature that is called Tempo Follower and will allow us to sync our session tempo with an external incoming signal. We will also look at Follow Action and the updates added to this feature with the release of Live 11, which is fun to use for both the studio and stage.

After Follow Action, we will take a small tour of the world of **Max for Live (M4L)**, which is a truly unique feature for Ableton Live users. To close off an exciting and informative chapter of fun music-making features and ways of playing music, we will also quickly explore how we can work with video in Live to compose sound for a motion picture.

Furthermore, we will discover the new addition of the Ableton family - the Ableton Note app, and we will discover how to use Ableton Cloud to transfer projects made in the Note app to the browser of Ableton Live.

This chapter will be a fairly mixed read with loads of fun and unique features, which can open up a lot of possibilities to users, possibilities that you might not have thought possible.

The chapter will consist of the following order of topics:

- Exploring Tempo Follower in Live 11
- Follow Action
- Introduction to M4
- Working with video in Live
- The Ableton Note app

Technical requirements

In order to follow along with this chapter, you will need the following:

- A computer with at least 8 GB of RAM and an Intel Core i5 processor
- A pair of headphones
- A copy of Live 11 Suite
- The Ableton Note app installed on an iOS device
- The **Chapter 13** Ableton Live project

Exploring Tempo Follower in Live 11

The Tempo Follower feature dropped with Live 11 and opened up some new ways in which we can sync Live's tempo with an external source. This feature is particularly useful if you are, for example, working with a drummer or have a rhythmical sound source that you want to sync your Live session tempo with.

You may have already tried or heard of syncing Live via MIDI or Ableton Link (if not, then this will be covered in *Chapter 15*), but this feature is slightly different, as, in this case, we are using an audio feed to sync Live's tempo with.

I already mentioned how to set up Live to "follow" a drummer that you might play with, but we can also use this feature to sync Live with a DJ performance.

Sounds exciting! Let's have a look at how we can set this up!

1. To set the incoming audio input source that you wish Live's tempo to follow, navigate to **Preferences | Link, Tempo, MIDI**.

2. In the **Tempo Follower** section (*Figure 13.1*), you can set **Input Channel (Ext. In)** to the input channel of your audio interface with the sound source that you'd like Live to connect to:

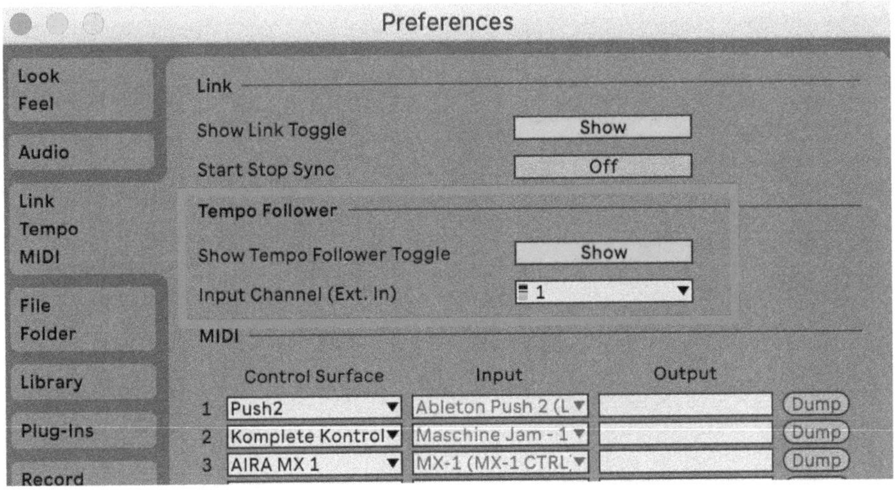

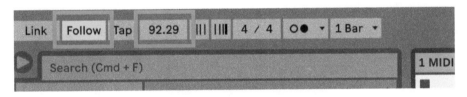

Figure 13.1 – Setting up Tempo Follower in Preferences

3. **Show Tempo Follower Toggle** should be switched to **Show**, so the **Follow** button will appear on the left side of the Control Bar (*Figure 13.2*).

Figure 13.2 – Follow button and the accordingly changing tempo in the Control Bar

4. In my example, I connected my Roland TR8 drum machine to my interface through input 1, and after starting to play the drum machine, Live's tempo started to follow it.

Now, we can enable the metronome if necessary and start playing along. This whole procedure can be super-useful if we use tempo-synced effects, for example. Try the arpeggiator while slowing down or speeding up the external source that Live is following in tempo – you will hear how the arpeggiation is also synced.

It is recommended to use rhythmical sources as the incoming signal for tempo-following, but it is, as always, recommended to experiment with other sound sources too to come up with something unique and weird perhaps.

As you can see, it is super easy to set up Tempo Follower. Even if you don't have a drummer at hand or an external device, just grab your microphone and use your own voice as the sound source for Live to follow and you can try this out immediately.

Follow Action

Follow Action allows us to assign an automated action to clips – for example, telling one clip to trigger another one, to repeat itself after its playback, or to stop, to name a few possibilities.

This can be used in multiple ways – for example, you can use this to play one backing track after another on stage, or create a randomized sequence of clips that trigger each other and record this generated sequence in the studio.

With Live 11, now you can also apply Follow Action to Scenes too! The Follow Action feature is only available in the Session View.

Let's try it out!

In this example, we are going to work with a bunch of one-shot guitar clips and create an automated sequence with Follow Action:

1. Open the **Chapter 13** project.

2. Head to and **solo** the track called **FOLLOW ACTION**.

    For this to work, we will need to create a selection of clips – a group of selected clips! (We can have multiple groups of clips set up with different Follow Action operations within the same track..

3. To make a selection, select the first clip, hold down *Shift*, and select the last clip. This should select all the clips from the first to the last, as that is what we will need for this example to work (*Figure 13.3*):

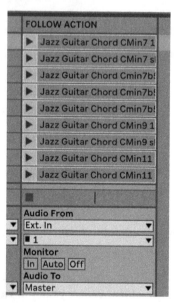

Figure 13.3 – Selected clips for Follow Action

4. Now, if you navigate to the bottom of the screen and display the Clip View, you can click on the **Follow Action** tab among the **Clips** tabs (*Figure 13.4*):

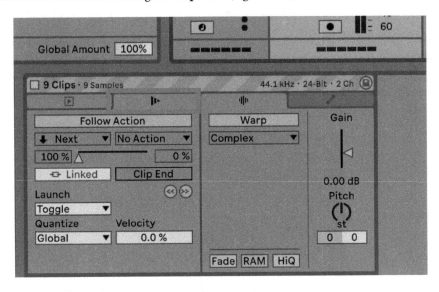

Figure 13.4 – The tab to show Follow Action in the Clip View

5. Now, click on the **Follow Action** button. Once the button turns yellow, you will notice that we now have two choosers active underneath the **Follow Action** button (which are currently displaying **Next** and **No Action** (*Figure 13.5*)):

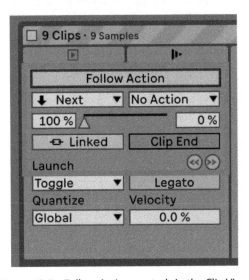

Figure 13.5 – Follow Action controls in the Clip View

The two choosers are called A and B. Here, you can select different actions to be applied to the selected clips.

For A, we are going to leave it as **Next**, and for B, we are going to choose **Previous**.

6. We have chosen two opposing actions, which can be confusing at first. The way we can decide and define which action will take place and for how long by using the **Chance** slider. This will change the percentage of chances for each action to happen when the clips are triggered. So, if we set the chance to **40%** for the **Next** action and **60%** for the **Previous** action, then, you guessed it, it will play the previous clip slightly more than the upcoming clip (*Figure 13.6*):

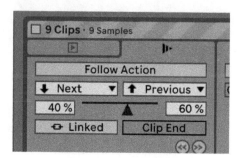

Figure 13.6 – Follow Action set to Next and Previous with defined chances

7. Under chances A and B, we have a button that is currently set to **Linked**. This means that the next action will happen after the clip that is currently playing has played through for its full length. We are going to set it to **Unlinked** by clicking on it.

8. Now, you will see the button next to it that used to say **Clip End** has changed to show us different **Follow Action Time** controls. Here, we can define how long the clips should play before the next action happens. It displays bars, beats, and sixteenths, respectively. We are going to set this value to **0.2.0**. When you do this, make sure you still have all the clips selected so that each clip will only play for two beats (*Figure 13.7*):

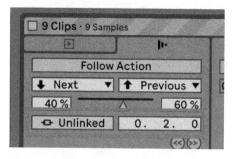

Figure 13.7 – Unlinked Follow Action set to play clips for two beats before the next action

Now, if you trigger one of the selected clips in the Session View, you should start seeing and hearing the Follow Action operations taking place within the selected clips. The clips are being launched by automated actions without you having to launch them.

Of course, you can specify this Follow Action Time for clips independently as well. Let's say you want one of the clips to play for a whole bar – then, you can set it that way.

Just select the clip and either type in the value, or use the **marker** in **Note Editor** to adjust this (*Figure 13.8*):

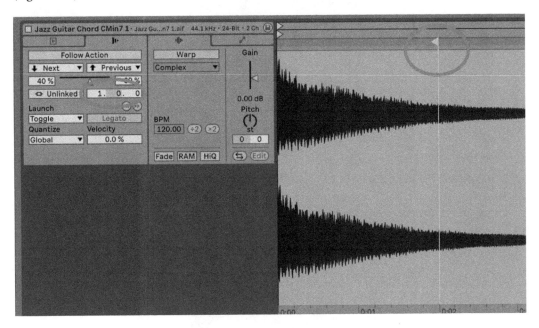

Figure 13.8 – Marker to adjust Follow Action Time for a clip in Note Editor

To determine which clip has a Follow Action operation assigned to it, you can check whether the launch button is stripy, which you can see in *Figure 13.9*:

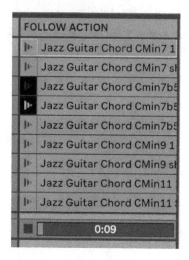

Figure 13.9 – Clip launch buttons indicating they have a Follow Action operation assigned to them

For this example, it also would have been highly suitable to only use the first chooser (A) and set it to **Other** instead of **Next**. Setting that to **100%** would have always made a random clip play, and it will always have been another one; no clips will repeatedly play multiple times in a row.

Let's actually quickly go through what each Follow Action does (*Figure 13.10*):

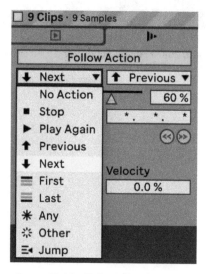

Figure 13.10 – Follow Action options

- **Stop**: This action will stop the clip after it has played

- **Play Again**: This will restart the played clip

- **Previous**: This will trigger the previous clip (the one above)

- **Next**: This will trigger the next clip (the one below)

- **First**: This will launch the first clip of the selected clip group

- **Last**: **Last** will launch the last clip in the selected clip group

- **Any**: With this, any clips can play in the selected clip group

- **Other**: Similar to **Any**, but with this action, no clip will play consecutively

- **Jump**: With this action, you can select a target clip to jump to after the current clip has played for the set Follow Action Time

Clip quantization with Follow Action

We haven't really covered clip launch modes and quantization besides a short overview in *Chapter 1*, but this will be looked at closer in *Chapter 15*. For now, just know that Follow Action will be defined by whatever is set under Follow Action Time unless **clip quantization** is set to other values than **None** or **Global**. Follow Action will avoid global quantization, but it will not avoid clip quantization, which we can set within the Clip View (*Figure 13.11*):

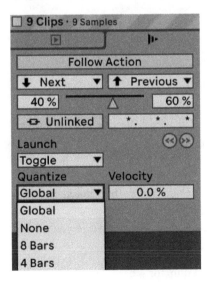

Figure 13.11 – Clip quantization settings

If you aren't familiar with clip quantization already, then skip ahead to *Chapter 15* so that the previous explanation will make full sense.

Follow Action applied to Scenes

With Live 11, the possibility to use Follow Action with Scenes has arrived.

It works exactly the same way as it does with clips, so everything we learned within this chapter already will be the knowledge you need to make Follow Action work with Scenes.

Now, let's have a look at how we can access this feature for Scenes:

1. Head to and **solo** the group called **SCENE FOLLOW ACTION** in the **Chapter 13** project.

2. Head to the Scene list on the right-hand side of the **Master**. Click on the **Master** track's title bar and then double-click on Scene 10, which is called **SCENE 1**. This will bring up the Scene View at the bottom of the screen on the left (*Figure 13.12*):

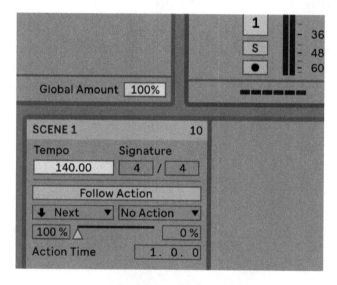

Figure 13.12 –The Scene View

3. Now when **SCENE 1** is selected, you can go ahead and switch on **Follow Action** in the Scene View.

4. We are going to set A (by the first chooser) to **Next**.

5. For **Action Time**, we will set it up for 4 bars (*Figure 13.13*):

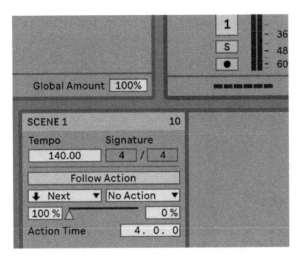

Figure 13.13 – Follow Action settings for Scene 10, called SCENE 1

6.   Now, select Scene 11, which is named **SCENE 2**, and in the Scene View, enable **Follow Action**, set A (the first chooser) to **Previous**, and for **Action Time**, again select 4 bars (*Figure 13.14*):

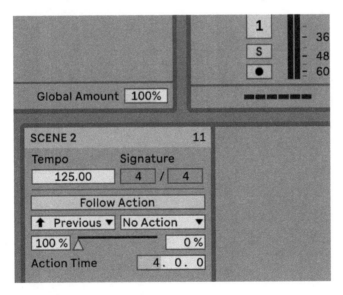

Figure 13.14 – Follow Action settings for Scene 11, called SCENE 2

7.   Press play and you should start hearing and seeing the Follow Action operations taking place. The scenes will trigger each other's launch after four bars of **Action Time**.

8.   Also, you can see the stripy scene launch buttons on the scenes for which Follow Action is set up (*Figure 13.15*):

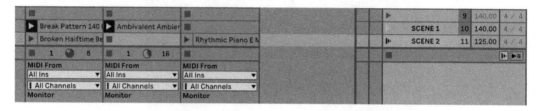

Figure 13.15 – Scene launch buttons for Scenes with Follow Action

> **Note**
>
> In the **Chapter 13** project, the scene launch buttons are also light blue, as these scenes have tempo changes applied to them, which you can see written in the box next to the scene names.

Disabling and deleting Follow Action

If you would like to **delete** your Follow Action settings, you can simply select the Clips or Scenes to which you wouldn't like Follow Action to apply anymore and disengage the **Follow Action** button in the Clip View or the Scene View. Furthermore, in the A and B choosers, you can select **No Action**.

You can also enable and disable Follow Action globally (without deleting anything) using the toggle underneath the Scenes (*Figure 13.16*):

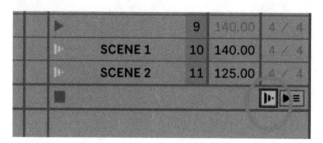

Figure 13.16 – Enabling/disabling Follow Action globally

Hopefully, by now, you have gained a good understanding of where and why you would like to use Follow Action. It can be a great tool to program intentional automatic actions, which can be useful for both production and performance, but it can also be set up in a more randomized way to create some surprising results – and don't forget, you can always **record the result of Follow Action** if it's applied to clips by routing the track with those clips to a brand new track and recording the output

(*Figure 13.17*). Alternatively, you can capture the result of Follow Action settings in a Scene in the Arrangement View.

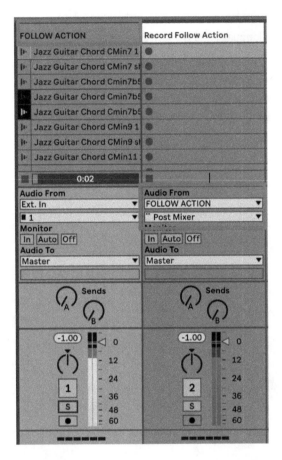

Figure 13.17 – The FOLLOW ACTION track is routed to a new track to record the result of Follow Action

We have arrived at the end of looking at this truly unique Ableton Live feature.

In the next section, you will be introduced to another unique feature, the amazing world of M4L!

Introduction to M4L

M4L allows you to build and modify devices for Live. This is super-useful if you have an idea for a device that you really wish existed or if there is an already existing M4L device that you'd like to modify to suit your needs better.

Most of these M4L devices can even look like "standard" Live devices. If you are not into development and learning to code, then you can download loads of M4L devices already developed by users for free or at very cheap prices from `https://maxforlive.com/`.

Max itself is a programming language and it connects to Ableton Live via M4L.

You can connect "objects." You can think of objects as modules of a modular synth. These objects process digital data, which can be audio, MIDI, video, and more. These objects are connected through "patch cables." This programming style implements a **visual programming language** (**VPL**) as you patch objects, and you can see the flow of data rather than just writing code.

M4L was developed by a company called Cycling 74 and is bundled with Live Suite. You will already find M4L devices and presets, as well as tutorials, within Live.

You can access these in the browser under the **Max for Live** tab (*Figure 13.18*):

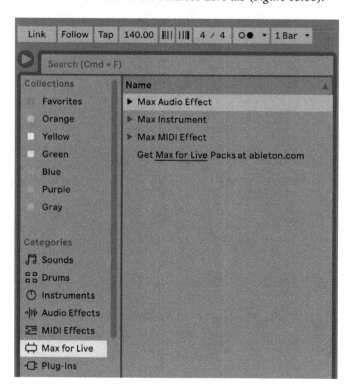

Figure 13.18 – M4L devices in the browser

Once you install Live Suite, M4L will be installed with it. The path of the installation can be found under **Preferences** (*Figure 13.19*):

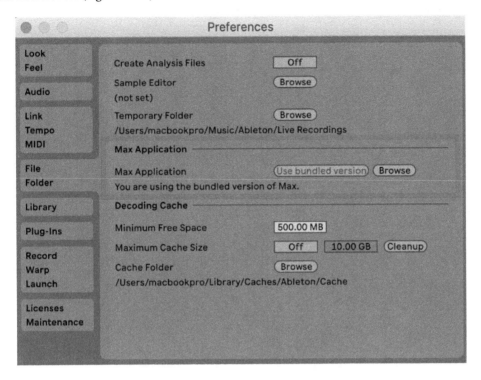

Figure 13.19 – M4L in Preferences

You can also use Max as an external application (the license for the standalone Max device is not included with Ableton Live) (*Figure 13.20*), and you can point Live to it through the **Browse** path, which you can see in the preceding screenshot (*Figure 13.19*).

Figure 13.20 – Max application

Once we load an M4L device, it may seem like it is a standard device, but there will be two indicators to differentiate an M4L device. Some of these M4L devices now even live among the main devices in the browser (*Figure 13.21*), meaning you do not even need to navigate to the M4L category.

The first indication of an M4L device will be the little icon just before the name of the device:

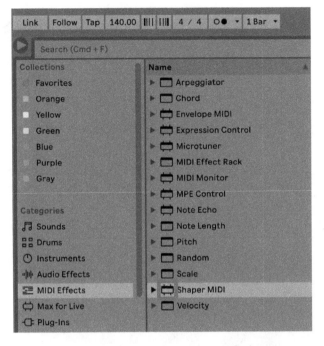

Figure 13.21 – Icon for an M4L device in the browser

The second indication will be the **Edit** button at the top-right corner of the device (*Figure 13.22*):

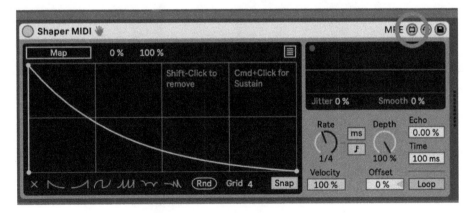

Figure 13.22 – The Edit button on an M4L device

Once you click on the **Edit** button, you can start editing the device:

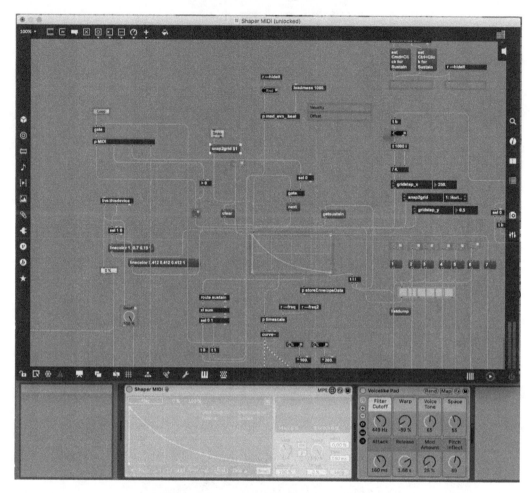

Figure 13.23 – Editing the Shaper MIDI M4L device

There are many resources on the internet about how to program with Max, and if you are interested in programming, it can be a lot of fun. If you would prefer to stick to just making music, you should still consider having a look at all the M4L devices created already out there so that you can customize Live and make your music-making experience better.

Adding and saving M4L devices in Ableton Live

Once you have downloaded an M4L device, you may be wondering how to get it into Ableton Live, and how you are going to use it in the future.

When you download an M4L device, the file's extension will be .amxd (*Figure 13.24*):

Figure 13.24 – Downloaded M4L device on my desktop

You can locate this downloaded file and drag and drop it into a track in Live. The device will load on the track.

The device will depend on its location, so if you move the downloaded file from the original location, then you may run into trouble and have to relocate the device.

It is suggested that once you have inserted the device onto a track in Live, you should save the device into your User Library as a **.adv** preset! You can do this by clicking on the floppy disk button at the top-right corner, then naming the preset in the browser (*Figure 13.25*):

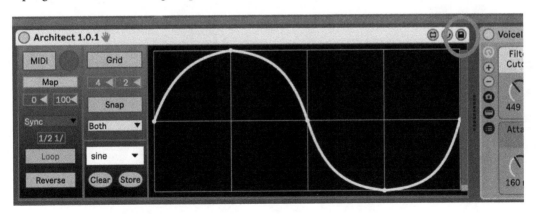

Figure 13.25 – Saving into User Library

You can also create an M4L folder on your computer and download/place all your devices into that folder. After that, you can add this folder to your browser by heading to **Places** and choosing **Add Folder....** (*Figure 13.26*):

Figure 13.26 – Adding a dedicated folder into the browser that has all the downloaded M4L devices in it

Loads of artists on stage have M4L devices programmed specifically for them to cater to the specific needs of their unique setups, because in this world, just because a device doesn't do exactly what you want doesn't mean that it cannot be modified to do what you want.

Here are some M4L device recommendations to try out:

- Granulator II:

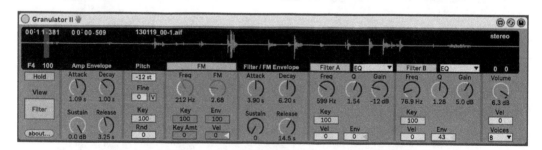

Figure 13.27 – Granulator II

This is a granular synthesis-based device that makes it super-easy to create lush textures and glitchy sounds.

You can download it from the Ableton website:

`https://www.ableton.com/en/packs/granulator-ii/`

- Modulators 21:

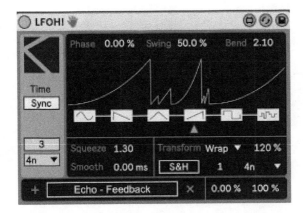

Figure 13.28 – LFOH! From Modulators 21 by K-devices

These are a bundle from K-devices to help you manipulate modulation signals for any available parameters within Live.

You can check out the bundle here:

`https://k-devices.com/products/modulators21/`

- Drum Synth:

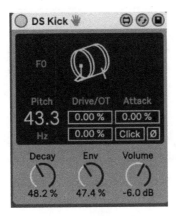

Figure 13.29 – Kick Drum Synth

There are eight super-simple Drum Synth devices to help you design drum sounds.

These devices come bundled with the Suite license – you can find them under the **Instruments** category in Live's browser.

- Microtuner:

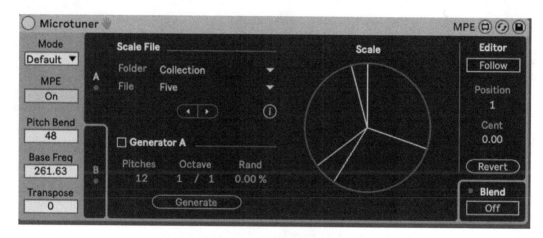

Figure 13.30 – Microtuner

This is a fairly new micro-tuning device that allows you to alter the tuning of virtual instruments. You can download it from the Ableton website:

`https://www.ableton.com/en/packs/microtuner/`

- Chord Generator:

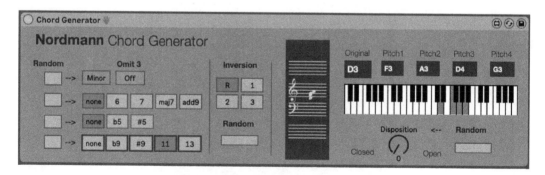

Figure 13.31 – Chord Generator by Nordmann

This is a very easy-to-use device to generate complex chords made by Nordmann.

You can download it from here:

`https://maxforlive.com/library/device/917/chord-generator`

- +1 High School Crush:

Figure 13.32 – High School Crush by CaligulaCuddles

This is a fun and easy-to-use bit crusher/downsampler device by CaligulaCuddles.

You can download it from here:

`https://maxforlive.com/library/device/5153/high-school-crush`

- +2 Inspired by Nature:

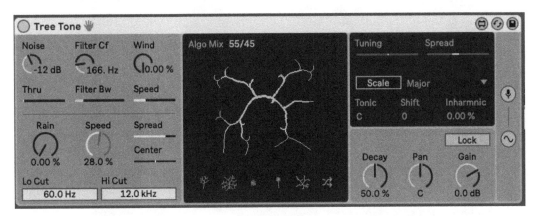

Figure 13.33 – Tree Tone from Inspired by Nature

This is a super-fun collection of visual M4L devices, which is a collaboration between Ableton and Dillon Bastan. There is just so much to discover here; devices to help you create generative soundscapes, random melodies, and lush evolving modulations.

You can download it from here:

`https://www.ableton.com/en/packs/inspired-nature/`

Make sure you take the time to explore some of the M4L devices, as there is truly just so much fun to be discovered.

Working with video in Live

I personally do loads of video tutorials, and for those, I tend to do the voice-over recording, dialog, music, sound effect editing, and mixing to sync to the motion picture in Live. It is super-easy to import and instantly start composing, recording, and editing the sound for video content.

Live will not turn into video editing software, so ensure that you have your final video edit ready to work with. However, you can import the final video and its corresponding audio, which you can quickly replace or add to using your current knowledge of the software. At the end, you can export a file that contains the video and the edited audio as well.

You can import video by dragging and dropping a video file into Live from your computer or browser.

If you drop it into the **Arrangement View**, straight away, you will see the waveform of the audio of the video on the timeline in a clip – the Video Window will also pop up, displaying the video (*Figure 13.34*):

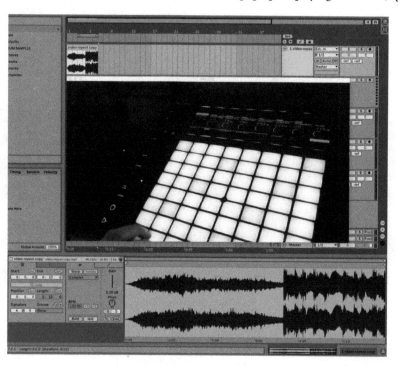

Figure 13.34 – Imported video in the Arrangement View

However, if you drop the video into the **Session View**, Live will warn you with a dialog box that the video will be treated like an audio clip (*Figure 13.35*):

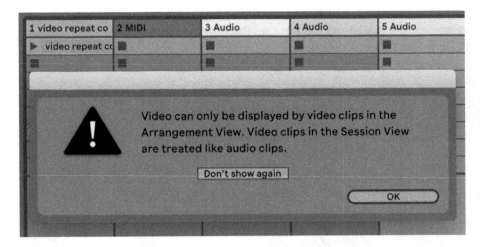

Figure 13.35 – Video imported into the Session View

You can use video in the Session View where Live is used as a real-time, live visual tool. If you are interested in exploring this, you can try Videosync for free at `https://videosync.showsync.com/`

Videosync will allow you to basically work with video just like you do with audio in Live.

Editing audio and video

Once the video is in the Arrangement View, we can apply basic editing techniques.

We can trim the clip, split it, and move the slices around – however, if we have a gap between clips, Live will display a black screen during the gaps.

We can also **warp** the clip, which can be super-useful for syncing purposes. I recommend going over the warping features again in *Chapter 3, Editing Audio and Warping*, and especially note the **Tempo Leader/Follower** option among the **Warp** settings in the Clip View!

We can also change what the **Time Ruler** display shows by *Ctrl + clicking* (*right-clicking* on Windows) on it (*Figure 13.36*). This can be super-important depending on what kind of video project you are working on!

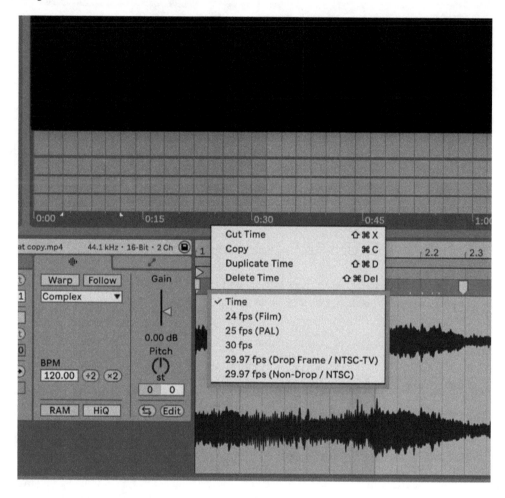

Figure 13.36 – Changing what Time Ruler is displaying

Live makes it super-easy to compose sound for videos, and with your existing knowledge of Live, you can get started straight away once you have set everything up to your preference!

Exporting your work

Once you are finished and you would like to export the video file with the audio attached to it, all you need to do is head to **File** | **Export Audio/Video**.

A dialog box will pop up, where you need to enable **On** for the **Create Video** option. Underneath this option, you can also choose from different **Video Encoder** settings (*Figure 13.37*):

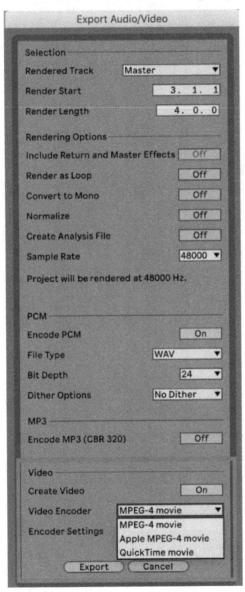

Figure 13.37 – Exporting video

You can also choose from different **Encoder Settings** options by clicking on the **Edit** button (*Figure 13.38*):

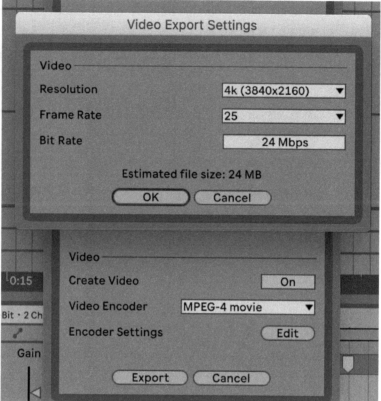

Figure 13.38 – Encoder Settings

Once all of these have been set by whatever specs you have been briefed to work with, you can hit the **Export** button so Live creates the video file to the chosen location on your computer.

Saving the project with video

Once you are finished, all you need to do is save the project as you normally would with the **Collect All and Save** command (**File | Collect All and Save**). Once this is done, the video file will be saved in the sample folder of the project folder within the **Imported** folder.

Before we wrap this chapter up, there is one more topic that I am really excited to talk about, which is the Note app.

Ableton Note app

Ableton has created a new iOS application called **Note**, which is the ideal tool for recording your musical ideas when you are on the move or away from your computer. This app is user friendly and easily accessible, making it effortless to capture your creative impulses.

With Note, you can generate beats, record melodies, and sample sounds from your surroundings, among other capabilities.

If you are using other devices, you can synchronize Note with them using Ableton Link. In *Chapter 15, Playing Live*, you will learn more about Ableton Link. Check out the Ableton website at `https://www.ableton.com/en/note/` for further instructions on using the Note app.

You may be wondering whether it's possible to transfer your Note projects to your computer and finish them in Ableton Live, especially since you are using an app developed by the same company. The answer is a resounding "yes"!

You can conveniently transfer your Note projects to Ableton Live using Ableton Cloud.

To use Note, you'll need a device that supports iOS 15 or higher, as well as Ableton Live 11.2.5 or a more recent version to use Ableton Cloud.

Now, let's have a look at how we can get started:

1. After installing Note from the App Store, when you open the application, it will prompt you to take a tour of the app.

2. Once you are finished, you already have the chance to enable Ableton Cloud on your iOS device. Tap on **Enable Ableton Cloud**. Alternatively, you can tap on the three white dots at the bottom left of the screen (*Figure 13.39*).

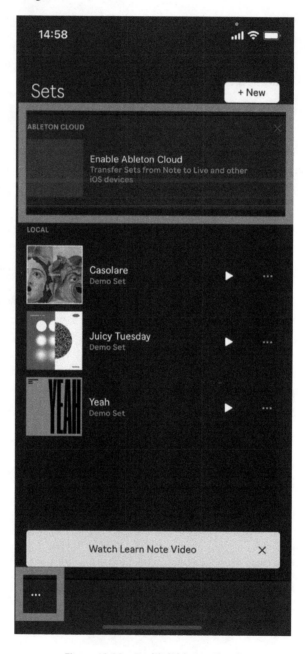

Figure 13.39 – Enable Ableton Cloud

3. Next, tap on **Ableton Cloud** to switch it **On** (*Figure 13.40*).

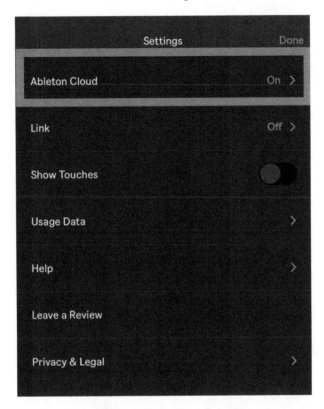

Figure 13.40 – Switching on Ableton Cloud.

4. The next screen will enable you to move the slider to the right so that Ableton Cloud will be turned on (*Figure 13.41*).

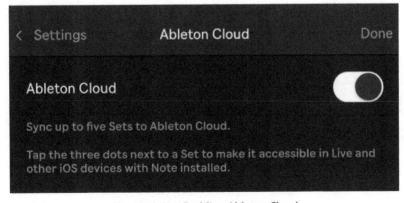

Figure 13.41 – Enabling Ableton Cloud

5. Now you will be redirected to the Ableton website in your mobile browser to connect to your Ableton user account (*Figure 13.42*).

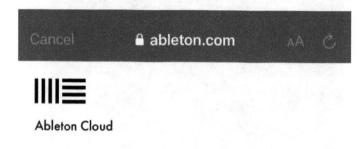

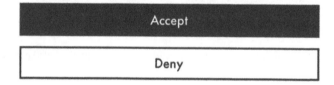

Figure 13.42 – Prompt to connect your Ableton user account

Once you are connected, you will be directed back to the Note app. Here, you can create your first set and sync it to Ableton Cloud.

I have created a set already (called **Set 1**), so let's sync it:

1. Tap on the three dots on the right side next to **Set 1** (*Figure 13.43*).

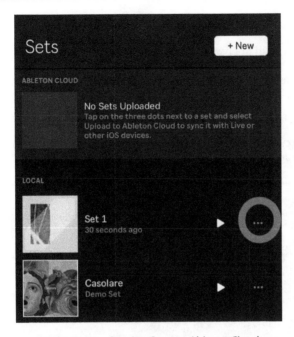

Figure 13.43 –.Syncing Set 1 to Ableton Cloud

2. Tap on **Upload To Ableton Live Cloud** (*Figure 13.44*).

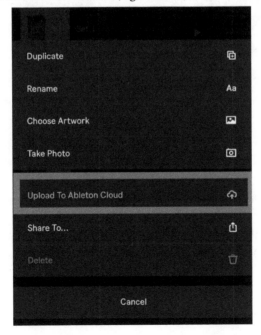

Figure 13.44 – Uploading to Ableton Cloud

And with that, we are done. You can upload up to 5 sets to Ableton Cloud!

Now let's enable Ableton Cloud in Live:

1. Once you have taken the preceding steps on your iOS device, and you have uploaded at least one set, you can head to your computer and open up Live.

2. Head to **Live | Preferences (Options | Preferences** on Windows).

3. Choose the **Library** tab. Here you can see the button that you can set to **On** for Live to **Show Cloud** (*Figure 13.45*).

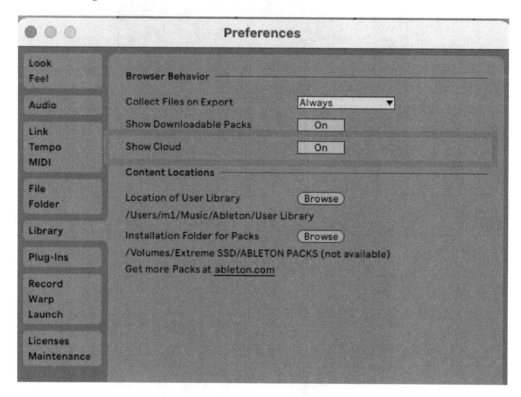

Figure 13.45 – Enabling the Show Cloud option in the preferences

4. In the browser under the **Places** section, you will find **Cloud**. If you click on it, Live will prompt you again to sign into your Ableton user account, but this time on your computer (*Figure 13.46*).

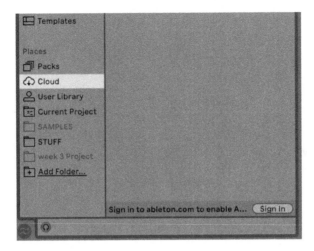

Figure 13.46 – Live prompting you to sign in to your Ableton user account

5. Once you have signed in, you will see the set you have uploaded to Ableton Cloud, synced to Live (*Figure 13.47*).

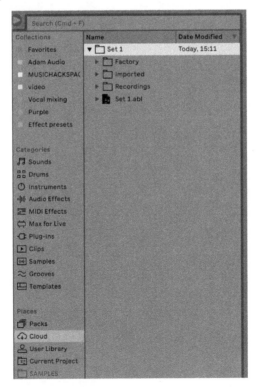

Figure 13.47 – Set from Notes shown in the browser

If I click now on the `Set 1.abl` file, Live will open the project I started in Note and I can continue happily creating and expanding the idea in Live.

With that, we have reached the end of this chapter.

Summary

In this chapter, we dove into some truly unique features of Live! We had a look at how we can make Live follow the tempo of an external audio source by using Tempo Follower, and we also discovered the amazing and updated Follow Action features.

We also introduced the world of M4L, which I hope managed to grab your attention enough to perhaps further explore this huge topic in the future, or just to comfortably work with and search for already-made M4L devices.

In addition, we also had a look at how we can work with video in Live. This is something that you can get started with super-easily, and in my opinion, sometimes composing for a motion picture can really give you a break from music while still working on music, and this is because you are visually stimulated too. Composing to a video clip also can help get you out of a creative block, which you might experience sometimes when you load up an empty project and no ideas start to flow. With a video in hand, your starting point will be the need to tell a story with the audio.

Lastly, we also examined the Ableton Note iOS app, and explored how we can transfer our Note project directly to the Ableton Live browser using Ableton Cloud. This allows us to easily open and continue working on our ideas in Ableton Live.

In the next chapter, we will dive into MIDI mapping, setting up external instruments, and working with MIDI CCs.

14

Exploring MIDI Mapping, External Instrument, and MIDI CCs

After looking at some of Live's unique and fun features, such as Tempo Follower and Follow Action, among others, in this chapter, we are going to start by learning more about **musical instrument digital interface** (**MIDI**) controllers and getting hands-on with MIDI mapping. MIDI controllers can be a great addition to your setup, especially if you are an instrumentalist or simply like a more tactile music-making experience. They can be considered for both the studio and the stage. MIDI controllers don't just allow you to play MIDI instruments or external synths; their usage can also be extended a lot by mapping parameters of Live to be controlled by your MIDI controller, which we will explore in this chapter.

We will also look at how you can hook up external synths to Live and what uses MIDI **continuous controllers** (**CCs**) have.

The chapter will consist of the following topics:

- MIDI controllers
- MIDI mapping in Live
- Using hardware synths with Live
- MIDI CCs

Technical requirements

In order to follow along with this chapter, you will need the following:

- A computer with at least 8 GB of RAM and at least an Intel Core i5 processor
- A pair of headphones

- A copy of Live 11 Suite

- **Chapter 14** and **Chapter 14.2** Ableton Live Projects

MIDI controllers

MIDI controllers send MIDI information to your software (in this case, Ableton Live), and external synths can be connected to mixing desks and even control lighting for shows.

There are many MIDI controllers available made by many different manufacturers in the market. They have become very popular and widely used because they can be accessed even on a super low budget. Because there are so many different types of MIDI controllers out there, we will look at a few things you can take into consideration when picking the best one for you or looking to upgrade.

If you have already done a quick search on the internet, you may have noticed that there are many different types of controllers available, sometimes even on the same MIDI controller device. There can be **keys**, **pads**, **faders**, **touchpads**, **wheels**, **encoders**, and **knobs**, to name the most popular ones.

You can get MIDI controllers that only have one type of the previously mentioned controllers, which means it is entirely up to your needs to pick which one is best.

Keys are obviously good for playing instruments, pads for finger drumming and triggering clips as well as sending on and off messages, faders to control volume, or any other parameters represented by a "slide" in Live. Knobs and encoders are useful for assigning effect parameters, sends, and touchpads to add some expression to your sounds.

We can further investigate these controls and what we need by looking at things such as whether the keys are weighted (**weighted keys** feel more like playing a proper piano and are a popular choice for pianists), and whether the keys or pads have **aftertouch** (aftertouch on a keyboard is a function where, when you press down the key and hold it down, you can feel a clicking kind of sensation. When that "click" happens, it can control parameters, such as vibrato, and volume, among others.) We can also look at whether the pads are **velocity-sensitive** (this means that the pad senses the force that you are hitting it with, which can control the volume of the sound).

When we look at faders, we can see whether we need them to be **motorized faders** (motorized faders can be moved by automation).

You can also see whether you can connect a sustain pedal to the MIDI controller, or whether it has MIDI in and out connections to send MIDI to and receive MIDI from other external devices through a five-pin MIDI cable (see *Figure 14.1*). MIDI will be sent and received between the controller and Live, via the **USB cable** you have connected the controller to the computer with:

Figure 14.1 – Five-pin MIDI cable to send and receive MIDI information

As I said, there are many different MIDI controllers out there made by different companies, and it is always worth reading about them in-depth, as some of them have very different features to offer.

Let's have a closer look at these controller types.

Control surfaces

There are MIDI controllers which are Control Surfaces. This means that once you connect them to your computer (and Live, in this instance), they will have some **pre-configured MIDI mappings** implemented, which means the physical controllers (buttons and knobs) will already be **assigned to parameters** in Live that are defined by a computer script. Some of them even come with designated buttons for **transport controls** (play, stop, and record).

Figure 14.2 – The Novation Launchkey MK3 MIDI controller – control surface

The MIDI controller in *Figure 14.2*, the Novation Launchkey MK3, is a great example of a MIDI controller with different types of controllers (keys, pads, buttons, and encoders), and is also a control surface as it has a really great integration to Live.

Most control surfaces are plug-and-play, which means you connect them to the computer and they will configure, ready to be used. However, sometimes you need to do some configuration yourself. This can be done by going to **Preferences | Link Tempo MIDI**, as shown in *Figure 14.3*:

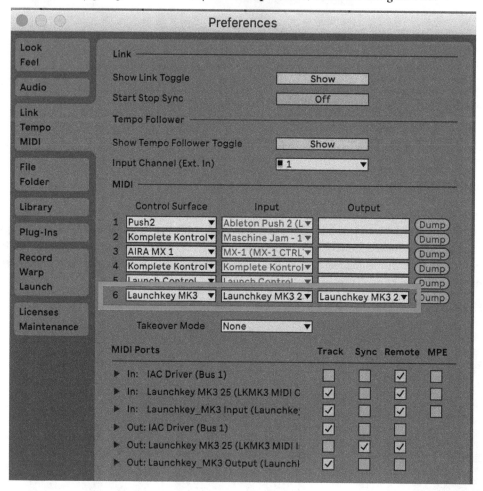

Figure 14.3 – Configuration of the Novation Launchkey MK3 in the Preferences tab

In *Figure 14.3*, you can see that under the **Control Surface** option, we can have up to six control surfaces connected to Live at any time. If you click on the tabs under the **Control Surface** option, you will see a huge list of control surfaces that we can use without installing any additional drivers. If your controller is not on the list, it might be a generic MIDI controller or an additional driver needs to be installed, meaning there is no pre-configured mapping available. Don't worry; you can manually map MIDI, which we will cover in the *MIDI mapping in Live* section of this chapter. Once the control surface is chosen or detected, Live will automatically configure the Input and Output of the control surface, which defines which ports the controllers will use to send and receive data. However, as you can see, it can be manually changed or assigned under the **Input** and **Output** tabs. If there are multiple options to choose from, you should read the controller's manual to see which ones you are supposed to be using. And with that, your controller is ready to be used and control Live with. We will look at other settings in this window in a moment when we will explore how to set up generic MIDI controllers.

Ableton Push is probably the best-configured control surface, specifically designed to exclusively integrate and control Live:

Figure 14.4 – The Ableton Push 2

It can even be thought of as an "instrument" to play Live with. More on Push in *Chapter 15, Playing Live*.

Generic MIDI controllers

Generic MIDI controllers do not come with any pre-configured MIDI mapping on plugging them in and connecting them to Ableton Live. However, you can create your own customized MIDI mapping. In this example, I will still use the Novation Launchkey MK3 control surface MIDI controller by turning it into a generic MIDI controller in the **Preferences** tab. With this, I can also give you a good example of how you can override MIDI mappings, even on controllers that have pre-configured mappings. Let's get started:

1. Connect the Launchkey and open up **Preferences | Link Tempo MIDI** in Live.

2. To disable the controller's pre-configured MIDI mapping, set **Control Surface** and **Input** and **Output** to **None**, as shown in *Figure 14.5*:

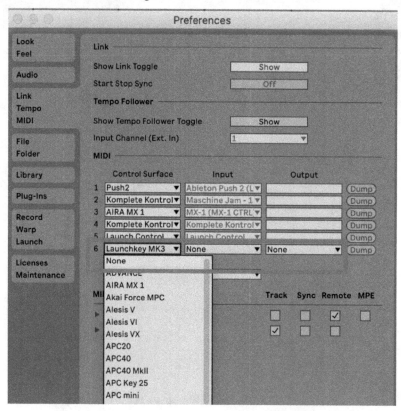

Figure 14.5 – Turning a control surface into a generic MIDI controller in the Preferences tab

Now, take a look at the **MIDI Ports** section, as shown in *Figure 14.6*:

We should see the inputs and outputs for any MIDI controllers we have connected. If they don't show up, you should check with the manufacturer of the controller to see whether you need to download any additional drivers:

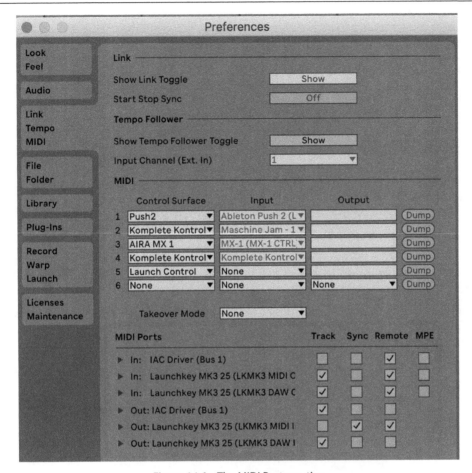

Figure 14.6 – The MIDI Ports section

3. Under the **Track** option, tick the **Track** option for the **In** port if you would like to play MIDI notes (trigger MIDI instruments) in Live.

4. If you are sending MIDI notes out from Live to another external device, then you need to tick the **Track** option for the **Out** port of the device.

5. Under the **Sync** option, if you tick **Sync** for the device's **In** port, then you can control Live's tempo through a connected external device. If you would like to sync an external device (for example, a drum machine, or a synth with a built-in arpeggiator) to Live's tempo, then you should tick the **Sync** option for the **Out** port of the device.

6. Under the **Remote** option, if you would like to receive MIDI control messages from a device to control Live, then you need to tick the device's **In** port.

7. If you would like to send control messages to the device from Live, then you also need to tick it for the **Out** port of the device.

This will be super important and make full sense in the next section of this chapter when we look at MIDI mapping.

And with that, we arrive at the end of setting up our generic MIDI controller to be used with Live.

In the next section, we will look at how we can create our own MIDI mapping with our MIDI controller, whether it is a control surface or a generic MIDI controller.

MIDI mapping in Live

MIDI mapping parameters in Live are actually really simple. In this section, I will walk you through how to set this up.

> **Important note**
>
> Remember what we learned at the end of the previous section; for MIDI mapping to work, you need to have **Remote** selected for at least the **In** port of the device under the **MIDI Ports** section in the **Preferences | Link Tempo MIDI** tabs!
>
> If your controller has a screen or lights that can display MIDI controls set to Live, then you should also have **Remote** ticked for the **Out** port of the device.

Follow these steps to set up MIDI mapping parameters in Live:

1. Navigate to the **PAD** track in the **Chapter 14** project file.
2. Display the Device View (which is, in this case, an Instrument Rack).
3. Now, press the **MIDI** button shown in *Figure 14.7* or hit *Cmd + M* (*Ctrl + M* on Windows):

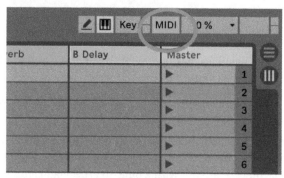

Figure 14.7 – MIDI map mode switch

Now, you will notice that loads of parameters, buttons, knobs, and faders became blue. These are the parameters and controls you can MIDI map to be controlled by a physical control on your MIDI controller.

4. For this example, let's select the **Filter Cutoff** macro, as seen in *Figure 14.8*:

Figure 14.8 – The frequency controller macro is selected to be MIDI mapped

You can see that there is a bracket around the parameter we selected, around the four corners. This indicates the selected parameter for MIDI mapping.

5. Now, move a knob on your MIDI controller.

You will notice that a number is written next to the parameter. It indicates which physical control you have mapped to, as shown in *Figure 14.9*:

Figure 14.9 – A MIDI-mapped parameter in the MIDI mode

6. Now, if you exit the MIDI mode by switching off the **MIDI** button or pressing *Cmd + M* (*Ctrl + M* for Windows) again, you will be physically controlling the **Filter Cutoff** macro with the knob on your controller that you mapped it to.

That is how simple it is to carry out MIDI mapping!

Of course, you can map multiple parameters at once while in MIDI mode. You can also map multiple parameters to the same physical controller (pad, encoder, knob, and fader) on your MIDI controller. Bear in mind, though, that mapping parameters to buttons can only trigger on and off states of parameters.

7. Go back to **MIDI Map Mode** and make sure you are displaying the browser. You will be able to see the **MIDI Mappings** list, as shown in *Figure 14.10*:

Figure 14.10 – List of MIDI Mappings in the browser area

We can see that we have two sliders to adjust the minimum and maximum values under **Min** and **Max**.

In this example, we have mapped the **Filter Cutoff** macro of the device rack that controls **Filter Cutoff** of the **Wavetable** device's **Filter 1**. Setting the minimum value (**Min**) to 50.0 Hz means that it doesn't matter how much we turn the physical knob on our MIDI controller to the left, **Filter Cutoff** will never fall below the value of 50 Hz. And vice versa, whatever we set for the **Max** value will be the maximum value that **Filter Cutoff** can be opened for. This is a great feature for performing on stage where you might have the computer screen off-stage, and you cannot see the screen and how much you are adjusting values. So, you are doing adjustments by ear; also, this way, you can make faster and more sudden movements with your physical controller as you know that your sound won't go away fully due to over-turning the knob and accidentally reaching such low frequencies that they become inaudible.

8. Even 50 Hz is a bit too low to hear properly, so depending on the kind of sound you are working with, you probably want to set this to around 100 Hz or higher.

In our next example, we will **delete the MIDI mapping**, which we can simply do by selecting the MIDI mapping in the **MIDI Mappings** list and hitting the delete key on the computer keyboard.

I also want to show you another cool feature that you can use in the **MIDI Mappings** list, which is "Invert Range"! Let's get started with the following steps:

1. We are still working with the same track, so let's map the **Filter Cutoff** macro to a knob on our MIDI controller.

2. This time, we also need to map the **Resonance** parameter of **Wavetable** Filter 1 to the exact same knob on our MIDI controller. See *Figure 14.11* and *Figure 14.12*:

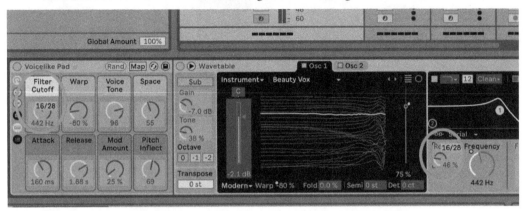

Figure 14.11 – Mapping two parameters to the same knob on the MIDI controller

Once we have mapped both parameters to the same knob, they will show up in the **MIDI Mappings** list:

C..	Note/Control	Path	Name	Min	Max
16	CC 28	PAD | Voicelike Pad	Filter Cutoff	50.0 Hz	20.5 kHz
16	CC 28	PAD | Voicelike P...	Filter 1 Resonance	0.0 %	125 %

Figure 14.12 – The two parameters mapped to the same knob on the
MIDI controller appearing in the MIDI Mappings list

Now, you will notice as you come out of **MIDI Mapping Mode** and move the physical knob on your MIDI controller that **Filter Cutoff** and **Resonance** are moving together. As you turn the knob to the left, **Filter Cutoff** opens up, and the **Resonance** parameter increases.

However, what if you wanted the exact opposite movement, where you move the same knob, and as **Filter Cutoff** opens, **Resonance** decreases? Well, this can be easily done!

3. Enable the **MIDI Mapping Mode** switch and head to the **MIDI Mappings** list; you can *Ctrl + click* (*right-click* on Windows) on the mapping of the **Resonance** parameter, and select **Invert Range**, as shown in *Figure 14.13*:

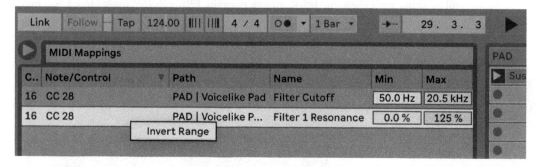

Figure 14.13 – Inverting the range of a mapped parameter to make it move in the opposite direction

Once you come out of **MIDI Mapping Mode** again and give it a try, you should now see the **Resonance** parameter decrease as you increase the frequency of **Filter Cutoff** by opening it up.

This is an area where you can get creative for both studio and stage with various types of devices.

We can also map the parameters of third-party plugins too, which we will discover in the next section.

MIDI mapping third-party plugins

We have looked at how to easily map native devices in Live, but what about third-party plugins? As you probably know, third-party plugins don't display the same way in Live as native devices; therefore, MIDI mapping parameters are also a little different.

I am going to use Serum by Xfer Records, but you could use any other third-party plugin, and it would work the same way. (For example, there is a similar third-party device to Serum called **Vital**, which is available for free. You can download it from here: `https://vital.audio/#getvital`.)

Let's have a look at how it is done:

1. Load Serum or your choice of a third-party plugin in Live.

2. Click on the **Show/Hide Plug-in Window** button to see Serum's interface. See *Figure 14.14*:

Figure 14.14 – Serum by Xfer Records loaded in Live

3. Now, to have access to the space where you can carry out the MIDI mapping, you need to click on the triangle button (the **Unfold Device Parameters** button) on the top bar of the device, next to the **Show/Hide Plug-in Window** button, as shown in *Figure 14.15*:

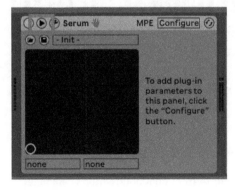

Figure 14.15 – Toggle triangle. The Unfold Device Parameters button to
gain access to parameter configuration for MIDI mapping

Since the third-party plugin parameters aren't displayed in the device area where we carry out the MIDI mapping of parameters, first, we need to add the parameters as instructed in the device area after clicking on the triangle button. You can see in *Figure 14.15* that Live is asking us to add plugin parameters to the panel by first hitting the **Configure** button.

4. Press the **Configure** button, then start selecting the parameters on Serum's interface.

5. Now, click on the parameters of Serum that you would like to configure for easy access and, in this case, to be able to MIDI map to your MIDI controller. You can see my example in *Figure 14.16*:

Figure 14.16 – Configuring Serum's parameters

6. Disable the **Configure** button to exit the configuration mode.

You can see that the parameters that you have configured are permanently visible in the device area and control the corresponding parameter on Serum.

Now you can go ahead and enter the MIDI mode and MIDI map the newly configured parameters to your MIDI controller, just as you learned in the previous section of this chapter. See *Figure 14.17* for an example of this:

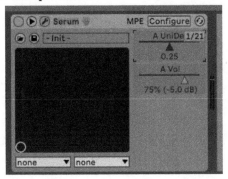

Figure 14.17 – In MIDI mode to MIDI map the configured parameters

Now, we have learned how to manage and create our own MIDI mappings. Next, we will need to head back to the **Preferences** tab to talk about something important!

Takeover modes

So, you created your MIDI mappings, went away with your controller to another studio, worked on another project with other MIDI mappings, and have now returned to your studio and loaded your original project.

This means that your physical knobs, for example, are not where you left them on your first project. Your mapped **Filter Cutoff** macro might be set all the way to the right, meaning the filter is fully open, but your knob on your MIDI controller (which is mapped to this macro) is all the way to the left – not matching the position of the parameter in the software assigned to it.

As soon as you move the knob, the mapped parameter in Live will jump to the position of the knob on your controller. This is obviously not ideal, especially not if you are on stage.

This happens when **Takeover Mode** is set to **None**. Let's go and change this!

Head to **Preferences | Link Tempo MIDI** and find the **Takeover Mode** option, as shown in *Figure 14.18*:

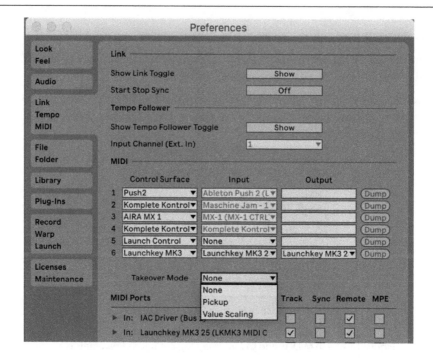

Figure 14.18 – Takeover Mode in the Preferences tab

If we set the **Takeover Mode** option to **Pickup**, it will cause nearly the opposite behavior that we experienced when this setting was set to **None**. The software will not do anything until the position of the knob on the controller gets moved and reaches the same value that the software is set to. When that happens, the control will be picked up.

If we set **Takeover Mode** to **Value Scaling**, the software will follow along with the hardware controller, but the software's movement will be scaled until they are back in sync. Imagine that your knob is set all the way to the left, but the software parameter that it's meant to control is set in the middle. If you start moving the knob, the assigned parameter in Live will also start moving, but in small-scaled increments until the knob catches up with the parameter in Live. It's like the parameter in Live is "waiting" for the hardware to catch up with it, so it's only moving slowly to allow this to happen until they are in sync with their positions again.

These settings should be taken into consideration, especially if you are prepping a set to be performed on stage, so you avoid parameters suddenly jumping everywhere due to not having the **Takeover Mode** option set to your needs.

We have arrived at the end of this section.

Before we move on to the next topic, though, I would like to show you something that I feel is relevant to what we have learned in terms of MIDI mapping: key mapping.

Key Mapping

Key mapping works in essentially the same way as MIDI mapping does in Live.

Key mapping allows you to map Live's parameters to your computer keyboard.

If you press the **Key** button in the top-right corner of the screen or hit *Cmd + K* (*Ctrl + K* for Windows), you will notice that all mappable parameters are not turning blue this time but turning orange instead, as shown in *Figure 14.19*:

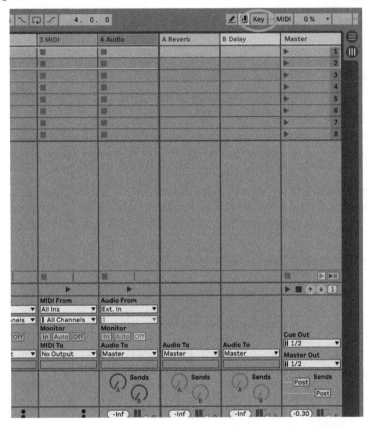

Figure 14.19 – The Key Mapping Mode switch – entering Key Map Mode

Similar to MIDI mapping, if you click on a parameter to map it, the parameter will have a bracket around it. Then, you just need to hit the key on your computer you would like to map it to.

In my example, I selected the **Session Record** button and mapped it to the *r* key on my computer keyboard, as seen in *Figure 14.20*:

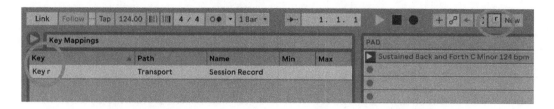

Figure 14.20 – Session Record button mapped to R on the computer keyboard

This means each time I hit the *r* key on my computer keyboard, the **Session Record** button will be triggered.

Important note

Make sure that you have the **Computer MIDI Keyboard** switch disabled, so Live isn't expecting MIDI notes from your computer keyboard rather than hotkeys (*Figure 14.21*).

Also, please be aware that you can map over existing keycommands. For example, the *A* key is already assigned to trigger **Automation** on and off, and *R* to reverse audio clips. If you key map something else to it, you will lose the functionality of the original hotkey.

So, now we have mapped *r* to triggel the **Session Record** button, you will no longer will be able to reverse clips using the *r* key, only by manually reversing the clip using the **Reverse** button in the Clip View or by pressing R (capitalized), as the reverse function is by default mapped to both r and R.

This is because key mapping is case-sensitive.

Figure 14.21 – Computer MIDI keyboard is disabled so key mapping can work

This feature can be super useful if you would like to create custom shortcuts fitting your own needs and workflow.

And with that, we are now ready to dive into working with external synths in Live!

Using hardware synths with Live

Connecting and using external synths with Live is super easy and super fun, in my opinion, as you are expanding your tool set for your music-making projects.

There are different ways you can manage external devices with Live, but we will look at the easiest and most convenient way: using an **External Instrument** device.

In this example, I will use my Moog Minitaur, one of my favorite synths:

Figure 14.22 – Moog Minitaur synthesizer

Let's see how to set this up in this section. First, we need to connect and configure the synth, so let's get started.

Configuring Live's audio and MIDI preferences

To configure Live's audio and MIDI preferences, do the following:

1. Open the **Chapter 14.2** project file. (Everything is already set up, so you can follow along.)

2. I connected the Moog to the computer with a USB cable. This synth supports MIDI over a USB cable, so I can send MIDI information from Live to the synth to sequence it. It also has a MIDI In and Out connection, so it is also possible to send MIDI information to the synth straight from a MIDI controller.

3. For this example, we will send MIDI to the synth from Live.

4. I took the audio out of the synth and connected it to my interface's first input, so we can route the audio from the synth to hear it from Live.

5. After that, I headed to **Preferences | Audio** to configure my interface and the audio input.

6. Next, I configured the MIDI preferences at **Preferences | Link Tempo MIDI**.

7. I enabled **Track** for the Moog's output **MIDI Port** to be able to send MIDI notes and MIDI CCs (more about MIDI CCs in the next section of this chapter). We can also enable **Sync** for the same output **MIDI Port** if our device has a built-in sequencer or effect. And we are going to leave **Remote** off. (We already learned what this does at the beginning of this chapter.) See *Figure 14.23* for these settings:

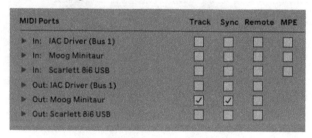

Figure 14.23 – Configured MIDI preferences

Now we are ready to set up our external instrument device.

Setting up External Instrument in Live

As I mentioned before, using an external instrument device is the most convenient way to use hardware with Ableton Live.

So, let's set it up:

1. Load **External Instrument** from the browser onto a new MIDI track, as shown in *Figure 14.24*:

Figure 14.24 – Ext. Instrument device loaded in Live

2. Now, simply choose under the **MIDI To** option the hardware synth (MIDI output port – in my case, **Moog Minitaur**), and underneath that, the MIDI channel, which should be set to **Ch.1**, as displayed in *Figure 14.25*. Now, you are going to send MIDI information to the hardware synth through channel 1:

Figure 14.25 – MIDI output port and channel setup

3. Under **Audio From**, you can select the input of your audio interface where you plugged in the hardware synth. For me, it was input 1, so I selected **1**. See *Figure 14.26*:

Figure 14.26 – Audio input setup to receive the outputted audio from the hardware synth

If you think the sound is a bit out of sync, you can use the **Hardware Latency** slide to adjust the timing. Furthermore, you can increase the input gain using the **Gain** knob.

And with that, we are all set up! Now we can go ahead and start sequencing!

If you arm the MIDI track that your External Instrument device lives on, and either use a MIDI controller to trigger this MIDI track and send that MIDI out of Live to the synth or just simply draw some notes into a clip, you will be able to see the MIDI notes hitting your hardware synth, and hear the sound coming back on the same track!

Figure 14.27 – Sequencing the hardware synth with MIDI notes programmed into a clip

Now, if you start playing with your synth, you will soon raise the question of how to record the audio of the synth since we are still using a MIDI track. Well, let's take a look at it in the next subsection.

Recording audio from the hardware synth into Ableton Live

Recording the audio can also be approached in different ways, but we will look at the most convenient one, which also gives you the most control.

It is super simple and quick, so follow me:

1. Create a new audio track.

2. In the input section (**Audio From**), pick the **Ext. Instrument** track to capture the output of that track:

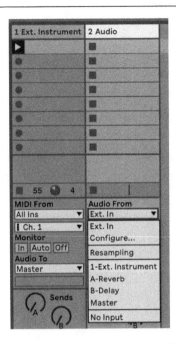

Figure 14.28 – Setting up a new audio track to record the audio from the hardware synth

3. Underneath where you chose the track's input, you can also pick from **Pre FX**, **Post FX,** and **Post Mixer**:

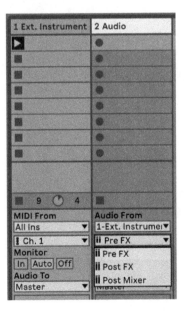

Figure 14.29 – Choosing between the Pre FX, Post FX, or Post Mixer settings

Let's quickly cover what the differences are:

- **Pre FX**: If you had effect processing (audio effect devices) on the **Ext. Instrument** track, then the sound will be captured *before* the audio effects, so effectively, you will be recording the clean signal that the synth outputted without the additional inserted effects.

- **Post FX**: Similarly, if you had effects inserted into the **Ext. Instrument** track, you will be capturing the sound with these effects included and recorded.

- **Post Mixer**: This option means that any changes you make at the mixer on the **Ext. Instrument** track while recording will also be captured (for example, changing volume, or muting the track).

For this example, I would suggest using **Pre FX** so that you aren't recording the effects (if you are using any). Then, you can put the effects onto the newly recorded track and later tweak them if you need to instead of committing to the effects by recording the audio with them included (**Post FX**).

4.   Now, make sure the monitoring is set to **Off** on this new audio track because you are already monitoring the **Ext. Instrument** track itself, and we wouldn't like to monitor the same audio twice. See *Figure 14.30* for an example of this.

5.   Next, arm the track and begin to record, as shown in *Figure 14.30*:

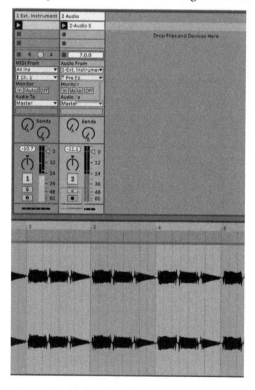

Figure 14.30 – New audio track's monitoring is turned Off, the track is armed, and recording is in process!

And with that, we have just successfully set up our hardware synth with Live.

In the next section, we are going to learn a bit more about MIDI CCs and how to use them for your music-making adventures.

MIDI CCs

A MIDI CC is a message category that adds extra functionality to a MIDI message.

We already saw that MIDI CC numbers get assigned to physical controls of MIDI controllers that we can map to a parameter in Live.

However, MIDI CCs can also be used to control the functions of some hardware synths.

In our example, we will control the filter cutoff of my Moog Minitaur using MIDI CC, without actually touching any knobs on the synth, and later record the filter cutoff movements manually from the synth and capture it into a clip envelope in Live!

Before we dive into that, let's look at a few more things about MIDI CCs.

We have 127 MIDI CC numbers, and they can have a value between 0 and 127. How these MIDI CCs have been implemented can vary between manufacturers, so it is recommended to check! It is like that for my Moog Minitaur, and how the MIDI CCs have been implemented can be found here: `https://midi.user.camp/d/moog/minitaur/`.

Now that we have learned a bit more about MIDI CCs and their role, we can dive in and see them in action! As I mentioned, we are going to control the filter cutoff of the Moog Minitaur from Live without actually touching the hardware synth itself.

Let's see how it's done!

1. Double-click **Clip** on the **Ext. Instrument** track that we are sending MIDI from to the hardware synth.

2. Display **Clip Envelopes** and choose **MIDI Ctrl** from the first option, as shown in *Figure 14.31*:

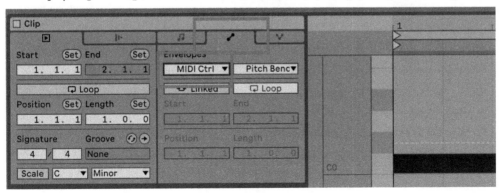

Figure 14.31 – Displaying MIDI Ctrl in Clip Envelopes

3.   At the next option (next to **MIDI Ctrl**), pick **CC19**. The reason for that is if you look at the documentation at the link for the Moog Minitaur, you will see that CC is assigned to control the filter cutoff of the hardware synth. Also, draw in some modulation to the envelope so you can hear its effect:

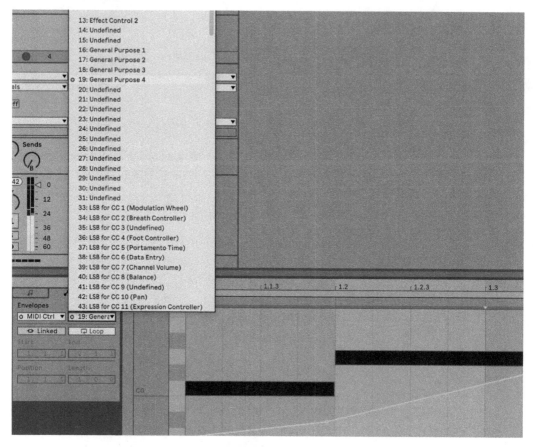

Figure 14.32 – MIDI CC19 controlling the filter cutoff of the
hardware synth, following the drawn clip envelope

Next, look at capturing the filter cutoff of the hardware synth into Live, so we can edit it if we want.

4.   Duplicate the MIDI clip we have been working with on the **Ext. Instrument** track.

5.   Delete the breakpoints we have created in the envelope for this CC19, but leave all the other settings the same, as we still will be working with CC19.

6.   Head to **Preferences | Link Tempo MIDI** and enable the **Track** option for the input **MIDI Port** for the hardware synth (*Figure 14.33*), as we would now like to receive data from the synth, not just send data to it:

MIDI Ports	Track	Sync	Remote	MPE
▶ In: IAC Driver (Bus 1)	☐	☐	☐	☐
▶ In: Moog Minitaur	☑	☐	☐	☐
▶ In: Scarlett 8i6 USB	☐	☐	☐	☐
▶ Out: IAC Driver (Bus 1)	☐	☐	☐	
▶ Out: Moog Minitaur	☑	☑	☐	
▶ Out: Scarlett 8i6 USB	☐	☐	☐	

Figure 14.33 – MIDI preferences set up for the hardware synth's input MIDI Port

7. Once we are set, we can go ahead and proceed as we would normally do to record automation or modulation into clip envelopes. The difference is that, this time, we are tweaking an actual hardware synth and recording the modulation of our physical touches from the synth itself through MIDI CC19:

Figure 14.34 – Recording the filter cutoff modulation into a clip envelope from the hardware synth

This is a simple process after grasping the basics of how to set up your preferences and the role of MIDI CCs. As I said, some parts can vary for different hardware synthesizers, but the manual will always reveal the differences, so I suggest always checking that out when trying to integrate with Ableton Live.

MIDI CCs can be further used internally to control third-party plugin parameters and to control Live's various parameters on different tracks (other than the one that you are working with to draw the modulation in). This can be done by setting up a virtual MIDI bus.

However, to use CCs to control your hardware synth, we have covered the necessary steps.

Summary

We have arrived at the end of another chapter.

We learned how to approach MIDI controllers, the different types, and how to map Ableton Live's parameters to physical controls on your MIDI controller.

Furthermore, we looked at how we can use the **Ext. Instrument** device in Live to integrate and control your hardware synthesizer with Ableton Live.

We also looked at how to use MIDI CCs to further control your synth.

In the next chapter, we will jump in to talking about playing live!

15

Playing Live

Ableton Live was originally designed as a loop arranger tool made to take studio production to the live stage. Now that the software has turned into a DAW, it of course still holds tools and features that provide a fluid performance workflow with many techniques and possibilities for performance that are hard to come by in other DAWs, or unique to Live altogether.

In this chapter, I have collected a couple of topics, considerations, techniques, and features that are specifically useful for Live Performance and will be helpful for you to improve your performance techniques or prepare your first set for performing live.

The chapter will consist of the following topics:

- Playing live with Ableton Live
- Clip Launch options
- Setting up dummy clips
- Syncing with Ableton Link and MIDI
- Cue Out and output routing
- Ableton Push and other controller considerations

Technical requirements

To follow along with this chapter, you will need the following:

- A computer with at least 8 GB of RAM and an Intel Core i5 processor at least
- A pair of headphones
- A copy of Live 11 Suite
- **Chapter 15** Ableton Live project
- **Chapter 15.2** Ableton Live project

Playing live with Ableton Live

There are multiple ways that live performance can be approached in Live and if you have ever dived into how accomplished artists use Live on stage, you most probably already came by the fact that some will use the **Session View** while others will use **Arrangement View**.

There is no right or wrong way to do it; it depends on your workflow and preferences.

When you perform with the Session View, how long parts of the set last is fully in your control, as you control that by launching **clips** and **scenes**. Performing with the Session View will also give you more opportunities for improvisation. However, this performance style will also require punctuality and focus to make sure everything is controlled the way you want it in terms of the structure being played back live, while you also might be busy with **effect manipulation** and playing **external instruments**.

Performing in the Arrangement View gives you the level of safety that you are playing along to a timeline so that you do not have to worry about making changes to your structure; that will happen as it was set up by you. This performing style allows you loads of safe spots for extensively playing external instruments, for example.

You can also combine the Arrangement View and Session View while performing; really you have many options to find the best way that suits you.

Which instruments, synths, and MIDI controllers you will play is also totally down to you depending on your skill sets and preference. I think this is the beauty of diving into the world of live performance; you get to experiment a lot, try out equipment and techniques, and really get to know yourself as a performer and find the limit of what you can and can't do on stage.

How MIDI works in Live is super easy and convenient, which is another reason why Live is a great choice to perform with. Not to mention **Device Racks** and what you can do with them, the ease of **MIDI mapping**, creative and unique effects, and how you can integrate external instruments and effects, just to name a few other benefits.

I think there are two very important aspects of a great performance—preparation and practice.

It doesn't matter how talented a musician you are, if your live set is not properly prepared so that you feel comfortable and have many techniques and tools implemented as your *range of weapons* to use on stage, you may always feel limited and maybe eventually bored.

It also doesn't matter how well you prepare your set if you haven't practiced enough, still feel unprepared, and get lost during the set in the tech stuff, or it frustrates you so much that it affects your musical talent.

So, I would say that it is important when you start out to elaborate on and explore what your key skills and strengths are and build a setup around them. A setup should not just keep you in your comfort zone so that you can shine through your existing musical skills but also push you a bit out of your comfort zone enough that you get excited about the constant development, new tech, and skills development.

When choosing your equipment, again, take into consideration your existing skills as well as what genre of music you are planning to perform. There are no rules for this, no right and wrong equipment, but there is the right equipment for you individually that makes it possible and exciting for you to perform your music. You should approach Live and all the features it has to offer in the same way when you are building your set.

Let's have a look at a couple of useful features, techniques, and considerations.

Clip Launch options

In this section, we are going to start looking at how Clip Launch modes work, as these modes are useful to know about, especially for live performance.

You can define how the clips behave in the Session View when you launch them either globally in **Preferences**, or individually for each clip in the Clip View.

As you have already learned and seen, you know that by default clips are set to **Trigger mode**, which means that when you launch the clip, the clip will start playing back, as we would expect. However, to stop the clip playing back, you need to click on an empty clip slot's **Stop** button (within the same track), or the **Clip Stop** button, which is located on the left side of the **Track Status** display (*Figure 15.1*):

Figure 15.1 – Clip Stop buttons

As I mentioned, this Clip Launch mode can be changed easily for the whole set **globally** (every single newly created clip within the same set after making the change) or **individually** for each clip within the Session View.

To change the default Clip Launch mode globally for every newly created clip, follow these steps:

1. Head to **Preferences** (**Live | Preferences** (**Options | Preferences** on Windows) or hit *Cmd +* , (*Ctrl +* , for Windows).

2. Navigate to the **Record Warp Launch** tab.

3. Under the **Launch** section, you will see the option to change **Default Launch Mode** (*Figure 15.2*):

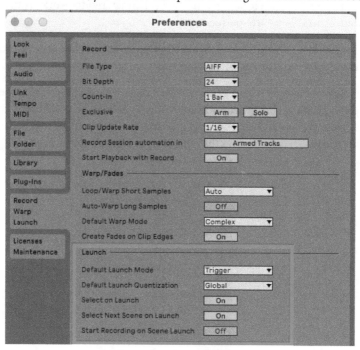

Figure 15.2 – Launch settings in Preferences

Here, you can choose from the different **Launch** modes:

- **Trigger**: The default mode, which was already explained previously.

- **Gate**: When you hold the mouse on the clip (or a pad representing this clip on a MIDI controller), it will play for as long as the mouse (or pad) is held on the clip launch button. As soon as you lift the mouse (or your finger) from the clip launch button (or the pad on the MIDI controller), the clip will stop playing back.

This can be used creatively, for example, you can set this mode to an individual clip of stuttered vocals and rhythmically trigger the clip while the set is playing back. We will look at how to change the **Launch** modes for individual clips later in this chapter.

- **Toggle**: Similarly to **Trigger**, once you launch the clip, it will start playing back. However, in order to stop the clip's playback, you do not need to trigger a Clip Stop button; you can just hit the same clip's **Launch** button again to stop the clip.

- **Repeat**: While holding down the clip's **Launch** button, the clip will be triggered repeatedly at its **Launch Quantization** value.

Underneath the **Default Launch Mode** settings, you can also change **Default Launch Quantization**.

Default Launch Quantization allows you to set all the newly created clip's quantize values. **Global** means that by default all clips will be quantized to the **Global Quantize** value, set next to the **Metronome** button (you can recap how global quantization works in the *Session View* section of *Chapter 1, Taking a Quick Tour of Ableton Live 11*). This can also be changed for each and every clip in the set individually.

Moving down within **Preferences**, you can switch **Select on Launch On** or **Off**, which means when you launch a clip or scene, it also will select the launched clip or scene. **Select Next Scene on Launch** means that once you launch a scene, the next scene in line will be selected afterward. This can be useful if you'd like to use the *Return* (*Enter* for Windows) key to keep on launching the next scenes one by one.

Start Recording on Scene Launch can also be set to **On** or **Off**, which decides whether the clip slots on armed tracks within the launched scene will automatically start recording or not. This feature can be useful if you are playing and live-looping (via clip slots) an instrument during your performance, as after launching the scene, you do not need to hit the Clip Record button within the clip slot to capture yourself playing. It is enough to just launch the next scene and start playing straight away. If you need more time to prepare your instrument after your scene launch, you can set up the **Global Quantize** value to, for example, two bars so that you have two bars before the launched scene will actually start playing back and simultaneously the recording of your instruments will also start.

> **Important note**
>
> These settings, of course, will be represented on the Control Surface MIDI controllers that you connect to Live and, for example, the selected **Launch** mode will be super important in terms of which pad to press to stop the playback of a launched clip.

Now, let's have a look at how we can configure the settings for individual clips in terms of launching.

Clip Launch modes for individual clips in the Session View

When you double-click on a clip, select the tab with the stripped launch icon on the **Clip** tab to display the appropriate settings (*Figure 15.3*):

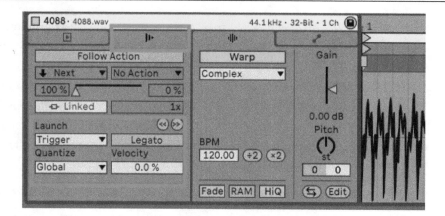

Figure 15.3 – Launch settings in the Clip View

The first setting we can change is the **Launch** mode. Here again, we can choose from **Trigger**, **Gate**, **Toggle**, and **Repeat** as we already learned previously—the difference here is that the chosen setting will only be applied to the selected clip.

Legato will allow the playback to pick up the previously launched clip's playback position. Let's say you played Clip 1, and you decide to launch Clip 2 halfway through playing back Clip 1. If **Legato** is turned on, then Clip 2 won't play back from the beginning of the clip upon launching as you would expect, but instead, it will start playing back from halfway through where Clip 1's playback left off.

This can be used super creatively to create chopped-up sequences by rhythmically switching between clips with **Legato** engaged, given the clips are properly warped.

Quantize will allow you to set clip launch quantization values for clips individually. **Global** means the clip launch will follow the **Global Quantize** value (set to next to the **Metronome** button). This set to **None** can be useful with **Launch** set to **Gate** so that you have full human control over the launch time.

The **Velocity** slide will allow you to let the velocity influence the clip's volume upon playback. If you are using a MIDI controller, you can apply your own force (velocity) where you press down the pad/key to trigger the clip. If the **Velocity** slide is set to **0**, then there is no influence on the clip's volume. If it is set to **100%**, the clip will play back silently if you apply less velocity.

If you head to **Chapter 15** project and look at the track called **CLIP LAUNCH OPTIONS**, you will see that I have set up a few clips with different settings for you to try out what we have learned so far.

In the next section of this chapter, we are going to discover something exciting and useful that allows us to have a more fluid workflow for live performance while managing our effect processing.

Setting up dummy clips

Dummy clips are clips with no actual sound, but their envelope settings control the effects and sounds of other tracks within Live.

Setting up dummy clips for your performance is super simple and allows a lot of creativity and possibilities to manage effect processing.

Let's say you are singing while you are performing and either for one part of your song or for each song you perform, you want multiple effect parameters to change at the same time. Here, dummy clips can be just what you want to use. Since you only have two hands to control the parameters through a MIDI controller and one mouse to click around with, how many parameters you are able to change at the same time can be limited.

We also learned about Macro Variations within Device Racks, which could be also used for this purpose. However, that is also limiting if you are looking to affect multiple tracks with the effect changes at the same time.

How this is going to work is that we will have to set up an audio track with audio effects, and then we will route the tracks' outputs, which we want to be affected by the effects to this new audio track. We will then program and write the effect parameter changes into the Clip Envelopes of multiple clips, which will be just there to hold these changes and implement them once we trigger these clips.

Follow me to set up some dummy clips:

1. Set up an audio track that you are going to sing through (for this example, I will put a vocal loop in to mimic the live vocals) – it's called **vox**.

2. Set up an audio track that you are going to use for your dummy clips (in the project, it's called **DUMMY CLIPS**).

3. On the **DUMMY CLIPS** track, add a bunch of **audio effects** that you would use. (I added **Auto Filter**, **Chorus Ensemble**, **Reverb**, and **Delay**.)

4. Insert a random audio clip into the **DUMMY CLIPS** track. Now, pull down the **Gain** of this clip in the Clip View since we don't want to have the sound of this clip; we would just like to write into its Clip Envelope (*Figure 15.4*):

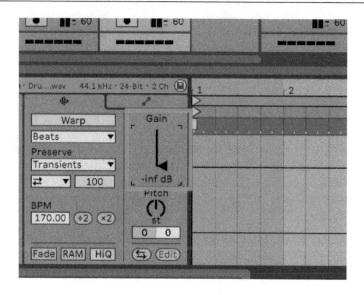

Figure 15.4 – Gain of the dummy clip pulled all the way down

5. Rename the clip Dummy Clip and duplicate this clip in the track two more times so that you end up with three of these dummy clips (*Figure 15.5*):

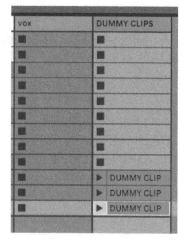

Figure 15.5 – Duplicated dummy clips

6. Set the **DUMMY CLIPS** track's **Monitor** option to **In**. You will see that the clips go gray.

7. On the **vox** track, set **Audio To** for the **DUMMY CLIPS** track so that we are now routing the output of the **vox** track through the **DUMMY CLIPS** track and its effect processing (*Figure 15.6*):

Figure 15.6 – Monitor is set to In for the DUMMY CLIPS track and the
vox track's output is routed to the DUMMY CLIPS track

8. Now let's go and set up the dummy clips. Select the first dummy clip, hit *Cmd + R* (*Ctrl + R*
    for Windows), and rename it Verse, the second clip Chorus, and the third Break Down
    (*Figure 15.7*):

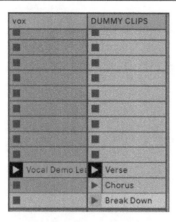

Figure 15.7 – Renamed dummy clips

9. Let's work out how we would want our vocals to sound during the verse:

I.   Double-click on the **Verse** clip and head to the Clip View.

II.   Select the **Envelopes** tab from the **Tool** tabs. Let's start with setting up **Dry/Wet** for the **Chorus Ensemble** device, as I would not like to apply any chorus for the vocals in the verse, so I will set it to **0%** in the Clip Envelope (*Figure 15.8*):

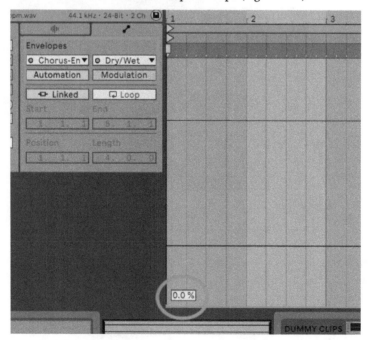

Figure 15.8 – Clip Envelope for Chorus Ensemble's Dry/Wet parameter for the Verse dummy clip

10. Let's set up **Reverb** and **Delay**'s **Dry/Wet** parameters with the same method as we did for the **Chorus Ensemble**. In the **Envelopes** tab, choose the **Reverb** device, and write the automation into the Clip Envelope for the **Dry/Wet** parameter with **20%** (*Figure 15.9*). Do the same for **Delay**'s **Dry/Wet** parameter too and set it to **15%**:

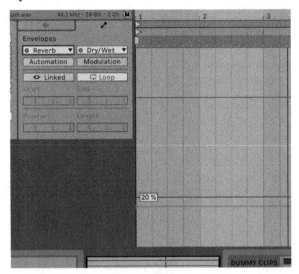

Figure 15.9 – Reverb's Dry/Wet parameter is written into Clip Envelope
automation and set to 20% in the Verse dummy clip

11. Now that we have set our **Verse** dummy clip, we are going to navigate to the **Chorus** dummy clip. Double-click on it and as we did for the **Verse** dummy clips, set up the following envelopes for the clip: **Chorus Ensemble**'s **Dry/Wet** parameter to **55%**, **Reverb**'s **Dry/Wet** to **22%**, and **Delay**'s **Dry/Wet** to **20%**.

12. Now if you play the clip on the **vox** track (or alternatively, you sing into the **vox** track live) and switch between the **Verse** and **Chorus** dummy clips, you should hear the changes of parameters of the effect devices that we wrote into the dummy clips' clip envelopes.

These dummy clips are just looping over and over again until you trigger the next dummy clip when you would like the effects to change. However, what if we want to write an effect parameter that gradually changes over a specific amount of time? Especially if the clip that we are using for the dummy clips is not long enough to implement the gradual change over the desired time? Well, if you remember what we learned before in this book about Clip Envelopes, then you might remember that we can unlink envelopes. Let's have a look how this would work in this scenario:

1. Navigate to the **Break Down** dummy clip, double-click on it, and head down to the clip envelope.

2.   Write the following clip envelope automation for the devices:

- **Chorus Ensemble**'s **Dry/Wet**: **30%**

- **Reverb**'s **Dry/Wet**: **20%**

- **Delay**'s **Dry/Wet**: **20%**

3.   For this **Break Down** dummy clip, we are also going to set **Auto Filter**'s low pass filter to gradually open up over 8 bars. Select **Auto Filter** from the envelope device chooser and then from the control chooser, select the **Frequency** parameter.

4.   The clip I inserted for this dummy clip is only four bars long, but I would like this parameter change to happen over eight bars. Therefore, let's unlink the envelope by setting the switch to **Unlinked** and setting **Length** to 8 . 0 . 0 bars. Now, we can write a gradually increasing automation lane for the **Frequency** parameter of **Auto Filter** (*Figure 15.10*):

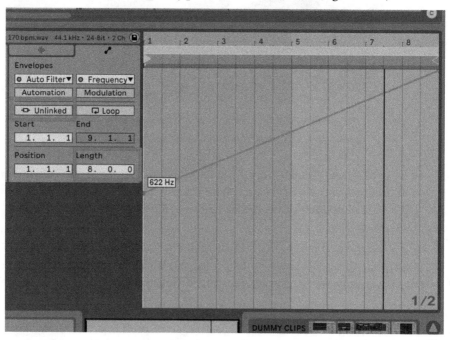

Figure 15.10 – Unlinked clip envelope set to eight bars

To make this dummy clip even more interesting, we will do the same as we just did with the **Auto Filter** parameter to the **Reverb** device's **Dry/Wet** parameter.

5.   Unlink the envelope, set it to eight bars, and write the clip envelope automation to gradually increase **Reverb** as **Auto Filter**'s **Frequency** cutoff gradually changes (*Figure 15.11*):

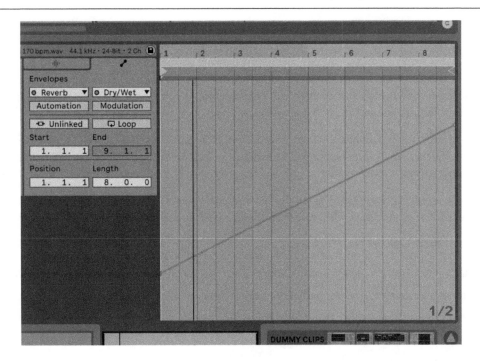

Figure 15.11 – Unlinked clip envelope to automate the Dry/Wet parameter of Reverb over eight bars

You can use dummy clips in many different ways – for example, you could route all your drum tracks through dummy clips with different **Beat Repeat**, **Auto Filter**, and **Saturator** parameter settings written into dummy clips throughout your set, use them on all your melodic elements, or route all your tracks to dummy clips with bespoke audio effect racks created for them, which would allow you to create a more dynamic performance with easily controlled but complex effect parameter changes.

In the next section, we will look at how we can sync multiple applications and computers together.

Syncing with Ableton Link and MIDI

There are multiple reasons why you might want to synchronize multiple devices and applications. It could be for collaborative purposes, to share the workload between multiple computers, to use multiple applications for creative purposes, or just for fun. In this section of the chapter, we will have a look at a few options to do this.

Synchronizing via Ableton Link

Ableton Link is a technology that enables you to keep multiple devices in sync with each other. This is super useful if you are playing with someone else or you are sharing the workload of your set over multiple devices, such as computers, iPads, and so on.

Link comes built into Live and there is also a growing list of applications from other manufacturers that are Link-enabled.

Link can be used over wireless or wired networks. Yes, it is that simple; you can use two computers, for example, yours and your collaborator's, run Live on both, join the same WiFi network, configure the necessary settings within Live, and you are ready to go!

When two devices or applications are linked together, you can stop and start playback for each device/application independently. The tempo will be synced on each device/application, as will the global quantization settings.

Using Link not only gives you many possibilities for complex setups and collaboration on stage but it is also super fun to get together with your friends and have a quick jam session.

Let's see how to set Link up:

1. Make sure all devices that you would like to link together are connected to the same network.

2. Now, we are going to make sure that the **Link** toggle button shows up in Live.

3. Head to **Live** | **Preferences** | the **Link Tempo MIDI** tab.

4. Enable **Show** next to **Show Link Toggle** (*Figure 15.12*):

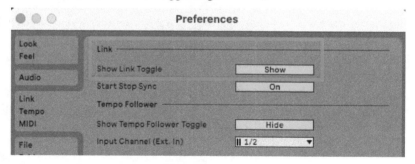

Figure 15.12 – Show Link Toggle option in Preferences

5. Now you can see the **Link** toggle in Live's control bar, and you can enable it (*Figure 15.13*):

Figure 15.13 – Link toggle in Live's control bar

6. In order to be able to sync starting and stopping playback across all linked devices/applications, make sure you head to **Live** | **Preferences** |the **Link Tempo MIDI** tab and enable the switch next to **Start Stop Sync** (*Figure 15.14*):

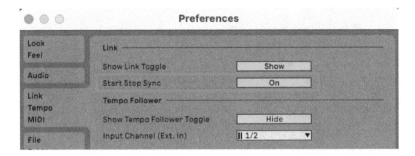

Figure 15.14 – Start Stop Sync enabled in Preferences

7. Once this is all set up, you can enable the **Link** button on all devices/applications. In the control bar, within the **Link** button (*Figure 15.15*), the number of connected devices will be indicated by a number (on this occasion, I linked the **Native Instruments Machine** application to Live to play them both in sync):

Figure 15.15 – Number of linked devices/applications indicated in the control bar

> **Important note**
> Make sure you enable the **Link** button in the other application too!

There are a couple of things to take into consideration when using Link.

When it comes to which instance of Live or application will dictate the initial tempo, it will be the one that joins the Link session first. After this, any of the Live instances or applications can change the tempo and all other joined applications and Live instances will follow.

However, if you are working with devices that don't support Link, you can still execute synchronization between devices via MIDI.

Synchronizing via MIDI

Let's see how to synchronize external devices to Live.

To make Live send out MIDI Clock messages to an external sequencer, set up and connect the external sequencer to Live to sync with MIDI. You can visit **Preferences** to make the necessary settings. Follow these steps:

1. Head to **Preferences | Link Tempo MIDI** tab.

2. Under the **MIDI Ports** section, enable **Out** next to the external device's name (destination) (*Figure 15.16*):

Figure 15.16 – Settings in Preferences to synchronize an external device to Live

MIDI Clock Sync Delay can be used to delay outgoing MIDI sync messages. This might be necessary if there is latency occurring by drivers to the outgoing messages.

MIDI Clock Type:

- **Song** mode: Live will send out **song position pointers** (**SPPs**) and continue messages as the play position changes over time.

- **Pattern** mode: Live will only send out start messages at the start of the following bar.

3. Now, the lower LED indicator next to the **Ext** button in the Control Bar will flash when Live sends out sync messages to the connected device (*Figure 15.17*):

Figure 15.17 – Lower LED indicator next to the Ext button in the Control Bar

Now let's have a look at how to synchronize Live with external MIDI devices:

To make Live sync from the external sequencer after it has been set up and connected, head back to **Preferences** and follow these steps:

1. Head to **Preferences | Link Tempo MIDI** tab.

2. Under the **MIDI Ports** section, enable **In** next to the external device's name (*Figure 15.18*):

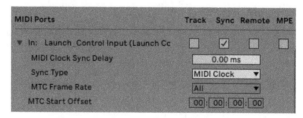

Figure 15.18 – Settings in Preferences to synchronize Live with an external device

- **MIDI Clock Sync Delay**: We just covered this; in this case, it is related to the incoming sync messages.

- **Sync Type**: Allows you to select the preferred incoming sync messages.

- **(MTC) Frame Rate**: This is only relevant if **MIDI Timecode** is selected as **Sync Type**.

We already learned how to set the Timecode format as the time ruler in the *Arrangement View in the Editing Audio and Video* section of *Chapter 13, Exploring Tempo Follower, Follow Action, Max for Live, Working with Video, and Ableton Note*.

- **(MTC) Offset**: This is also only relevant if **MIDI Timecode** is selected as **Sync Type**. Live will interpret the SMPTE time offset as the start time of the arrangement.

3. Activate external sync via the **Ext** button in the control bar when the external sync source is enabled in **Preferences**, as we learned previously. This time, the upper LED indicator will flash next to the **Ext** button when Live receives sync messages (*Figure 15.19*):

Figure 15.19 – Upper LED indicator and Ext button

One last important thing to note before we head to the next section of this chapter is that if **Link** is enabled, Live will be able to send MIDI clock information, but it will not be able to receive it!

In the next section, we will go back to talking about cues and look at output routing options!

Cue Out and output routing

In this section, we will investigate how you can take advantage of the **Cue Out** function to, for example, be able to hear the metronome in your headphones without your audience hearing it.

We are also going to have a look at how you can set up an external mix and a separate mix for you in your headphones, which can be extremely helpful when you are singing or playing an instrument during your performance, as you might want to hear yourself singing or playing louder than you want your audience to hear you in order to nail all the notes.

This is all possible within Live if you know your routing options.

We already briefly talked about what **Cue Out** does in Live and how you can turn the **Solo** buttons into **Cue** buttons. You can recap this in the *I/O on Master Track* section of *Chapter 1, Taking a Quick Tour of Ableton Live 11*.

What I really want to talk about here is using **Cue Out** to send the metronome into your headphone mix without your audience hearing it!

What you will need is an audio interface with multiple outputs. In this example, I am using the Focusrite Scarlett 8i6, but any other brand and make that has at least four outputs will do.

Open **Chapter 15.2** Ableton Live project and follow me!

The metronome is automatically routed through **Cue Out**, which you can find in the **I/O section** of **Master** (*Figure 15.20*):

Figure 15.20 – Cue Out on Master's I/O section

In the preceding figure, **Cue Out** is routed to the same output as **Master Out**, which is, in this case, **1 / 2**. This means the metronome plays to your speakers and/or your headphones, just like each track of the music you are making in Live.

By adjusting the **Preview/Cue** volume, you can adjust the volume of the metronome too (*Figure 15.21*):

Figure 15.21 – Preview/Cue volume

Now, in order to separate the metronome from the rest of the music (with the metronome going to the headphones and the music going to the speakers), all we need to do is change the outputs for **Master Out** (the music) and **Cue Out** (the metronome).

Go to **Preferences** and within the **Audio** tab, make sure you enable multiple outputs to use. **1/2** is going to be dedicated to the metronome (most of the time, the **Headphones Out** plug is automatically routed within your interface's app or hardwired to **1/2**), and we will set **3/4** for "front of house," the music going to the speakers, which will not have the metronome sound, included as it is routed to the separate **Headphones Out** (*Figure 15.22*):

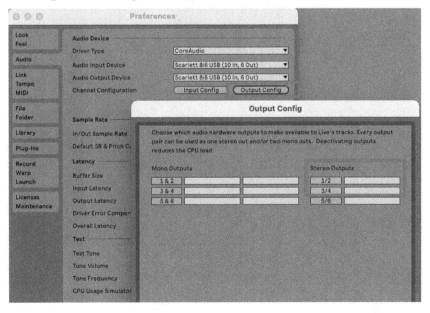

Figure 15.22 – Live's output configuration

We can also rename the outputs accordingly by typing in the boxes next to the outputs' names (*Figure 15.23*):

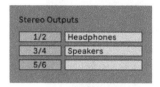

Figure 15.23 – Outputs renamed

Make sure your speakers are now connected to the **3/4** output on your audio interface.

Now if we go back to Live, you can simply choose these outputs separated for your **Master Out** (music) and your **Cue Out** (metronome) (*Figure 15.24*):

Figure 15.24 – Cue Out and Master Out routed to separate outputs

Now if you enable your metronome, you can check that **Master Out** (the music) is going out to your speakers, and if you check your headphones, you will hear the metronome through **Cue Out**. There is only one problem now – that although the metronome is not hitting the speakers (and potentially your audience), your headphone mix only includes the metronome so you aren't monitoring your music through it, which is not very useful.

All you need to do now is press on the **Solo** button above the **Preview/Cue** volume knob to turn your **Solo** buttons (**Solo** mode) into **Cue** buttons (**Cue** mode) (*Figure 15.25*):

Figure 15.25 – Cue mode enabled

Once that is done, now you can cue the desired tracks you would like to monitor to your headphones through the **Cue Out** output (*Figure 15.26*):

Figure 15.26 – Tracks sent to the headphones through Cue Out

With that, we have successfully created a headphone mix with the metronome included via **Cue Out** but not heard through the speakers via **Master Out**.

However, there are some limitations presented with this technique. We won't be able to control the volume of the various tracks of your project heard via the headphones.

If you are on stage, for example, and you are singing, you want to hear your vocals louder in your headphones than your audience does. Or if you are playing guitar, you might wish to hear the drums that you are following louder than the audience, as well as your guitar.

If that is the case, I will show you another technique for how you can have a different mix in terms of volume balance, as well as for your headphones and your audience!

Follow along:

1. Create two extra return tracks.

2. Call one of them **FOH** (front of house) and the other one **HEADPHONES** (*Figure 15.27*):

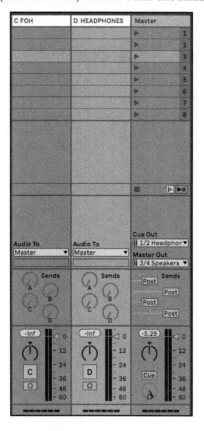

Figure 15.27 – Two new Return Tracks called FOH and HEADPHONES

3. Now, you will see these new Return Tracks become **C FOH** and **D HEADPHONES**.

4. **Cue Out** is still set to the **1/2 Headphones** output, which hears the metronome, so we will route the **D HEADPHONES** Return Track instead of **Master** to **1/2 Headphones**. The **C FOH** Return Track will be routed to **3/4 Speakers** instead of **Master** (*Figure 15.28*):

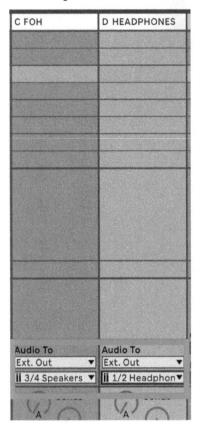

Figure 15.28 – C FOH and D HEADPHONES' outpus are routed appropriately

5. Navigate to the tracks in your set and set the output of each of them to **Sends Only** (*Figure 15.29*). This will ensure that nothing is going to **Master** anymore since we are using the two new Return Tracks to create a separation between the headphone mix that you hear and the FOH mix that your audience hears.

Figure 15.29 – The output of the tracks in the live set is set to Sends Only

At this point, you still cannot hear anything, as we told the tracks to output audio only through **Sends/Returns** and we have routed the Return Tracks (C and D) to the appropriate output, but we haven't sent the tracks (VOX CHOPS and DRUMS) to the Return Tracks (C and D) yet.

Let's do that; **Send D** will send the audio to the **D FOH** Return Track, which is going to the speakers, and **Send C** will send the audio to the **C HEADPHONES** Return Track.

Now, it is up to you how much of each track is being sent where.

I sent the entirety of each track through **Send D** to the **D FOH** Return Track, and I sent a little more of the **VOX CHOPS** track through **Send C** to **C HEADPHONES** (my headphones) than I did of the **DRUMS** track (*Figure 15.30*):

Figure 15.30 – Tracks sent to the appropriate Return Tracks to monitor via Send C and D

We are nearly done, but here is another little detail; as you can see in the preceding figure (*Figure 15.30*), I am sending the **VOX CHOPS** track through **Send A** and **Send B** to return **A Reverb** and **B Delay**, so we will need to make sure that these Return Tracks are sent to both the audience (FOH) and the headphones.

Let's set that up quickly:

1. Navigate to the output of the **A Reverb** Return Track and the **B Delay** Return Track. Set their output to **Sends Only** (*Figure 15.31*):

Figure 15.31 – Outputs set to Sends Only

2. Once that is done, you can send the **Reverb** and **Delay** Return Tracks to both your audience (FOH) via **Send C** and your headphones via **Send D** (*Figure 15.32*):

Figure 15.32 – Reverb and Delay are sent to the FOH and HEADPHONES Return Tracks via Sends C and D

Now, if you have done everything correctly, your session should look like this:

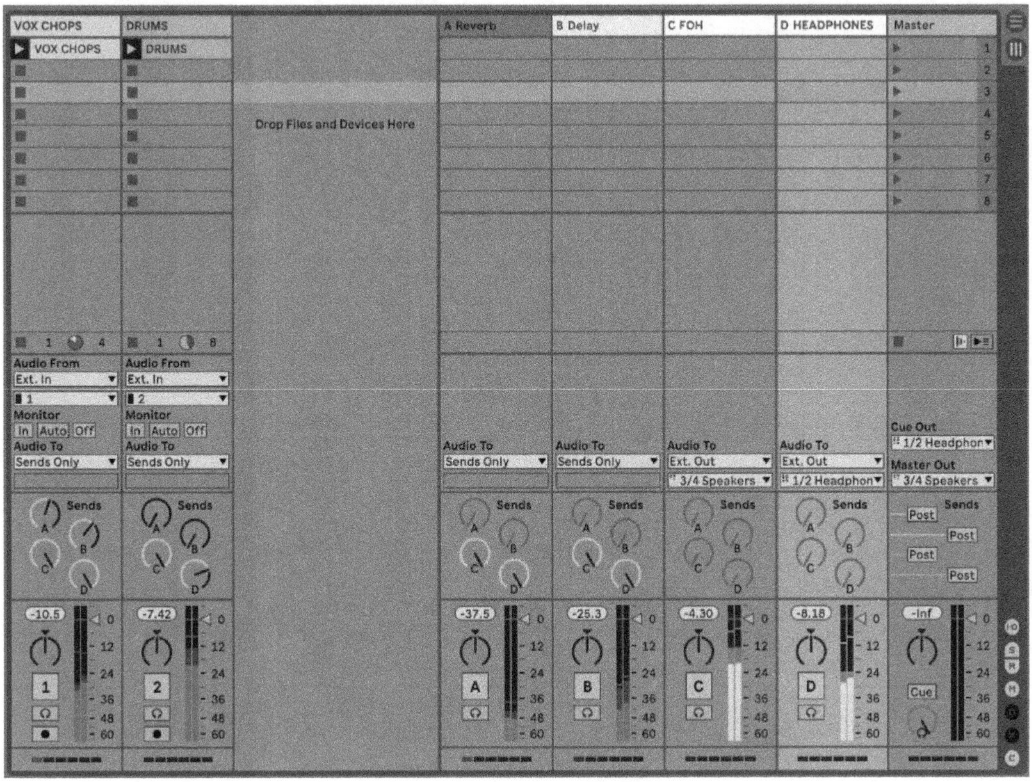

Figure 15.33 – The final settings

Now, let's move on to the last section of this chapter and talk a little bit about Ableton Push 2 and other MIDI controller considerations!

Ableton Push and other controller considerations

We already mentioned Ableton Push 2 (*Figure 15.34*) previously in this book when we looked at MIDI controller types, but I wanted to make sure that we dedicated a bit more time to looking at what Push is, as I truly believe that it is wonderful to have a dedicated MIDI controller to control the universe of Live with seamless integration, which enables you to treat it like an "instrument." Nothing like Push integrates so well with Ableton Live!

Figure 15.34 – Ableton Push 2 in my studio

Ableton Push 2 is the improved version following the success of Ableton Push 1.

Push allows you to lay down ideas even quicker than just using Live on its own. It also gives you an amazing tactile experience, as you literally feel like your music is at your fingertips. The improved display of Push 2 allows you to be able to barely look at your computer screen when you are using it.

You can use Push 2 to step-sequence or play all your drums and melodies in real time with the velocity-sensitive pads.

You can slice and dice loops and samples and tweak them just by using Push.

Furthermore, you can tweak not only your samples but also your effects via the display and the encoders.

You don't even need to use your computer to navigate Browser; you can also do that through Push 2's display.

It is also possible to record your arrangement from the Session View with Push 2, as well as get stuck in the mixer to adjust levels, pans, and sends.

And of course… you can have fun with it and use it for your live performance to navigate your set's structure, live loop, manipulate effects, and, of course, play instruments all on stage!

There is no way to tell whether it has more use in the studio or on stage, as it is equally powerful for fulfilling your needs on both occasions.

You can check out some videos on the Ableton website to see the beast in action: `https://www.ableton.com/en/push/learn-push/`.

When it comes down to choosing your MIDI controller, there are multiple things to take into consideration. Again, we already talked about this in the *MIDI controllers* section of *Chapter 14, Exploring MIDI Mapping, External Instruments, and MIDI CCs*, but it's worth another mention here while we are on this topic again.

Many other manufacturers offer great MIDI controllers, such as Novation, Native Instruments, Akai, and more.

Most of these manufacturers are combining keys, pads, faders, and knobs, so it is really down to you to do some research and find the perfect MIDI controller or controllers! It is fairly common that artists will use more than one MIDI controller on stage, based on their needs.

Just look at your skills, preferences, and intentions for playing live; are you more of a key or pad player? Do you prefer to use both – maybe pads for drums and keys for melodies? Do you need something to extensively navigate your clips and scenes? Do you need extra knobs for effect manipulation? Do you want to use faders?

Once you have figured out the answers to these questions, it is time to research and let the fun begin!

Summary

We have arrived at the end of another chapter. In this chapter, we dived into features and considerations for performing live using Ableton Live, such as approaching live performances by looking at the two views that Live has to offer, as well as Clip Launch options to customize how clips are set up for playback in your set. We covered dummy clips and how to use them, and also explored the word of syncing using Ableton Link and MIDI.

Furthermore, we looked at how to use **Cue Out**, which allows you to separate the metronome from the music in your project so that you can include the metronome in a headphone mix that is not heard by your audience through the speakers. We took the headphone mix topic even further and investigated the possibility of setting up a headphone mix that includes the metronome but with additional control over the volume of each track going into the headphone mix, which differs from what the audience hears through the speakers, by using Sends and Return Tracks in a very specific way.

Lastly, we took some more time to talk about MIDI controller considerations, with a focus on Push 2.

In the next chapter, we are going to look at some exciting and advanced mixing techniques, as well as how to approach mixing your track and preparing it for mastering.

16

Interesting Mixing Techniques in Live 11

Mixing down your track is an important part of the creative process. This is the stage where you blend all the tracks of your project by balancing levels, panning, frequencies, and dynamics, as well as applying creative processing to sounds to create the desired sound characteristics and a sense of depth in your song. In this process, you bring out the best of your sounds and create a cohesive balance between them. Mixing is usually done by a mixing engineer, but it is not unusual in the modern age for the producer to mix their own songs down, so it is definitely a good skill to master to be self-sufficient. Sometimes, with certain genres (specifically in electronic music), some parts of mixing start while the track is still being produced as part of the sound design process, or it is necessary to make elements of a track sound genre appropriate within the production process.

Mixing is a huge topic, and there are many books written about this one topic alone; therefore, in this chapter, we will look at some specific techniques and how to apply them in Ableton Live.

This chapter will include the following key topics:

- Approaching a track mixdown
- Split-band processing
- Sidechained reverbs
- Parallel compression
- Mid-side EQ
- Preparing your mix for mastering

Technical requirements

To follow along with this chapter, you will need the following:

- A computer with at least 8 GB of RAM and an Intel Core i5 processor
- A pair of headphones
- A copy of Live 11 Suite
- The **Chapter 16** Ableton Live project

Approaching a track mixdown

Let's start by covering the basics and how you could approach mixing down your track. The order of these processes can be quite important to achieve a fast and fluid workflow.

Volume balance

The first thing that is super important and a significant part of mixing down a track is to balance the volume between each element of your track. At this stage, you can identify, for example, whether there is further need for volume automation for certain parts or elements of your track, as well as make sure that you have enough headroom at your Master track's meter and ensure that each element of your track is audible at all times.

If you are working on a track that you started a fairly long time ago and are revisiting it weeks later to do the final mixdown, it can be a good idea to rebalance the volume mix from scratch. If you are hired to mix someone's song, and you are being sent the stems of their track, you will need to balance the volume between the tracks while also familiarizing yourself with the stems.

To pull all the faders down in Live is super simple. You can select all the tracks (or groups) in your project, and once all of them are selected, you can move the faders of all tracks together (*Figure 16.1*).

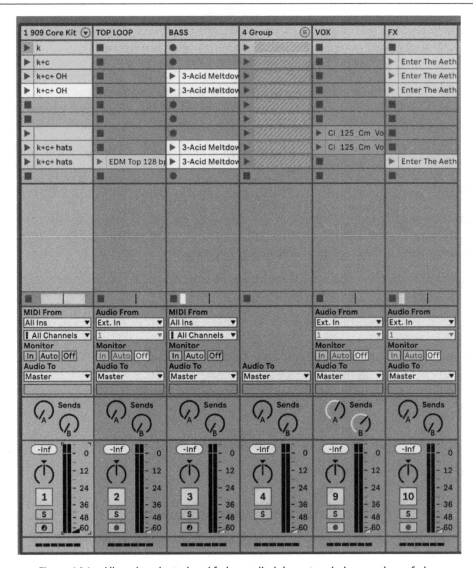

Figure 16.1 – All tracks selected and faders pulled down to rebalance volume faders

This is also useful if you are clipping on the Master tracks and would like to adjust the volume faders together while maintaining the volume balance between each track.

It is a good idea to first balance the volume between each of the drum tracks, followed by the bass to create a great foundation for the track and identify early whether there is frequency masking between the kick drum and the bass.

Following these elements, you can add all the other instruments and, finally, the vocals. This order can change based on which mixing engineers you ask; some prefer to start with the vocals and balance everything around them.

While you are balancing the volume faders, ensure you are checking your master's meter and leaving enough headroom to apply processing to each sound later where necessary. But of course, as we mentioned, you can adjust the volume faders later without losing the balance between them.

Once you are done with the volume balance, it is a good idea to move on to looking at each sound's panning.

Panning

With panning, you can control which side of the stereo field the track is panned to. With this, you can widen or narrow sounds and mixes. There are general rules, such as bass-heavy sounds should be mono and panned in the center to avoid muddying up the mix.

We can also control the stereo position of each left and right channel of a track independently. To do that, you can enable **Select Split Stereo Pan Mode**.

Simply *Ctrl + click* (*right-click* on Windows) on the panner and choose this option (*Figure 16.2*).

Figure 16.2 – Select the Split Stereo Pan Mode option by Ctrl + clicking on the panner

Once we are done with our volume balance and panned each sound where we desire, we should already have a fairly dry but balanced mix.

We can now move on to cleaning up sounds with an **equalizer** (**EQ**).

Subtractive EQing

Subtractive EQing means you are removing unwanted frequencies from each sound.

This involves subtracting frequencies using notch-filtering to remove unpleasant resonant frequencies (*Figure 16.3*).

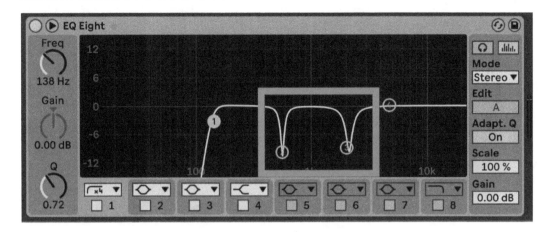

Figure16.3 – Notch filtering applied in EQ Eight

This process also involves using low, high, and band pass filters (*Figure 16.4*).

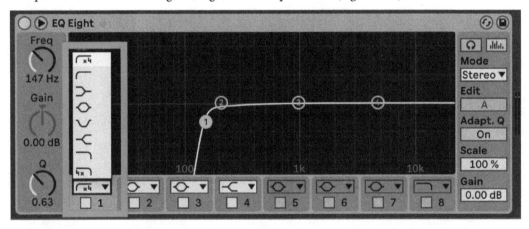

Figure 16.4 – Choosing from filter types in EQ Eight

A good example of this is, if you are working with female vocals, you can probably cut all frequencies below 150 Hz (given that the singer doesn't have a really deep voice), and most probably, cutting those frequencies will make no difference in the vocals' sound characteristics, but those frequencies you cut is where all the noise and rumble lives. Not removing these frequencies from sounds that don't have fundamental frequencies at that frequency range will cause them to add up and get in the way of your bass. You can use an EQ frequency chart from a simple Google search to reference which instruments should be sitting at what frequency range.

Once you have cleared up all unwanted frequencies of your sounds, we can start looking at the dynamics.

Compression

So far, we have balanced the volume between all the tracks and the panning and cleared up the sounds. However, as you look at some of the sounds individually, you might realize that some of them are quite dynamic. Thus, it is really hard to find the right volume balance for them, and they fluctuate in volume as there are big differences between the quieter and louder parts. Dynamic controllers, such as a compressor, can easily control this. A compressor will reduce the dynamic range by reducing the volume of louder parts of an audio signal and amplifying the quieter parts.

In Live, you can use the **Compressor**, **Glue Compressor**, and **Multiband Dynamics** to apply compression to your sounds.

Once the dynamics are controlled on a track basis, we can look at applying EQing again.

Additive EQing

Additive EQing means that, unlike subtractive EQing, here you are boosting frequencies.

You might feel like the vocals sound a bit dull or dark, so you decide to boost some of the higher frequencies (*Figure 16.5*). Maybe you find your bass a bit too subby; of course, you can apply some saturation or noticeable distortion to create more harmonics and overtones, but sometimes it is enough just to boost some of the lower mid-range with an EQ.

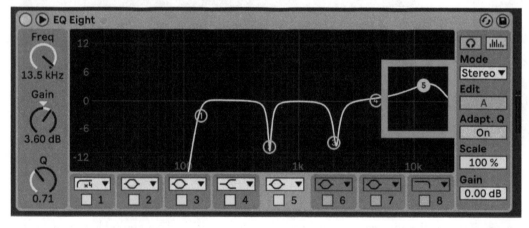

Figure 16.5 – Additive EQing boosting high frequencies

The reason why you might like to use a separate EQ for additive EQing is that when you are boosting frequencies, you are essentially making the sound louder, changing the level of the output of the EQ device. So, if you already have a compressor after the EQ where you are about to boost frequencies, you will need to reset it as it was set up to the level of the sound before you applied the frequency boost. So, to avoid this, you can simply use another EQ after your compressor to apply the frequency boost.

Once you are done, you can compress again if needed or apply a limiter or other dynamic controllers.

Creative effects

After you have taken control of the frequencies and the dynamics of your sounds, it is time to apply creative processing to your controlled and balanced sounds to create depth and add spice to your sounds.

You can think of any fun devices – choruses, delays, reverbs; it's time to get creative!

Now we have looked at a basic approach to getting started with mixing, let me show you a few quite specific and advanced mixing techniques and how they are done in Ableton Live!

Split-band processing in Live

The idea here is to take a sound with a fairly wide frequency range and process the frequency bands separately and accordingly.

Let's take as an example a fat Reese bass. Since it is a bass sound, it is obviously heavy in low frequencies, but these basses are also really rich in the mid-range.

You might also want this bass to sound super huge and spacey, but we know that we can't really have a bass stereo, nor have reverb on it; otherwise, it will muddy up our entire mix.

Well, this is where splitting this bass into two by frequency ranges and processing them differently can get you that big fat spacey sound that you are looking for without mudding up your mix.

Let me show you how it is done in Live using **Audio Effect Rack**. You can use the **Chapter 16** project file to follow along:

1. Create or pick the bass sound you desire in Live. (In the **Chapter 16** project, we are working with the track called **Reese Split Bass**.)

2. Drop and empty **Audio Effect Rack** onto the track. (If you need to refresh on how Audio Effect Racks work, it is explored in depth within *Chapter 8, Exploring Device Racks in Live 11*.)

3. In **Audio Effect Rack**, drop in an **EQ Eight** device. Now you should see the **Chain** that the **EQ Eight** is sitting on (*Figure 16.6*).

Figure 16.6 – An EQ Eight device in Audio Effect Rack

4. Now, you can *Ctrl + click* (*right-click* on Windows) on **Chain** and choose the **Duplicate** option (*Figure 16.7*).

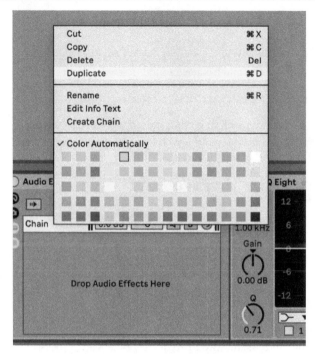

Figure 16.7 – Duplicating Chain in Audio Effect Rack

5. Now we have two chains, and we can go ahead and rename the first one `Sub` and the second one `Mids` (*Figure 16.8*). (To rename a **Chain**, simply click on it and hit the *Cmd + R* (*Ctrl + R* or *Ctrl + click* for Windows) and choose the **Rename** option.)

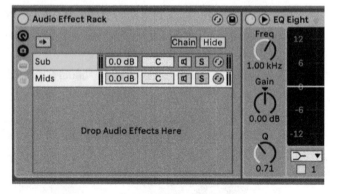

Figure 16.8 – The two chains named in Audio Effect Rack

Now we are ready to split the sound by its frequency bands, and it will be done by the two EQ Eight devices on the chains.

6. Navigate to the **Sub** chain and solo the chain (by hitting the Solo button (**s**) on the chain) and cut all the frequencies above 80–100 Hz (*Figure 16.9*).

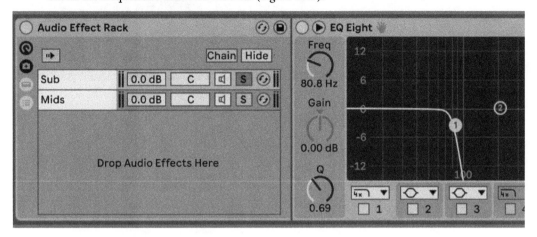

Figure 16.9 – The soloed Sub chain and the frequency cut applied on its EQ Eight device

7. Now, navigate to the **Mids** chain, make sure that this chain is only soloed this time, and on this chain apply the opposite frequency cut in the EQ Eight device; cut everything below 80–100 Hz (*Figure 16.10*).

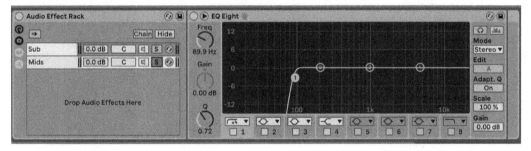

Figure 16.10 – The soloed Mids chain and the frequency cut applied on its EQ Eight device

And with that, we now have the same bass but split over two chains by the EQ devices. This split enables us to apply effect processing independently to the frequency bands of the same bass sound. In my opinion, it is a genius technique and one of the keys to creating huge sounds for certain electronic genres without compromising the clarity of your overall mix.

Now you can start applying different effect processing to each chain. In my example, I applied a **Utility** device to the **Sub** chain, which I switched to **Mono** (*Figure 16.11*) to ensure my lower bass frequencies were kept nice and centered.

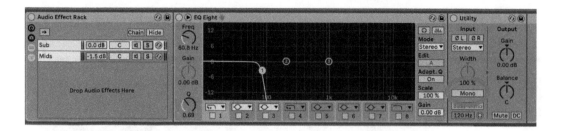

Figure 16.11 – Utility device switched to Mono on the Sub chain

To the **Mids** chain, I applied some **Saturation**, **Chorus**, and **Reverb** without affecting the lower bass frequencies with these effects.

This technique can be applied to heavy lead synth and pad sounds, or to anything, in fact, where you feel like the sound is taking up multiple frequency ranges, and each band and your overall mix would benefit from different processing to maintain the clarity of the sound.

Now let's move on to the next section and discover how and why we would want to sidechain reverbs!

Sidechained reverb

Sidechaining reverbs is something I personally found super useful in certain situations for vocal processing. For example, sometimes you can find yourself in a situation where you have found a lush reverb, and you really want to use it on your vocals, but for some reason, you just don't seem to be able to set it right. If you add a bit more, it makes your vocals sound too washed out; if you add a bit less, then it seems to sound too dry. In this case, of course, you can look for a different type of reverb and settings, but maybe you can also try to sidechain the reverb. The sidechain will duck down (reduce in volume) each time the vocals come on, and when there are no vocals in the playback, the reverb level comes back up. This can also be used very creatively in slower tracks with more spaced-out vocals (in terms of having long spaces between words or phrases), so the increased level of reverb can beautifully fill out these spaces.

Let's see how to set this up in Live!

1. In the **Chapter 16** project, navigate to the **Sidechained Reverb** track; this track has some vocals playing back.

2. Insert **Hybrid Reverb** and a **Compressor** device onto a **Return Track**.

3. After ensuring that **Hybrid Reverb** is set to **100%** with the **Dry/Wet** knob, send a significant amount of the vocals (called a **Sidechained Reverb** track) via the **Sends** section of the Mixer to the Return Track where you inserted **Hybrid Reverb** and the **Compressor** device. (To refreshyourself on how Sends and Return Tracks work, visit *Chapter 7, Discovering Some of Live 11's Creative Audio Effects,* and refer to the *Understanding the difference between Insert Effect Chains and Return Tracks* section.)

4. Group **Hybrid Reverb** and the **Compressor** device into an **Audio Effect Rack**. Now open and enable the **Sidechain** section on **Compressor** (*Figure 16.12*).

(To refresh on sidechain compression, you can refer to the *Sidechaining techniques* section in *Chapter 7, Discovering Some of Live 11's Creative Audio Effects*).

Figure 16.12 – The Hybrid Reverb and Compressor devices grouped into an Audio Effect Rack, and the Sidechain section is open and enabled in the Compressor device

Now, in the **Sidechain** section, from the **Audio From** drop-down menu pick the track that we are working with (**Sidechained Reverb**), which has the vocals playing as the external sidechain source (*Figure 16.13*).

Figure 16.13 – Selecting the external sidechain source

5. Once this is done, you can now adjust the **Compressor** device's **Threshold, Attack, Release, Ratio, and Out** controls to control the sidechain effect.

This technique can be a great weapon for corrective and creative processing purposes.

In the next section, we will work further with the Compressor and look at how we can apply parallel compression in Ableton Live.

Parallel Compression

The process of parallel compression (also called New York -style compression) blends a dry audio signal together with a *copy* of this signal heavily compressed. It can give a really nice excitement and flavor to sounds. It is a widely used technique and can give some real spice to, for example, drums and vocals.

Let's see how it is done in Live:

1. Navigate in the **Chapter 16** project to the **DRUMS** track.

2. Insert a new **Return Track**. (In this project, this will be Return C.)

3. Insert the **Compressor** device onto this new **Return Track**.

4. Send the drums via **Sends C** all the way to the **Return Track** with the **Compressor** device on it (*Figure 16.14*).

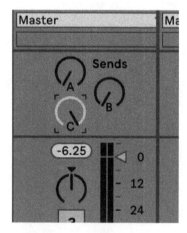

Figure 16.14 – The DRUMS track sent all the way to Return Track C

5. Now you can hit the **Solo** button on Return Track C and set up the **Compressor** device on this **Return Track** to compress the signal really-really heavily! Go really heavy-handed and over the top with the compression!

6. Once it is done, you can pull down the volume fader of Return Track C, remove solo from it, and slowly mix and blend in the heavily compressed signal to the original uncompressed signal (the **DRUMS** track) (*Figure 16.15*).

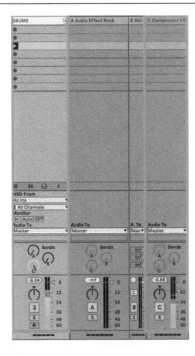

Figure 16.15 – The original uncompressed signal (DRUMS) mixed with
the heavily compressed signal (Return C Compressor)

You can also add further processing to the **Return Track** with the **Compressor** device on it to add some further flavor to blend in. In my example, I applied the **Overdrive** device to add some distortion (*Figure 16.16*).

Figure 16.16 – Additional distortion added to Return Track C

We have just learned how to apply parallel processing to our drums. In the next section, we will look at another interesting mixing technique; mid-side EQing.

Mid-side EQing

Mid-side EQing enables us to equalize an audio signal's mid and side components independently. This provides us with much greater control of the stereo image and can clear up mixes super quickly.

In this example, we will apply this technique to our Master track.

In Live, it is actually super simple to set up; let me show you how in the following steps:

1. In the **Chapter 16** project, launch the **Mid-side EQ** scene.

2. Apply the **EQ Eight** device on the **Master track**.

3. Now, it's time to turn our old **EQ Eight** device into a mid-side EQ.

4. Under **Mode** choose the **M/S** option instead of **Stereo**.

5. Under the **Edit** section, you can choose between **M** (mid) and **S** (side) (*Figure 16.17*).

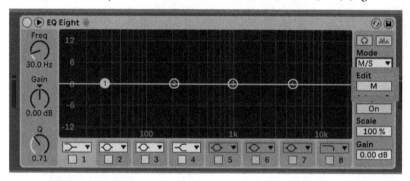

Figure 16.17 – Switching between mid and side under the Edit section of the EQ Eight device

6. Now, we will take the opportunity to ensure that there is no low-frequency bleed into our side/stereo signal. Simply switch to **S** (side) under the **Edit** section and apply a high-pass filter, around 150 Hz (*Figure 16.18*).

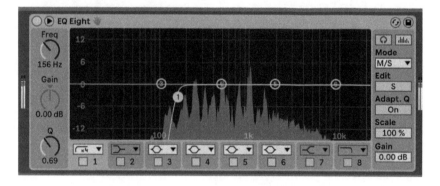

Figure 16.18 – A high-pass filter applied to the side

7.   Here, you can also apply a little bit of boost on the top end on the side if you feel it is necessary to brighten the sound up a little bit.

8.   Now, switch to **M** (mid) under the **Edit** section and apply a little boost, around 80 Hz (*Figure 16.19*).

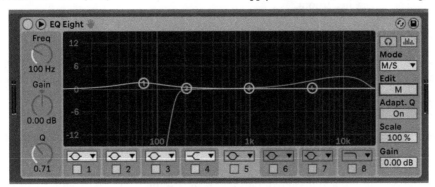

Figure 16.19 – A little low frequency boost applied to the mid

If you now bypass the **EQ Eight** device with the processing applied to the Master track, you should hear the difference. Notice how much more separation and clarity you have now. This EQ technique can also be applied on a track-to-track basis for sounds that occupy multiple frequency ranges at once.

Let's move on to the last section of this chapter and talk a little bit about how you can prepare your mix for mastering and what mastering is.

Preparing your mix for mastering

When you have finished the production of your song, you will notice that it is still quieter than all the other songs released out there. The reason behind it is that your song isn't mastered yet. The mastering process will put the final touches and polish to your song in terms of sonic characteristics, and it will be mastered to a loudness standard. This is also a standardization process, so your song will be able to compete with other songs on streaming platforms, DJ sets, and radio, and you will have the appropriate formats for however you desire to release your song (vinyl and digital formats). The mastering stage is also where metadata is applied to your song.

However, an incorrectly prepared mix can limit what the mastering engineer can do. Mastering engineers work with the stereo bounce of your track, and they will not have access to your production project file, so you need to make sure the mix is exported correctly and there is enough headroom left on your Master track's meter for the mastering engineer to apply further processing to your mix.

Mastering is a huge topic, and there are numerous books written about it. Here, I just want to make sure that you prepare your mix properly for the mastering engineer to do their job if it isn't you who will be mastering the song and you have little to no knowledge of the mastering process.

As I previously mentioned, probably the most important aspect of exporting your mix for mastering is that you leave enough headroom for the mastering engineer to do their job. What this means is that your mix should peak on the Master track's meter between -3 dB and -6 dB (True Peak), which will provide the necessary headroom.

Let's take it step by step:

1. Ensure that your mix sounds the way you want it to sound; don't expect the mastering engineer to make your vocals louder or your bass to hit harder; if that's what you desire, then achieve it at the mixing stage. Use **reference tracks** to ensure your mix sounds genre-appropriate and is what you want.

   It is fairly simple to set up reference tracks in Live. Let's have a look at how to set one up:

   I. Create a new audio track.

   II. Import a mixed and mastered track into your session that has the sound characteristics that you are trying to achieve in your mix.

   III. You need to make sure that the reference track's output is not routed to the Master, as you probably already have processing on your Master track. If the reference track is outputted through the Master track's effect processing then you will alter the sound of the reference track too.

   IV. So, set the reference track's output directly through your main output (to your speakers/ headphones) instead of the Master (*Figure 16.20*).

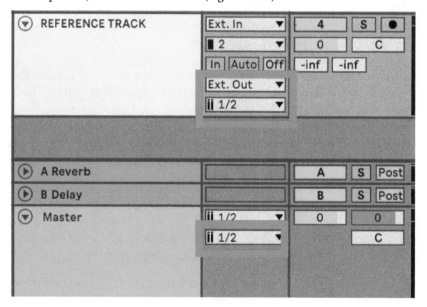

Figure 16.20 – Setting the reference track's output directly through the main external output

Now you can solo the reference track quickly to check the difference between the sound of the reference track and your mix.

You can also make the soloing more comfortable and effective by mapping the reference track's solo button to a key on your keyboard. In my example, I mapped the . key to the solo button of the reference track (*Figure 16.21*). You can recap how key mapping works in *Chapter 14*.

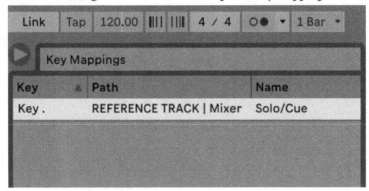

Figure 16.21 – The reference track's Solo button is mapped to the . key on the computer keyboard

Alternatively, there are third-party plugins that you can also use for track referencing inside Live (for example, ADPTR AUDIO Metric AB).

2. Make sure that when you are exporting your mix, you aren't cutting any reverb tails at the end of the song, and the sounds are properly faded out (if that's how your song ends). You can take a recap on how to export audio out of Live in the *Getting your work out* section of *Chapter 1, Taking a Quick Tour of Ableton Live 11*.

3. Make sure that your meter on the Master track is peaking between -3 dB and -6 dB without any heavy limiting or bus compression!

4. Make sure when you export your track, your sample rate is set to the sample rate that you used in the project throughout the recording and production process. This should be 44.1 kHz unless you are working on audio for films, which is then 48 kHz.

5. Make sure the bit depth is set to at least 24 bits (or above), and you do not apply dithering because that's what the mastering engineer will do when they convert the bit depth to 16 bits during their final export.

Mastering is also an art form of the music production world, and it requires extensive training and practice to truly *master* (pun intended) this process.

And with that, we have arrived at the end of this chapter.

Summary

In this chapter, we discussed the process of a track mixdown, and how you can approach it.

We also discussed advanced mixing techniques and how they can be carried out in Ableton Live, such as split-band processing to process sounds that engage multiple frequency ranges to maintain clarity.

We also looked at sidechaining reverbs for corrective and creative applications, parallel compression to bring more flavor to our sounds, and mid-side EQing to take further control of the stereo field.

Furthermore, we talked about how you can prepare your mix for mastering to ensure that your mastering engineer can do the best possible job as you provide them with the appropriate export of your mixed song.

In the next chapter, we will look at how to manage your files and troubleshoot in Ableton Live.

17
Troubleshooting and File Management

Now that we have looked at some useful and creative mixing techniques, we have arrived at the last chapter of this book. In this chapter, we are going to look at some troubleshooting techniques. We are going to explore how to replace missing files, which is super important if we might have made a mistake during our file management process, and now, we are facing missing samples. Sometimes, we also can end up with an unnecessarily large project that takes up loads of disk space because we have piled up some unused files. This can be aided easily by removing these unused files.

And finally, if you are looking to use third-party plug-ins, you will find out how to manage them properly.

These topics might not be the most exciting ones; however, they are a crucial part of maintaining a fluid and stress free workflow and being able to troubleshoot with ease when needed.

The chapter will consist of the following topics:

- Missing samples
- Unused files
- Managing third-party plug-ins

Technical requirements

In order to follow along with this chapter, you will need the following:

- A computer with at least 8 GB of RAM and an Intel Core i5 processor
- A pair of headphones
- A copy of Live 11 Suite

Managing missing files

Missing files in a project is a common problem that can happen to any of us. This can be due to incorrect saving (not saving samples upon saving a project or a file management error), not using the **Collect All and Save** commands, or misplacing the saved sample folder in our project file. When any of these things happen, and we open the set (the .als file), Live will give us a message indicating that it is unable to locate the files (*Figure 17.1*):

Figure 17.1 – Live's warning that there are missing files in a project

When this happens, you can also see that the missing files are grayed out and appear offline in your project. Luckily, it is very simple to run a quick search on your computer or on an external storage device where the files might be. For this, we are going to use the **File Manager** (*Figure 17.2*):

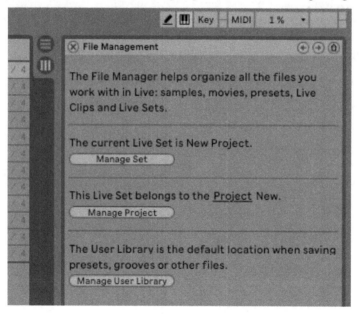

Figure 17.2 – The File Manager in Live

Let's talk a bit more about the File Manager before we dive into replacing the missing files. The File Manager allows us to manage all the files that belong to our project. Since it is possible that numerous files are being referenced from various locations other than your project folder (maybe you haven't hit **Collect All and Save** yet), the File Manager enables us to view and manage all the files of our project and where they are located.

To view the File Manager, simply go to **View | File Manager** (*Figure 17.3*):

Figure 17.3 – Locating the File Manager

In the File Manager, we have three options to choose from:

- **Manage Set**, which is specific to the current set we are working at
- **Manage Project**, which allows us to manage all the sets and files within the project folder
- **Manage User Library**, where we can deal with the files related to our user library

Now that we know a little bit more about the File Manager, let's go back to replacing missing files.

We can click on the orange message (*Figure 17.1*), which will open straight away in the File Manager and show you the list of missing files (*Figure 17.4*):

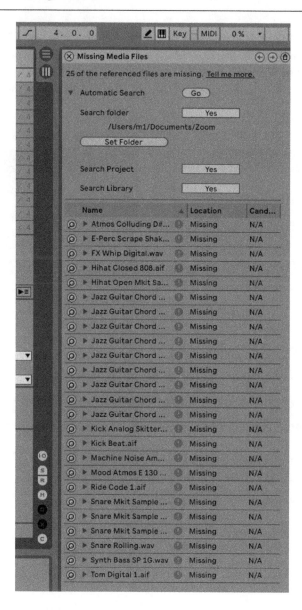

Figure 17.4 – A list of missing files in the File Manager

At the top part of the File Manager, you have some options for where you can search for the files on your computer.

Once you set the location in your file directory and click on **Yes** next to **Search folder**, you can hit the **Go** button.

Once you run the search, you will be notified by Live whether the search was successful and the files got replaced (*Figure 17.5*):

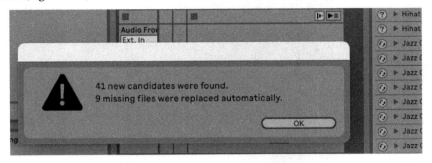

Figure 17.5 – Replacing missing files in Live

If you hover your mouse over the list of missing files, Live will show you at the bottom of the File Manager from what location it is trying to reference the file (the original location).

You can also manually pick to repair the file by clicking on the small magnifying glass (the **Find File** button), which then will take you to the browser, where you can select the file quickly, just like with **Hot-Swap**.

Once you are done, you can hit the **Save** button at the bottom of the File Manager to collect and save all the replaced files in your project folder.

So, in this section, we learned how to manage missing files; in the next section, let's check out how to reduce our project's file size and remove unused files.

Managing unused files

As I mentioned before, it is not unlikely that we end up with unused files eventually in our project that can take up unnecessary space, increasing our project's file size.

This can be especially annoying and something to look out for when you are collaborating with someone and you are transferring the project folder back and forth online.

To see whether you have unused files that you would like to remove, do the following:

1. Go to **View | File Manager**.
2. Click on **Manage Project**.
3. Navigate to the middle of the File Manager to **Unused Files** (*Figure 17.6*):

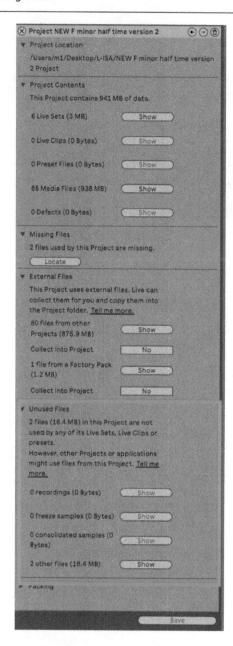

Figure 17.6 – Unused Files in the File Manager

As *Figure 17.6* shows, there are two unused files.

4.   Click on **Show** to view them in the browser (*Figure 17.7*):

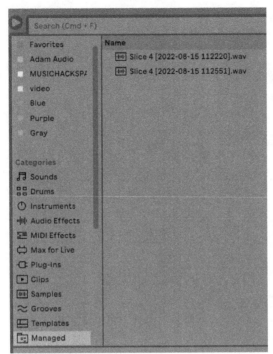

Figure 17.7 – A list of unused files displayed in the browser

5.   Once you see the list of unused files in the browser, you can simply decide to select all or some of them and then delete them.

6.   Live will ask you to confirm whether you'd like to move the files to the trash.

And with that, you are done; you have removed the desired unused files.

In the last section of this chapter, we will discover how we can manage our third-party plug-ins (made by other manufacturers) in Live.

Managing third-party plug-ins

Besides the native Live devices, you might wish to use third-party plugins.

As we have already learned in this book, you can find these plug-ins in the browser under the **Plug-Ins** tab (*Figure 17.8*):

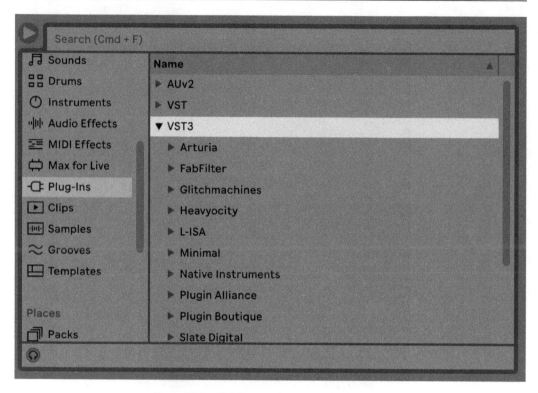

Figure 17.8 – Third party plug-ins in the browser

When you install or uninstall plug-ins, Live will not detect them and, therefore, will not show the changes in the browser until you close and reopen Live.

It is necessary to activate your plug-in sources if no plug-ins are showing up in the browser.

To do so, and to carry out other plug-in-related settings, head to **Live** | **Preferences** | **Plug-Ins** (**Options** | **Preferences** | **Plug-Ins** on Windows) or hit *Cmd + ,* (*Ctrl + ,* for Windows) (*Figure 17.9*):

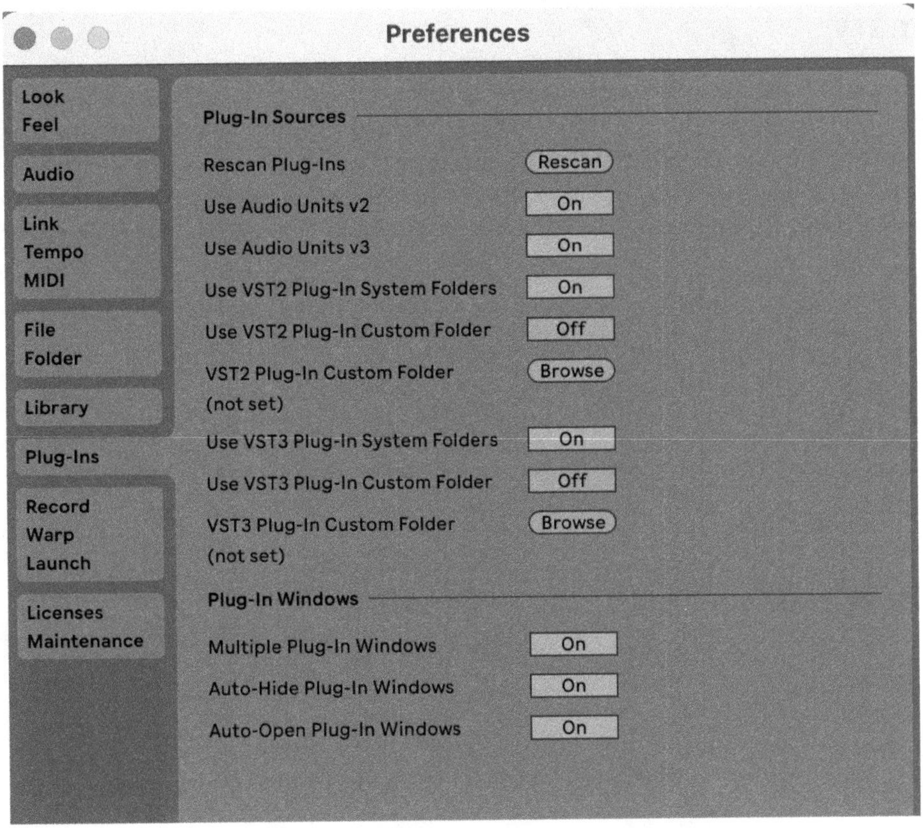

Figure 17.9 – The Plug-Ins tab in Live's Preferences

In **Preferences** (*Figure 17.9*), you can also set custom folders where you might also store VST2 and VST3 plug-ins (**Use VST2 Plug-In Custom Folder** and **Use VST3 Plug-In Custom Folder**). In my case, I am only using and storing my VSTs in the original system folder. You can use the custom folder in addition to your plug-ins in the system too; you do not have to choose either. To set your custom folder where you are storing additional plug-ins, just simply hit the **Browse** button and set the folder within the directory.

Once you have made changes, you can always hit the **Rescan** button next to **Rescan Plug-Ins**.

Under **Plug-In Windows**, you can set up the behavior of the third-party plug-in windows. As you can see, they open up in a new window as opposed to native devices. These window management settings are not about troubleshooting, but rather, can provide a more pleasant window management to your liking.

Summary

In this chapter, we looked at some troubleshooting techniques if you are having to deal with common problems. These can happen to anyone, and knowing how to use the File Manager will give you the confidence to oversee and be in control of all the files belonging to your project. Reducing file size is also crucial in the modern world to make file transfers easier. And, of course, everyone likes to use some new cool additional plug-ins to add some extra spice to the already amazing selection of Live devices.

Index

www.packtpub.com

Subscribe to our online digital library for full access to over 7,000 books and videos, as well as industry leading tools to help you plan your personal development and advance your career. For more information, please visit our website.

Why subscribe?

- Spend less time learning and more time coding with practical eBooks and Videos from over 4,000 industry professionals

- Improve your learning with Skill Plans built especially for you

- Get a free eBook or video every month

- Fully searchable for easy access to vital information

- Copy and paste, print, and bookmark content

Did you know that Packt offers eBook versions of every book published, with PDF and ePub files available? You can upgrade to the eBook version at packtpub.com and as a print book customer, you are entitled to a discount on the eBook copy. Get in touch with us at customercare@packtpub.com for more details.

At www.packtpub.com, you can also read a collection of free technical articles, sign up for a range of free newsletters, and receive exclusive discounts and offers on Packt books and eBooks.

Other Books You May Enjoy

If you enjoyed this book, you may be interested in these other books by Packt:

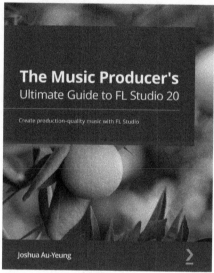

The Music Producer's Ultimate Guide to FL Studio 20

Joshua Au-Yeung

ISBN: 978-1-80056-532-6

- Get up and running with FL Studio 20
- Record live instruments and vocals and process them
- Compose melodies and chord progressions on the Piano roll
- Discover mixing techniques and apply effects to your tracks
- Explore best practices to produce music like a professional
- Publish songs in online stores and promote your music effectively

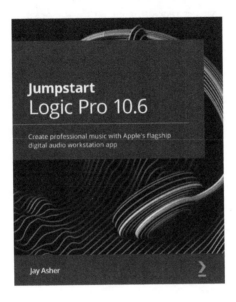

Jumpstart Logic Pro 10.6

Jay Asher

ISBN: 978-1-80056-277-6

- Get to grips with Audio and MIDI and how they are different, along with covering Apple Loops

- Record and edit audio, such as your voice or guitar

- Create and edit MIDI parts, using Logic Pro's software instruments

- Develop realistic drums and electronic drums with Logic Pro 10.5's amazing Drummer

- Explore the new Step Sequencer, Live Loops, and Quick Sampler that were included with version 10.5

- Edit your arrangement and prepare the parts for mixing

- Discover the principles of good mixing, including automation, pre-mastering, and final bouncing

Packt is searching for authors like you

If you're interested in becoming an author for Packt, please visit authors.packtpub.com and apply today. We have worked with thousands of developers and tech professionals, just like you, to help them share their insight with the global tech community. You can make a general application, apply for a specific hot topic that we are recruiting an author for, or submit your own idea.

Hi!

I am Anna Lakatos, author of *The Music Producer's Creative Guide to Ableton Live 11*. I really hope you enjoyed reading this book and found it useful for increasing your productivity and efficiency in Ableton Live.

It would really help me (and other potential readers!) if you could leave a review on Amazon sharing your thoughts on *The Music Producer's Creative Guide to Ableton Live 11*.

Go to the link below or scan the QR code to leave your review:

`https://packt.link/r/1801817634`

Your review will help us to understand what's worked well in this book, and what could be improved upon for future editions, so it really is appreciated.

Best Wishes,

Anna Lakatos

Download a free PDF copy of this book

Thanks for purchasing this book!

Do you like to read on the go but are unable to carry your print books everywhere? Is your eBook purchase not compatible with the device of your choice?

Don't worry, now with every Packt book you get a DRM-free PDF version of that book at no cost.

Read anywhere, any place, on any device. Search, copy, and paste code from your favorite technical books directly into your application.

The perks don't stop there, you can get exclusive access to discounts, newsletters, and great free content in your inbox daily

Follow these simple steps to get the benefits:

1. Scan the QR code or visit the link below

https://packt.link/free-ebook/978-1-80181-763-9

2. Submit your proof of purchase

3. That's it! We'll send your free PDF and other benefits to your email directly

CPSIA information can be obtained
at www.ICGtesting.com
Printed in the USA
LVHW020145090623
749170LV00011B/7

9 781801 817639